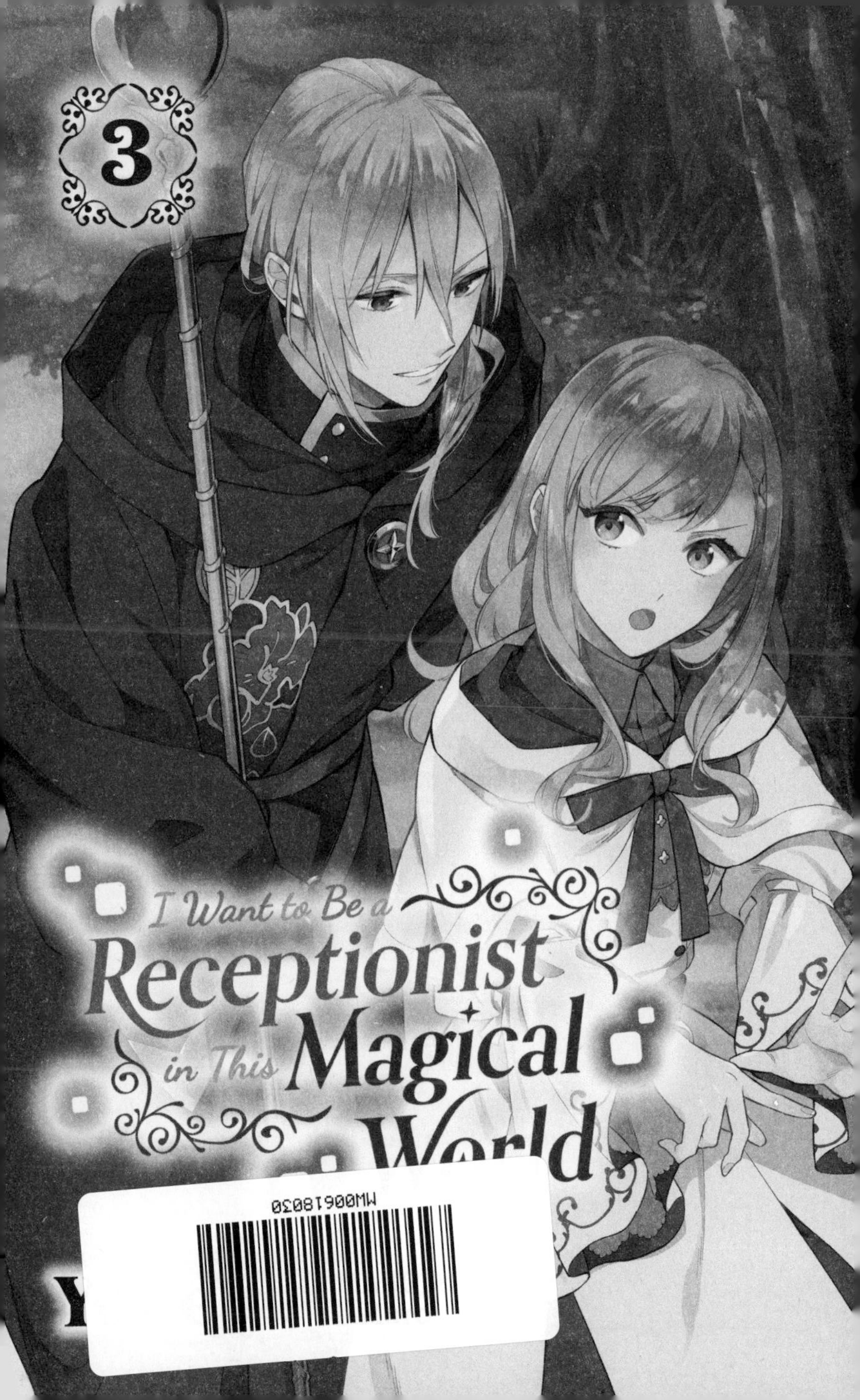
3
I Want to Be a
Receptionist
in This Magical
World

Contents

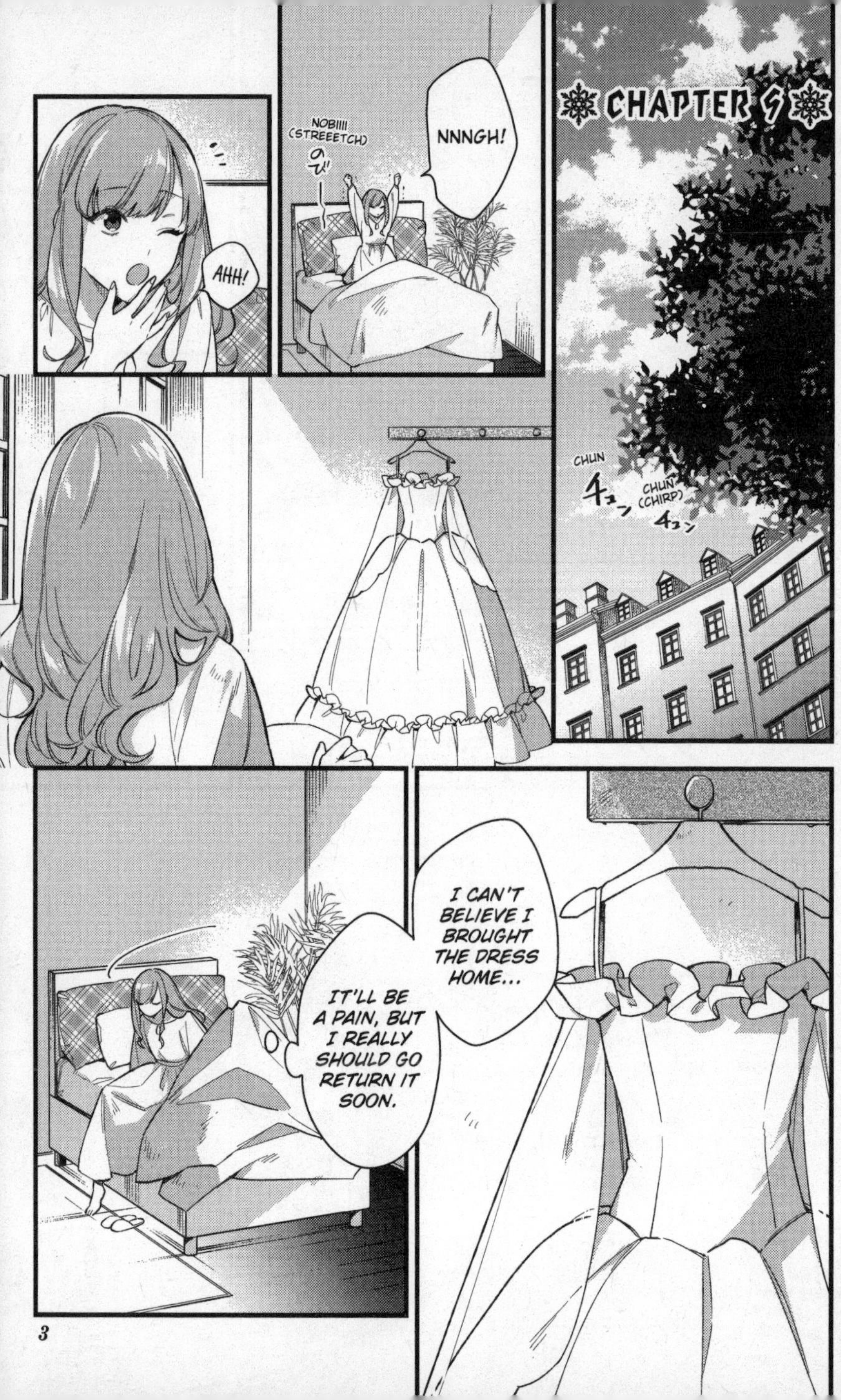
CHAPTER 5
CHUN チュン CHUN (CHIRP) チュン
NNNGH!
NOBIIII (STREEETCH) のび～～
AHH!
I CAN'T BELIEVE I BROUGHT THE DRESS HOME...
IT'LL BE A PAIN, BUT I REALLY SHOULD GO RETURN IT SOON.

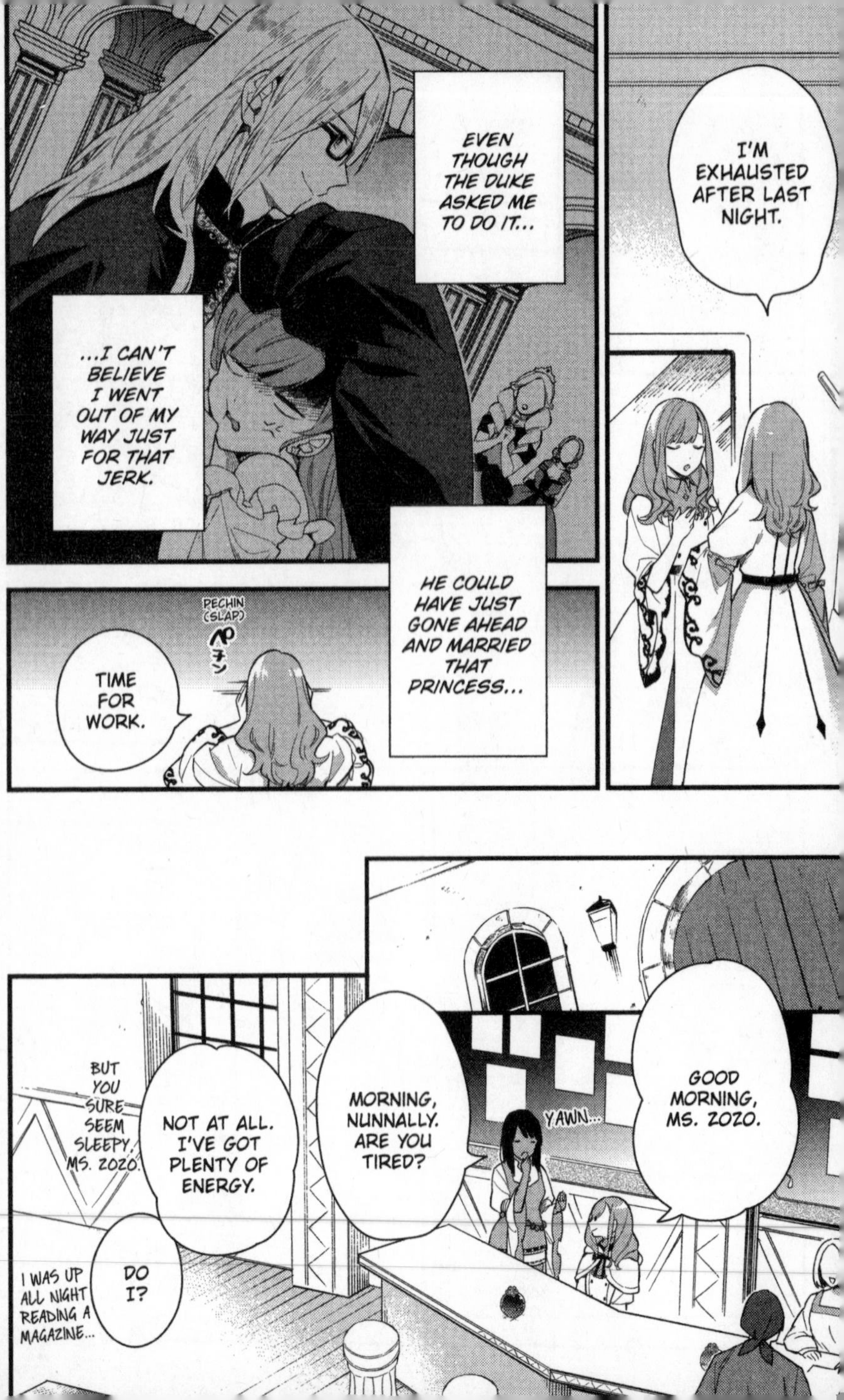
I'M EXHAUSTED AFTER LAST NIGHT.
EVEN THOUGH THE DUKE ASKED ME TO DO IT...
...I CAN'T BELIEVE I WENT OUT OF MY WAY JUST FOR THAT JERK.
HE COULD HAVE JUST GONE AHEAD AND MARRIED THAT PRINCESS...
PECHIN (SLAP)
TIME FOR WORK.
GOOD MORNING, MS. ZOZO.
YAWN...
MORNING, NUNNALLY. ARE YOU TIRED?
NOT AT ALL. I'VE GOT PLENTY OF ENERGY.
BUT YOU SURE SEEM SLEEPY, MS. ZOZO.
DO I?
I WAS UP ALL NIGHT READING A MAGAZINE...

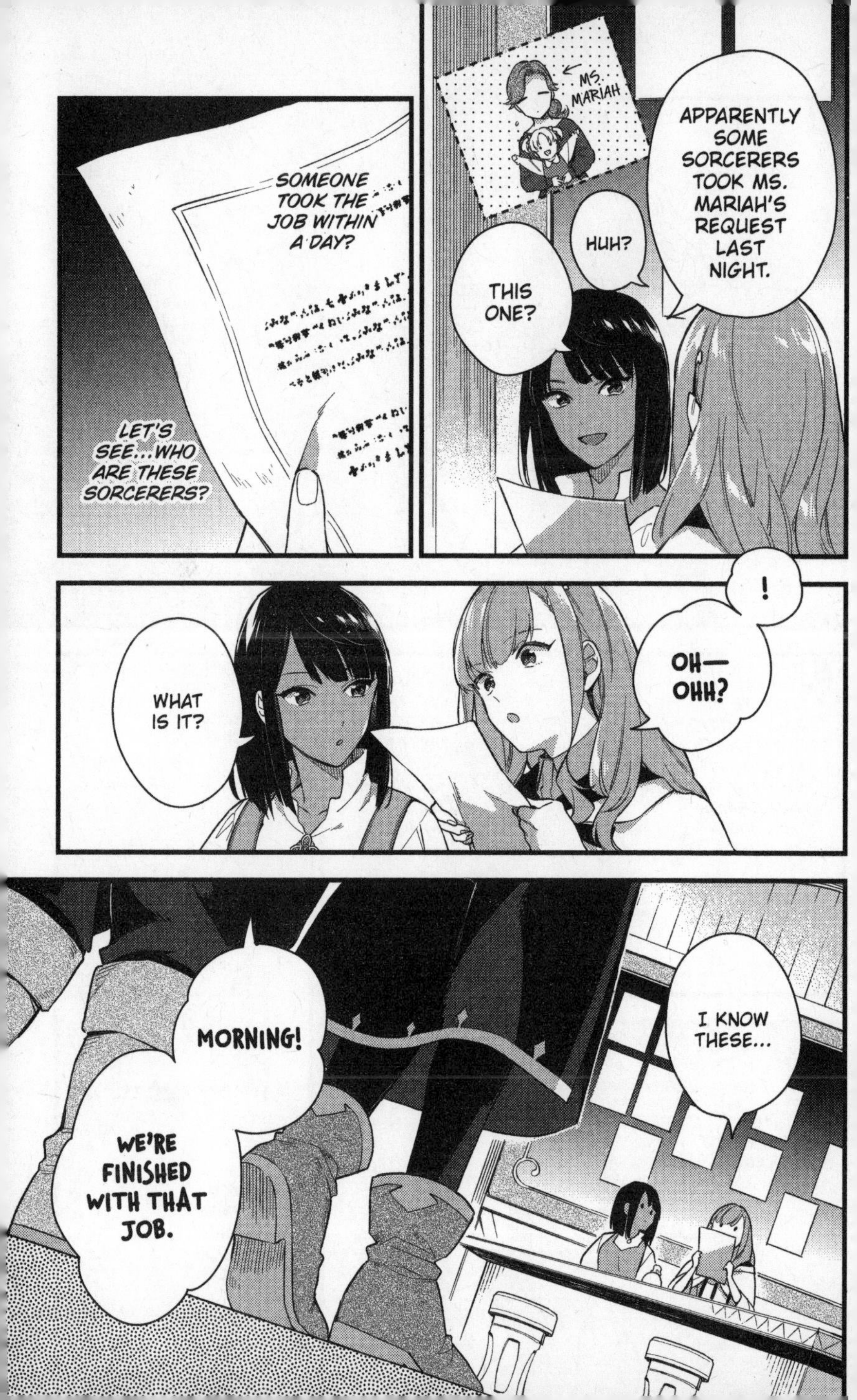
APPARENTLY SOME SORCERERS TOOK MS. MARIAH'S REQUEST LAST NIGHT.
MS. MARIAH
HUH?
THIS ONE?
SOMEONE TOOK THE JOB WITHIN A DAY?
LET'S SEE...WHO ARE THESE SORCERERS?
!
OH— OHH?
WHAT IS IT?
I KNOW THESE...
MORNING!
WE'RE FINISHED WITH THAT JOB.

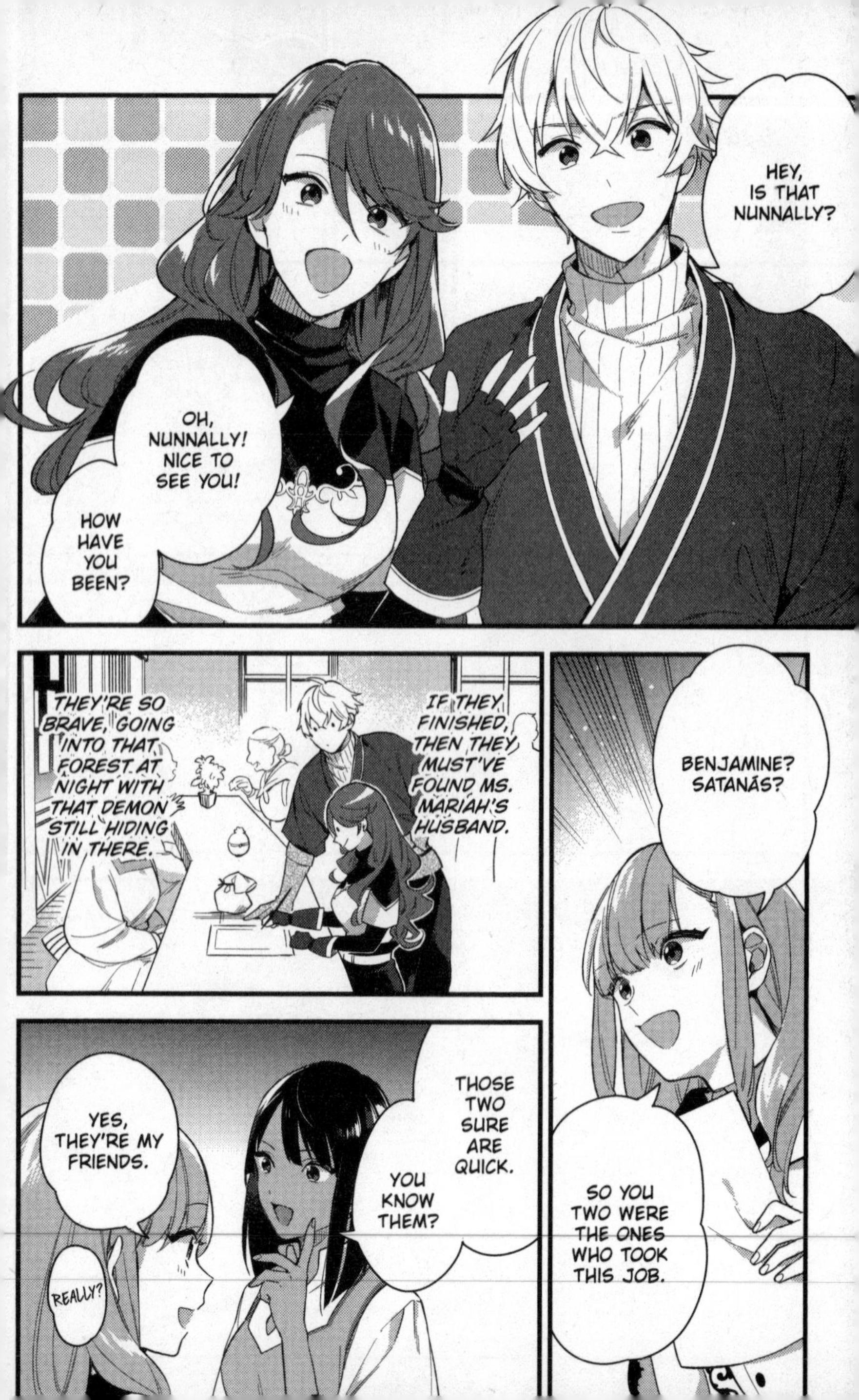
HEY, IS THAT NUNNALLY?
OH, NUNNALLY! NICE TO SEE YOU!
HOW HAVE YOU BEEN?
BENJAMINE? SATANÁS?
IF THEY FINISHED, THEN THEY MUST'VE FOUND MS. MARIAH'S HUSBAND.
THEY'RE SO BRAVE, GOING INTO THAT FOREST AT NIGHT WITH THAT DEMON STILL HIDING IN THERE.
SO YOU TWO WERE THE ONES WHO TOOK THIS JOB.
THOSE TWO SURE ARE QUICK.
YOU KNOW THEM?
YES, THEY'RE MY FRIENDS.
REALLY?

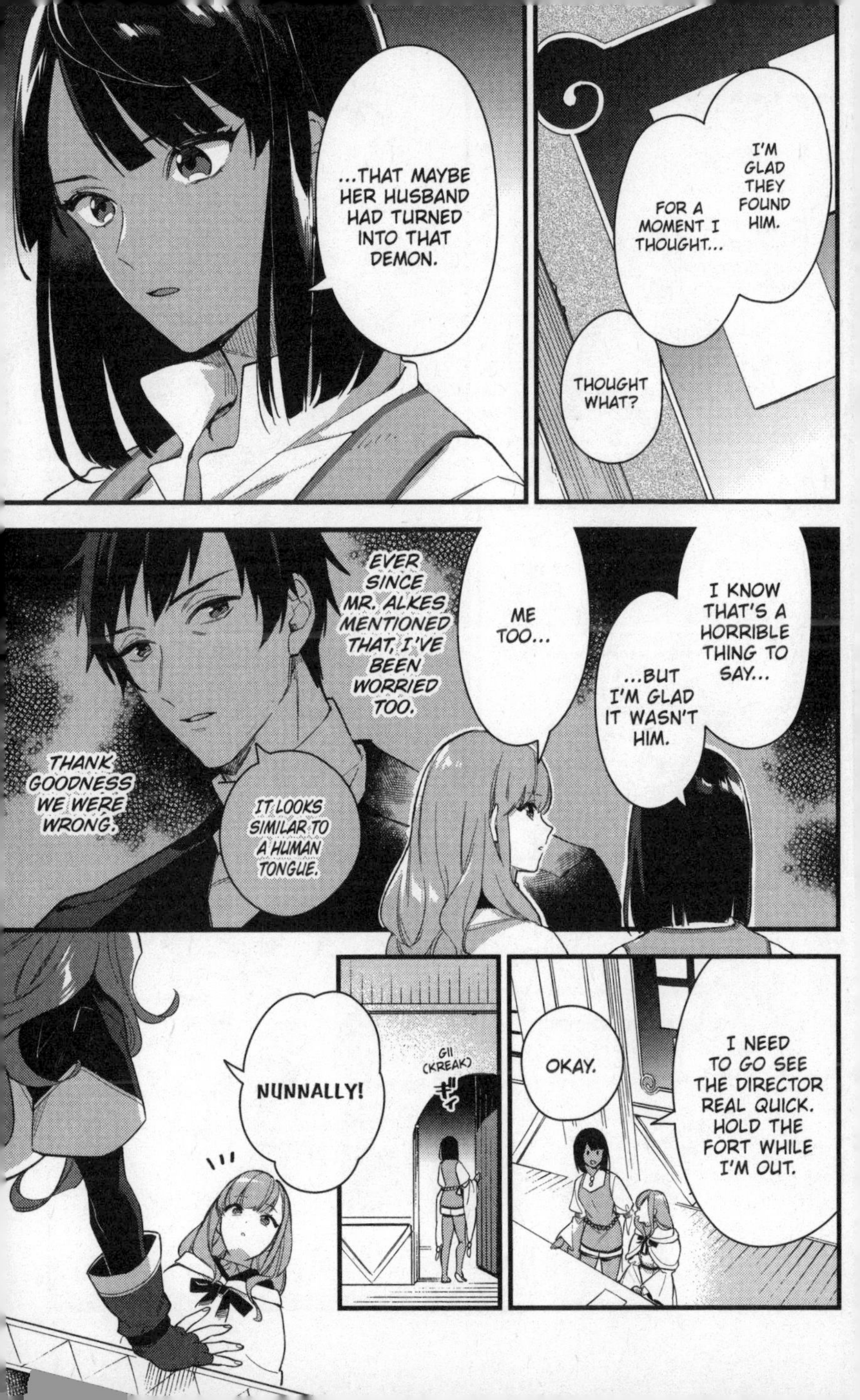
I'M GLAD THEY FOUND HIM.
FOR A MOMENT I THOUGHT...
THOUGHT WHAT?
...THAT MAYBE HER HUSBAND HAD TURNED INTO THAT DEMON.
I KNOW THAT'S A HORRIBLE THING TO SAY...
...BUT I'M GLAD IT WASN'T HIM.
ME TOO...
EVER SINCE MR. ALKES MENTIONED THAT, I'VE BEEN WORRIED TOO.
IT LOOKS SIMILAR TO A HUMAN TONGUE.
THANK GOODNESS WE WERE WRONG.
I NEED TO GO SEE THE DIRECTOR REAL QUICK. HOLD THE FORT WHILE I'M OUT.
OKAY.
GII (KREAK)
NUNNALLY!

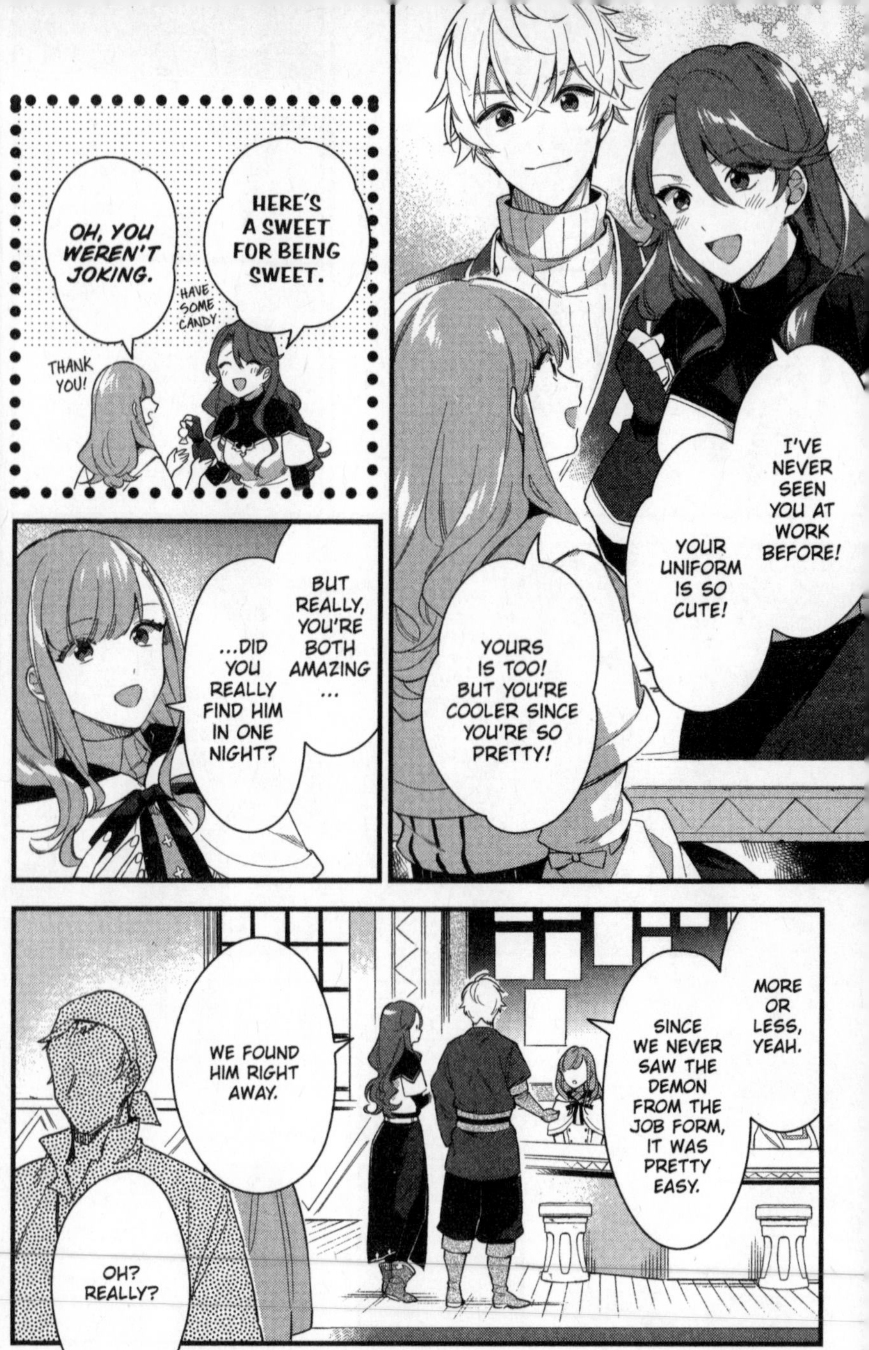
I'VE NEVER SEEN YOU AT WORK BEFORE!
YOUR UNIFORM IS SO CUTE!
YOURS IS TOO! BUT YOU'RE COOLER SINCE YOU'RE SO PRETTY!
HERE'S A SWEET FOR BEING SWEET.
HAVE SOME CANDY
OH, YOU WEREN'T JOKING.
THANK YOU!
BUT REALLY, YOU'RE BOTH AMAZING ...
...DID YOU REALLY FIND HIM IN ONE NIGHT?
MORE OR LESS, YEAH.
SINCE WE NEVER SAW THE DEMON FROM THE JOB FORM, IT WAS PRETTY EASY.
WE FOUND HIM RIGHT AWAY.
OH? REALLY?

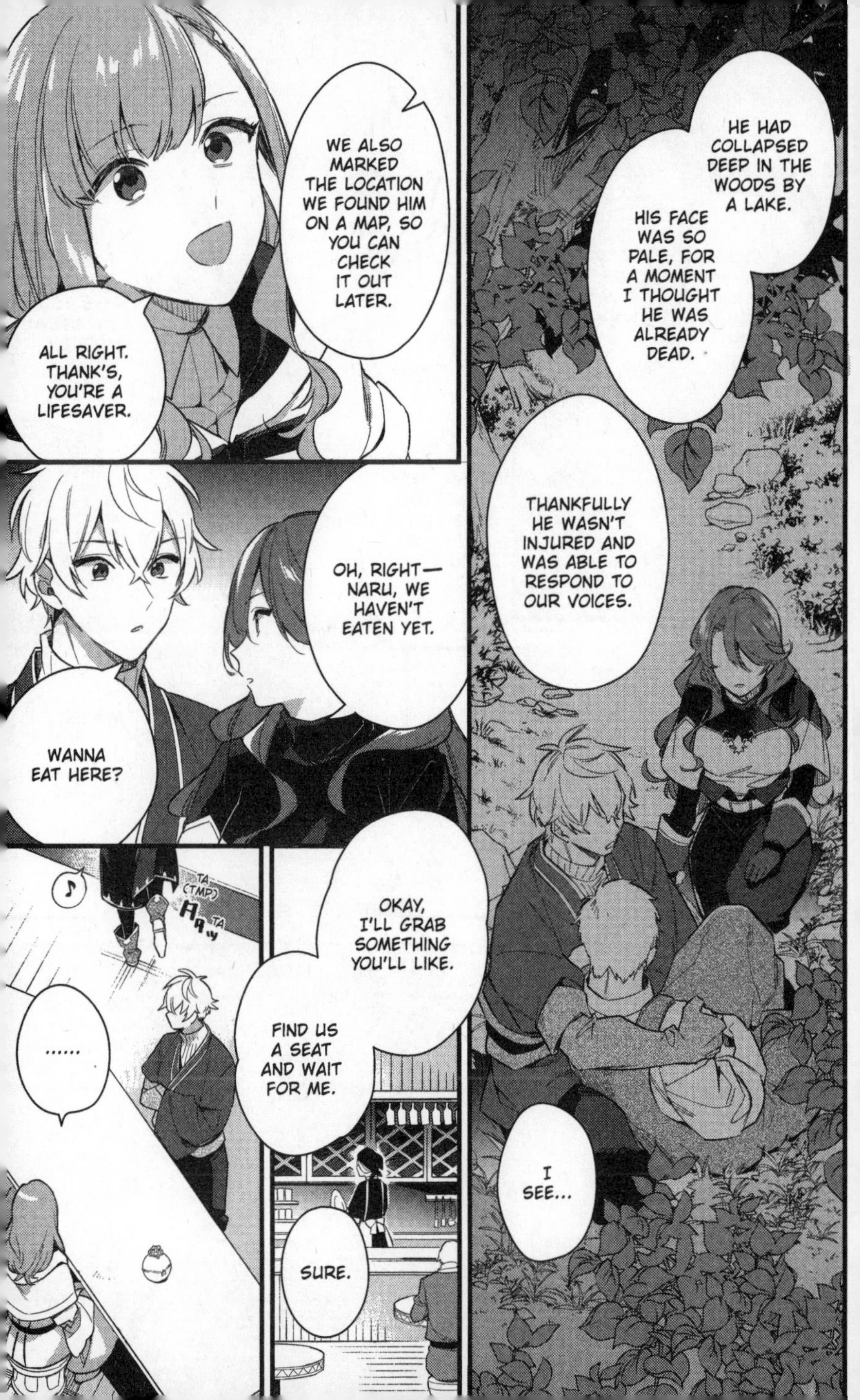
HE HAD COLLAPSED DEEP IN THE WOODS BY A LAKE.
HIS FACE WAS SO PALE, FOR A MOMENT I THOUGHT HE WAS ALREADY DEAD.
THANKFULLY HE WASN'T INJURED AND WAS ABLE TO RESPOND TO OUR VOICES.
I SEE...
WE ALSO MARKED THE LOCATION WE FOUND HIM ON A MAP, SO YOU CAN CHECK IT OUT LATER.
ALL RIGHT. THANK'S, YOU'RE A LIFESAVER.
OH, RIGHT— NARU, WE HAVEN'T EATEN YET.
WANNA EAT HERE?
OKAY, I'LL GRAB SOMETHING YOU'LL LIKE.
FIND US A SEAT AND WAIT FOR ME.
SURE.
♪
TA TA (TMP)
......

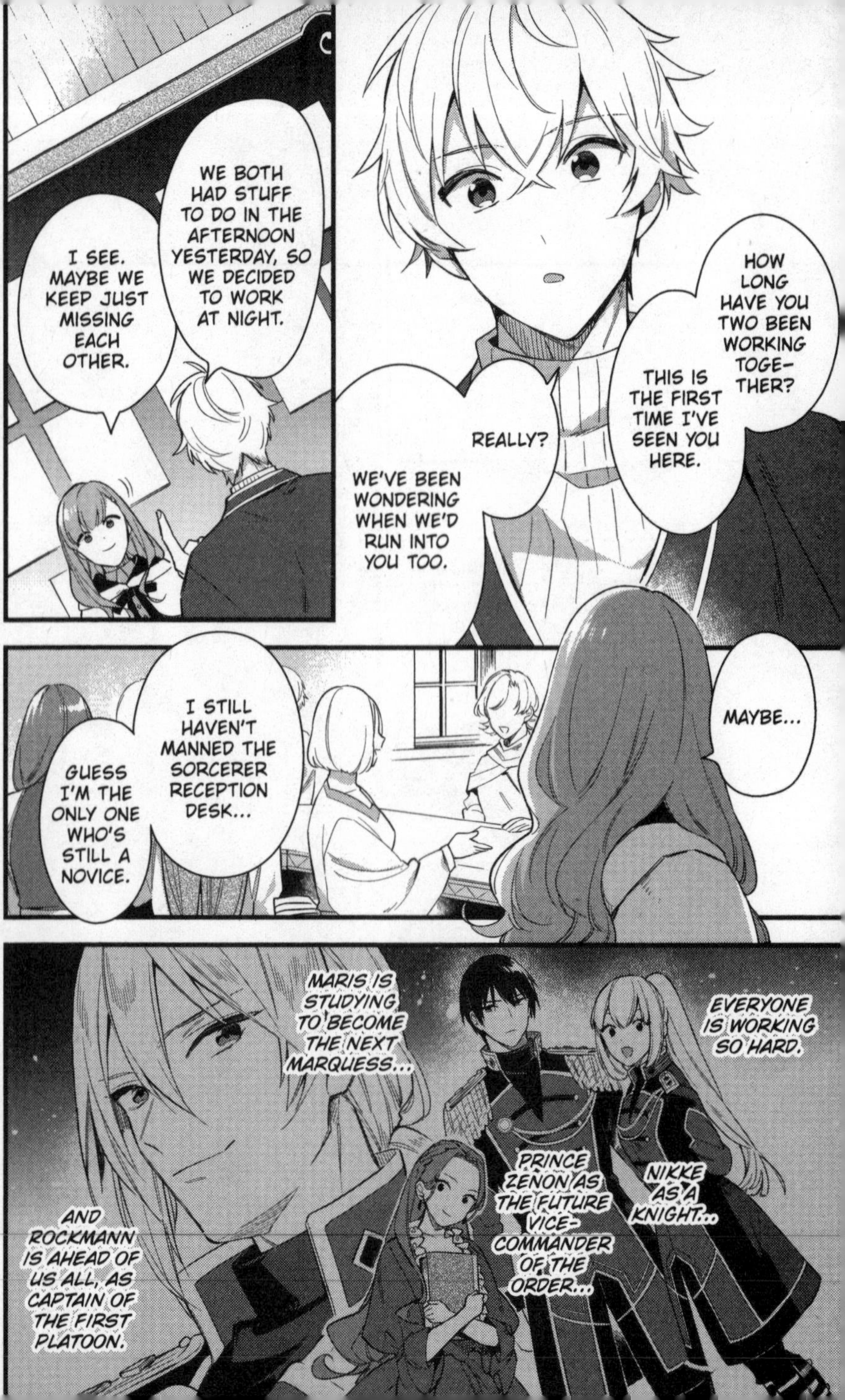
HOW LONG HAVE YOU TWO BEEN WORKING TOGE-THER?
THIS IS THE FIRST TIME I'VE SEEN YOU HERE.
REALLY?
WE'VE BEEN WONDERING WHEN WE'D RUN INTO YOU TOO.
WE BOTH HAD STUFF TO DO IN THE AFTERNOON YESTERDAY, SO WE DECIDED TO WORK AT NIGHT.
I SEE. MAYBE WE KEEP JUST MISSING EACH OTHER.
MAYBE...
I STILL HAVEN'T MANNED THE SORCERER RECEPTION DESK...
GUESS I'M THE ONLY ONE WHO'S STILL A NOVICE.
EVERYONE IS WORKING SO HARD.
MARIS IS STUDYING TO BECOME THE NEXT MARQUESS...
NIKKE AS A KNIGHT...
PRINCE ZENON AS THE FUTURE VICE-COMMANDER OF THE ORDER...
AND ROCKMANN IS AHEAD OF US ALL, AS CAPTAIN OF THE FIRST PLATOON.

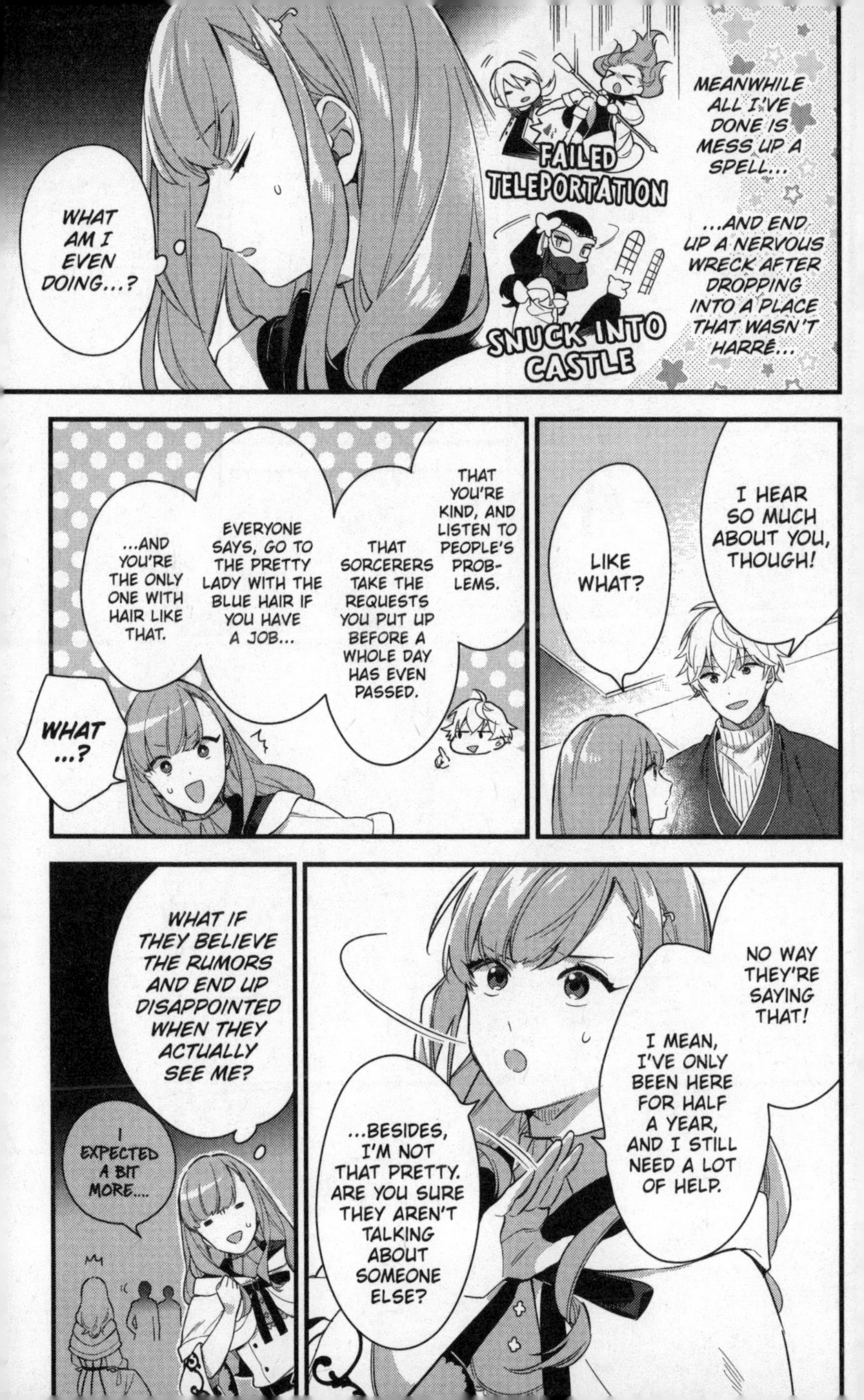
MEANWHILE ALL I'VE DONE IS MESS UP A SPELL...
FAILED TELEPORTATION
...AND END UP A NERVOUS WRECK AFTER DROPPING INTO A PLACE THAT WASN'T HARRÉ...
SNUCK INTO CASTLE
WHAT AM I EVEN DOING...?
I HEAR SO MUCH ABOUT YOU, THOUGH!
LIKE WHAT?
THAT YOU'RE KIND, AND LISTEN TO PEOPLE'S PROB-LEMS.
THAT SORCERERS TAKE THE REQUESTS YOU PUT UP BEFORE A WHOLE DAY HAS EVEN PASSED.
EVERYONE SAYS, GO TO THE PRETTY LADY WITH THE BLUE HAIR IF YOU HAVE A JOB...
...AND YOU'RE THE ONLY ONE WITH HAIR LIKE THAT.
WHAT ...?
NO WAY THEY'RE SAYING THAT!
I MEAN, I'VE ONLY BEEN HERE FOR HALF A YEAR, AND I STILL NEED A LOT OF HELP.
...BESIDES, I'M NOT THAT PRETTY. ARE YOU SURE THEY AREN'T TALKING ABOUT SOMEONE ELSE?
WHAT IF THEY BELIEVE THE RUMORS AND END UP DISAPPOINTED WHEN THEY ACTUALLY SEE ME?
I EXPECTED A BIT MORE...

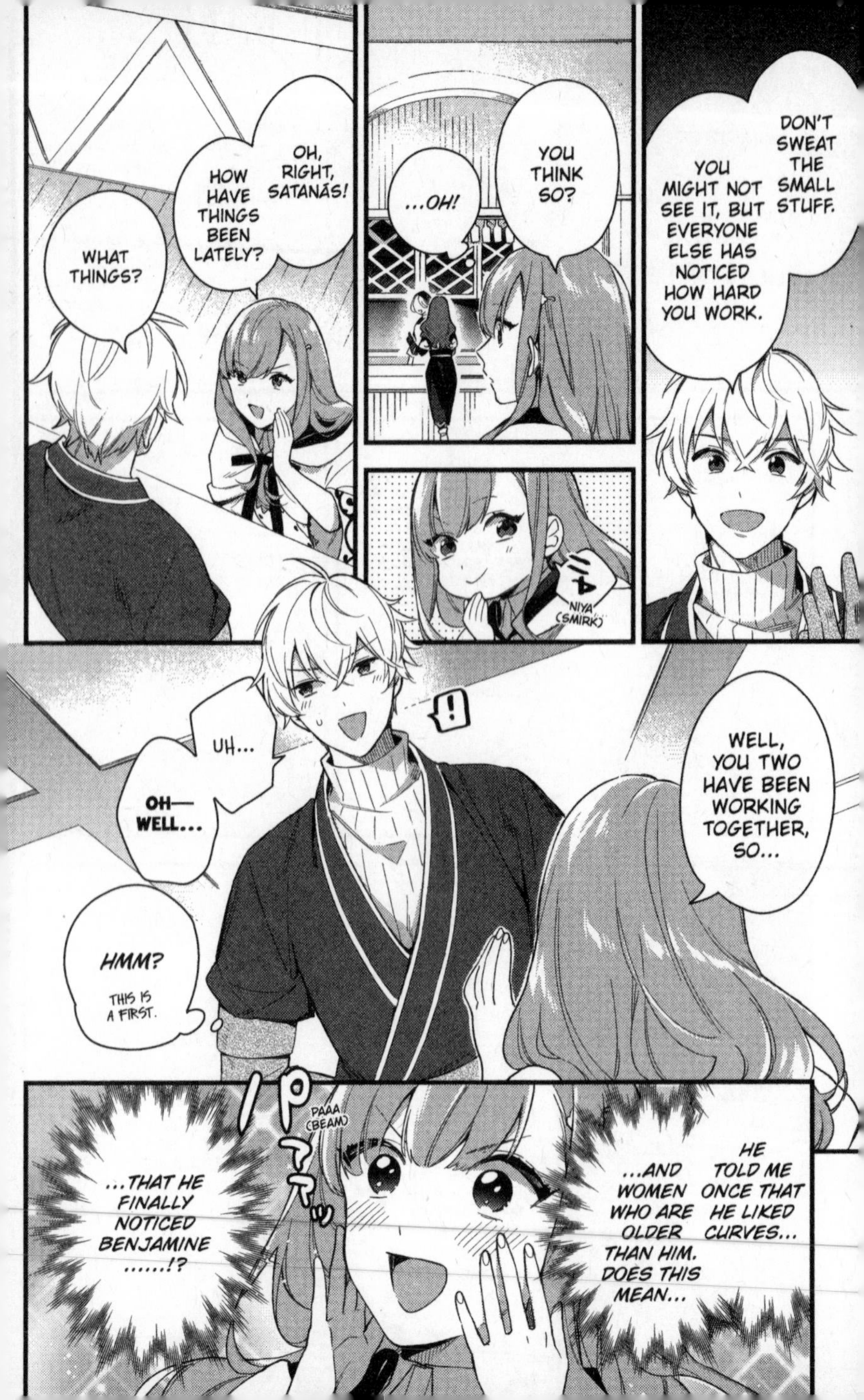
DON'T SWEAT THE SMALL STUFF.
YOU MIGHT NOT SEE IT, BUT EVERYONE ELSE HAS NOTICED HOW HARD YOU WORK.
YOU THINK SO?
...OH!
NIYA (SMIRK)
OH, RIGHT, SATANÁS!
HOW HAVE THINGS BEEN LATELY?
WHAT THINGS?
WELL, YOU TWO HAVE BEEN WORKING TOGETHER, SO...
!
UH...
OH— WELL...
HMM?
THIS IS A FIRST.
HE TOLD ME ONCE THAT HE LIKED CURVES...
...AND WOMEN WHO ARE OLDER THAN HIM. DOES THIS MEAN...
PAAA (BEAM)
...THAT HE FINALLY NOTICED BENJAMINE ......!?

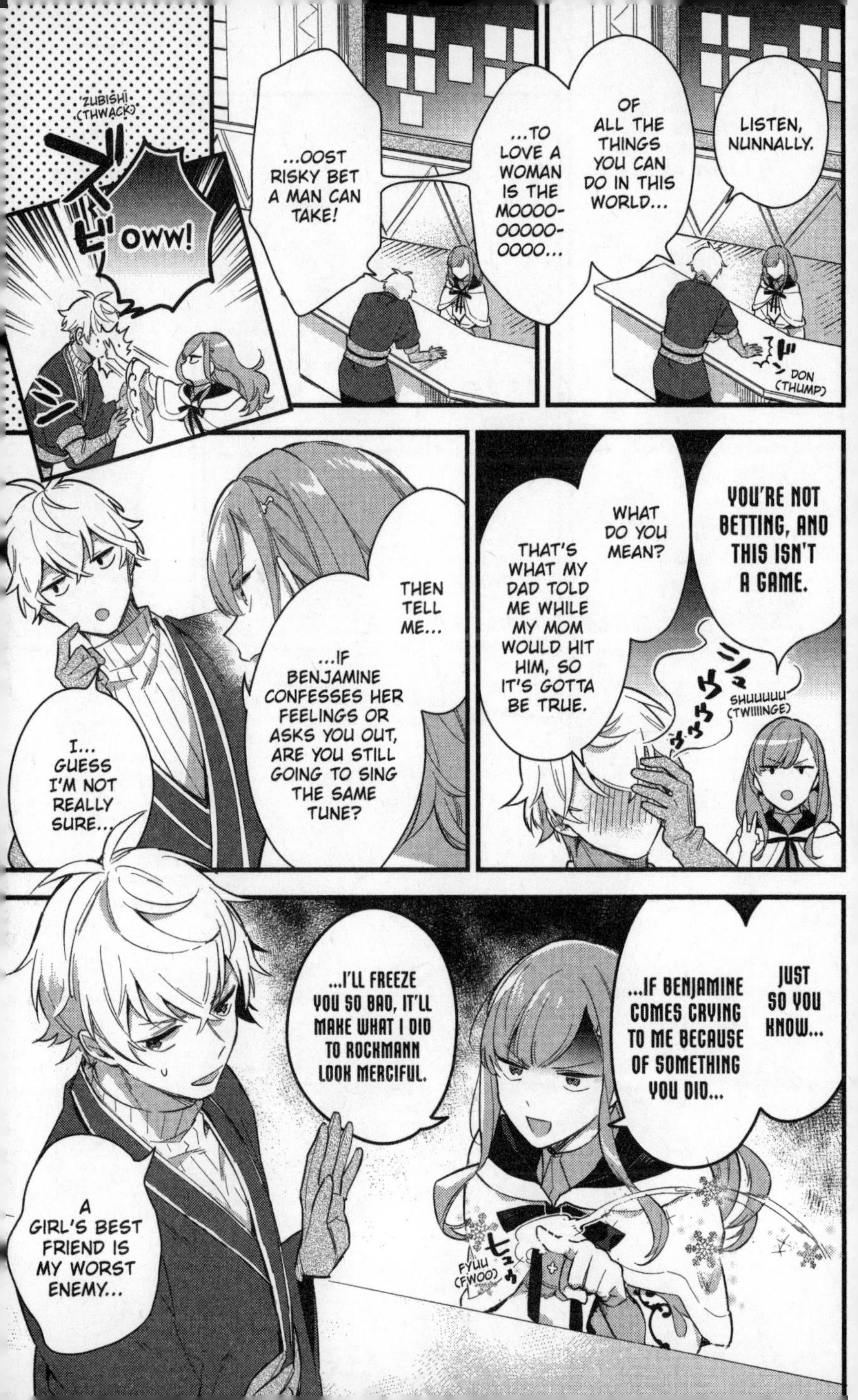
LISTEN, NUNNALLY.
DON (THUMP)
OF ALL THE THINGS YOU CAN DO IN THIS WORLD...
...TO LOVE A WOMAN IS THE MOOOO-OOOOO-OOOO...
...OOST RISKY BET A MAN CAN TAKE!
ZUBISHI (THWACK)
OWW!
YOU'RE NOT BETTING, AND THIS ISN'T A GAME.
WHAT DO YOU MEAN?
THAT'S WHAT MY DAD TOLD ME WHILE MY MOM WOULD HIT HIM, SO IT'S GOTTA BE TRUE.
SHUUUUU (TWIIIINGE)
THEN TELL ME...
...IF BENJAMINE CONFESSES HER FEELINGS OR ASKS YOU OUT, ARE YOU STILL GOING TO SING THE SAME TUNE?
I... GUESS I'M NOT REALLY SURE...
JUST SO YOU KNOW...
...IF BENJAMINE COMES CRYING TO ME BECAUSE OF SOMETHING YOU DID...
...I'LL FREEZE YOU SO BAD, IT'LL MAKE WHAT I DID TO ROCKMANN LOOK MERCIFUL.
FYUU (FWOO)
A GIRL'S BEST FRIEND IS MY WORST ENEMY...

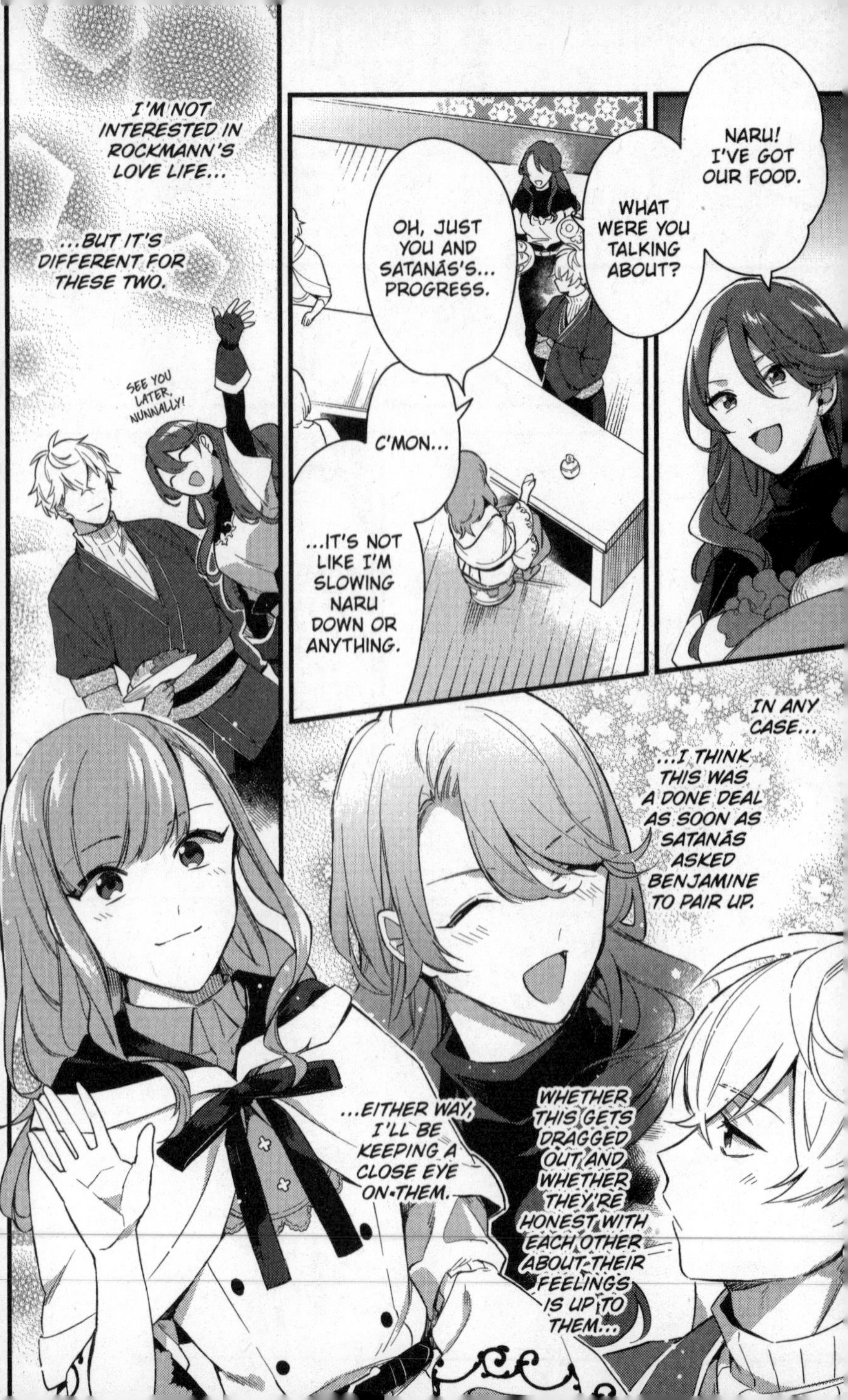
NARU! I'VE GOT OUR FOOD.
WHAT WERE YOU TALKING ABOUT?
OH, JUST YOU AND SATANÁS'S... PROGRESS.
C'MON...
...IT'S NOT LIKE I'M SLOWING NARU DOWN OR ANYTHING.
I'M NOT INTERESTED IN ROCKMANN'S LOVE LIFE...
...BUT IT'S DIFFERENT FOR THESE TWO.
SEE YOU LATER, NUNNALLY!
IN ANY CASE...
...I THINK THIS WAS A DONE DEAL AS SOON AS SATANÁS ASKED BENJAMINE TO PAIR UP.
WHETHER THIS GETS DRAGGED OUT AND WHETHER THEY'RE HONEST WITH EACH OTHER ABOUT THEIR FEELINGS IS UP TO THEM...
...EITHER WAY, I'LL BE KEEPING A CLOSE EYE ON THEM.

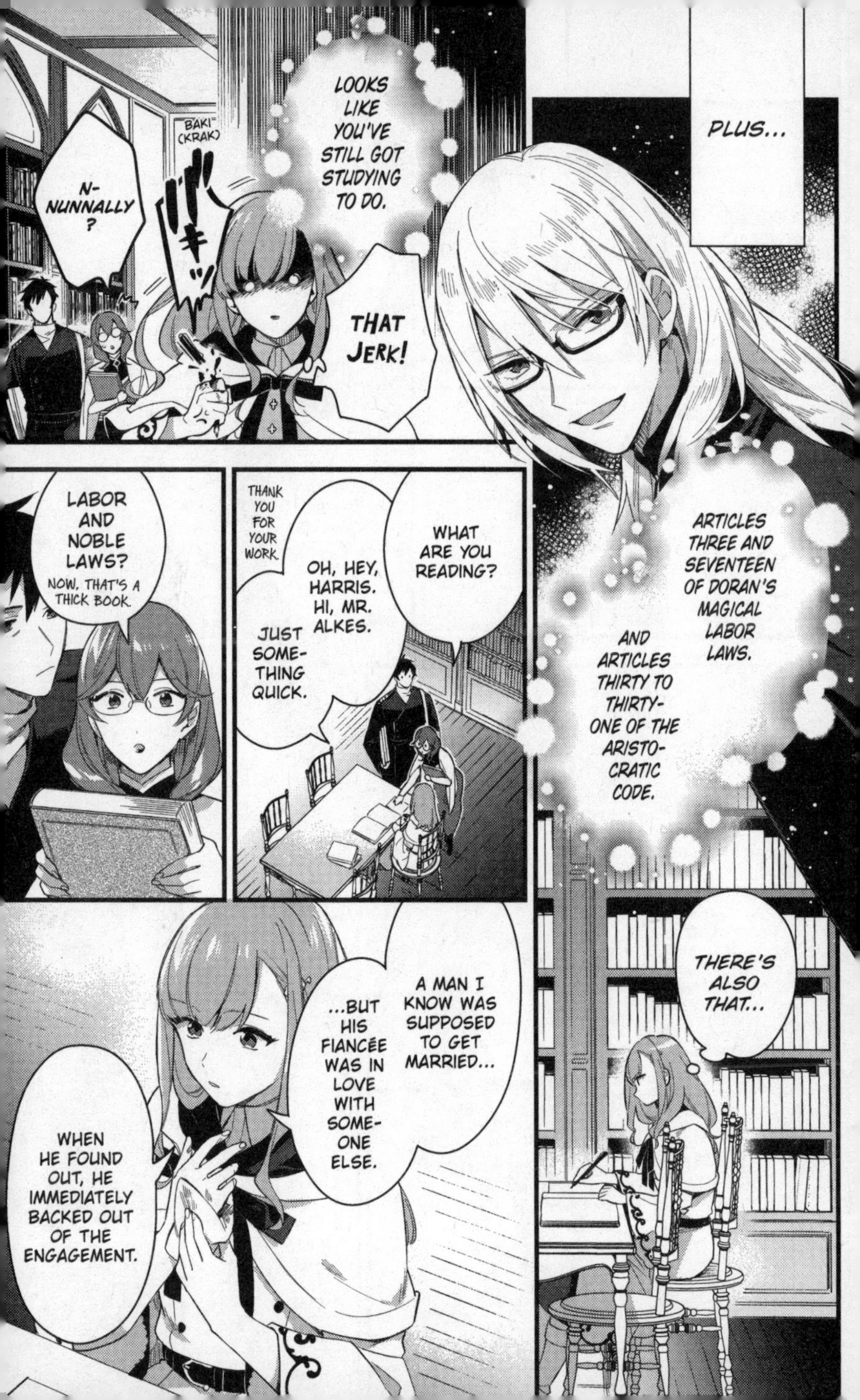
PLUS...
ARTICLES THREE AND SEVENTEEN OF DORAN'S MAGICAL LABOR LAWS.
AND ARTICLES THIRTY TO THIRTY-ONE OF THE ARISTO-CRATIC CODE.
THERE'S ALSO THAT...
LOOKS LIKE YOU'VE STILL GOT STUDYING TO DO.
THAT JERK!
BAKI (KRAK)
N-NUNNALLY?
WHAT ARE YOU READING?
OH, HEY, HARRIS. HI, MR. ALKES.
THANK YOU FOR YOUR WORK.
JUST SOME-THING QUICK.
LABOR AND NOBLE LAWS?
NOW, THAT'S A THICK BOOK.
A MAN I KNOW WAS SUPPOSED TO GET MARRIED...
...BUT HIS FIANCÉE WAS IN LOVE WITH SOME-ONE ELSE.
WHEN HE FOUND OUT, HE IMMEDIATELY BACKED OUT OF THE ENGAGEMENT.

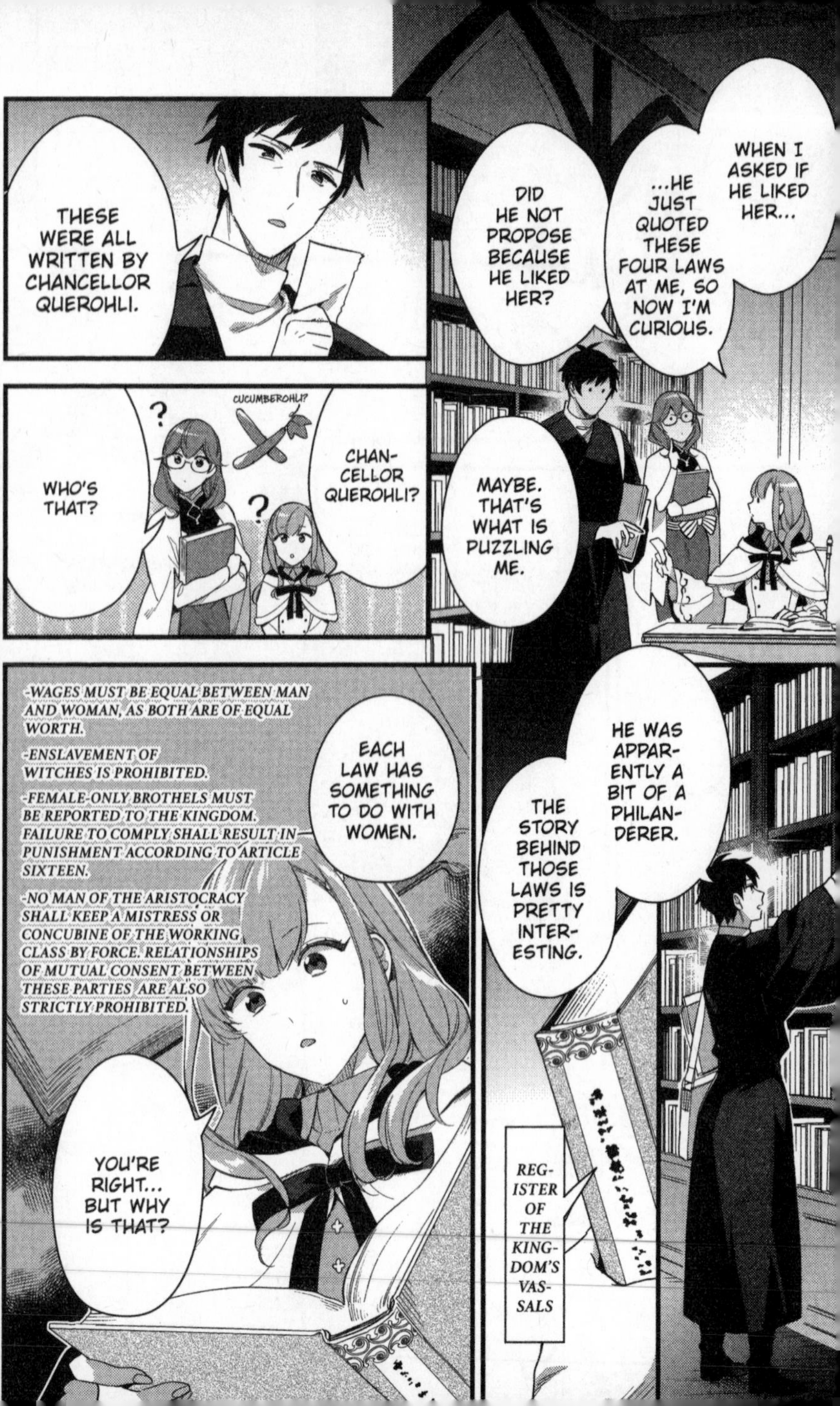
WHEN I ASKED IF HE LIKED HER...
...HE JUST QUOTED THESE FOUR LAWS AT ME, SO NOW I'M CURIOUS.
DID HE NOT PROPOSE BECAUSE HE LIKED HER?
MAYBE. THAT'S WHAT IS PUZZLING ME.
THESE WERE ALL WRITTEN BY CHANCELLOR QUEROHLI.
CHAN-CELLOR QUEROHLI?
CUCUMBEROHLI?
WHO'S THAT?
HE WAS APPARENTLY A BIT OF A PHILANDERER.
THE STORY BEHIND THOSE LAWS IS PRETTY INTERESTING.
REGISTER OF THE KINGDOM'S VASSALS
-WAGES MUST BE EQUAL BETWEEN MAN AND WOMAN, AS BOTH ARE OF EQUAL WORTH.
-ENSLAVEMENT OF WITCHES IS PROHIBITED.
-FEMALE-ONLY BROTHELS MUST BE REPORTED TO THE KINGDOM. FAILURE TO COMPLY SHALL RESULT IN PUNISHMENT ACCORDING TO ARTICLE SIXTEEN.
-NO MAN OF THE ARISTOCRACY SHALL KEEP A MISTRESS OR CONCUBINE OF THE WORKING CLASS BY FORCE. RELATIONSHIPS OF MUTUAL CONSENT BETWEEN THESE PARTIES ARE ALSO STRICTLY PROHIBITED.
EACH LAW HAS SOMETHING TO DO WITH WOMEN.
YOU'RE RIGHT... BUT WHY IS THAT?

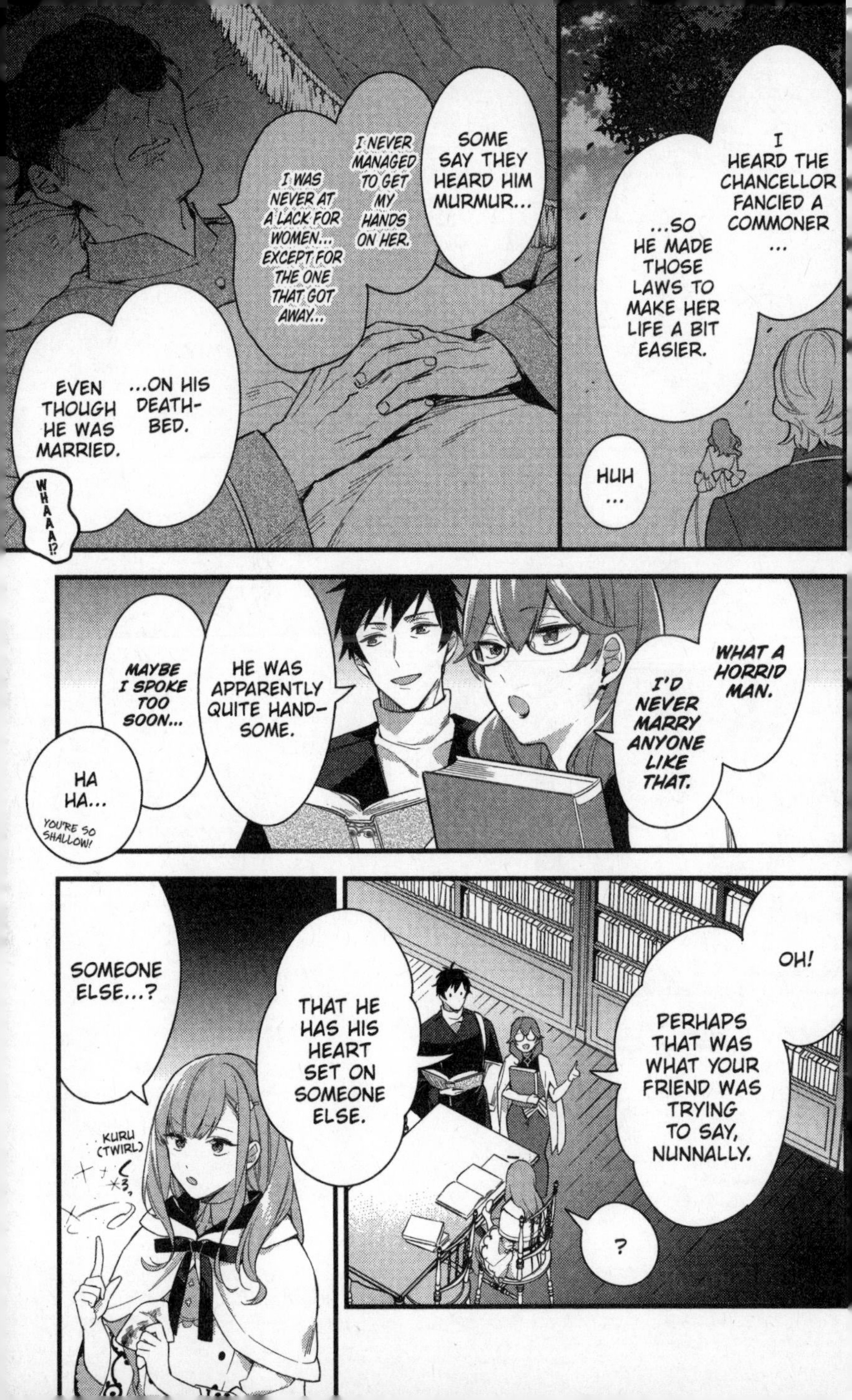
I HEARD THE CHANCELLOR FANCIED A COMMONER ...
...SO HE MADE THOSE LAWS TO MAKE HER LIFE A BIT EASIER.
HUH ...
SOME SAY THEY HEARD HIM MURMUR...
I NEVER MANAGED TO GET MY HANDS ON HER.
I WAS NEVER AT A LACK FOR WOMEN... EXCEPT FOR THE ONE THAT GOT AWAY...
...ON HIS DEATH-BED.
EVEN THOUGH HE WAS MARRIED.
WHAAAA!?
WHAT A HORRID MAN.
I'D NEVER MARRY ANYONE LIKE THAT.
HE WAS APPARENTLY QUITE HAND-SOME.
MAYBE I SPOKE TOO SOON...
HA HA...
YOU'RE SO SHALLOW!
OH!
PERHAPS THAT WAS WHAT YOUR FRIEND WAS TRYING TO SAY, NUNNALLY.
?
THAT HE HAS HIS HEART SET ON SOMEONE ELSE.
SOMEONE ELSE...?
KURU (TWIRL)

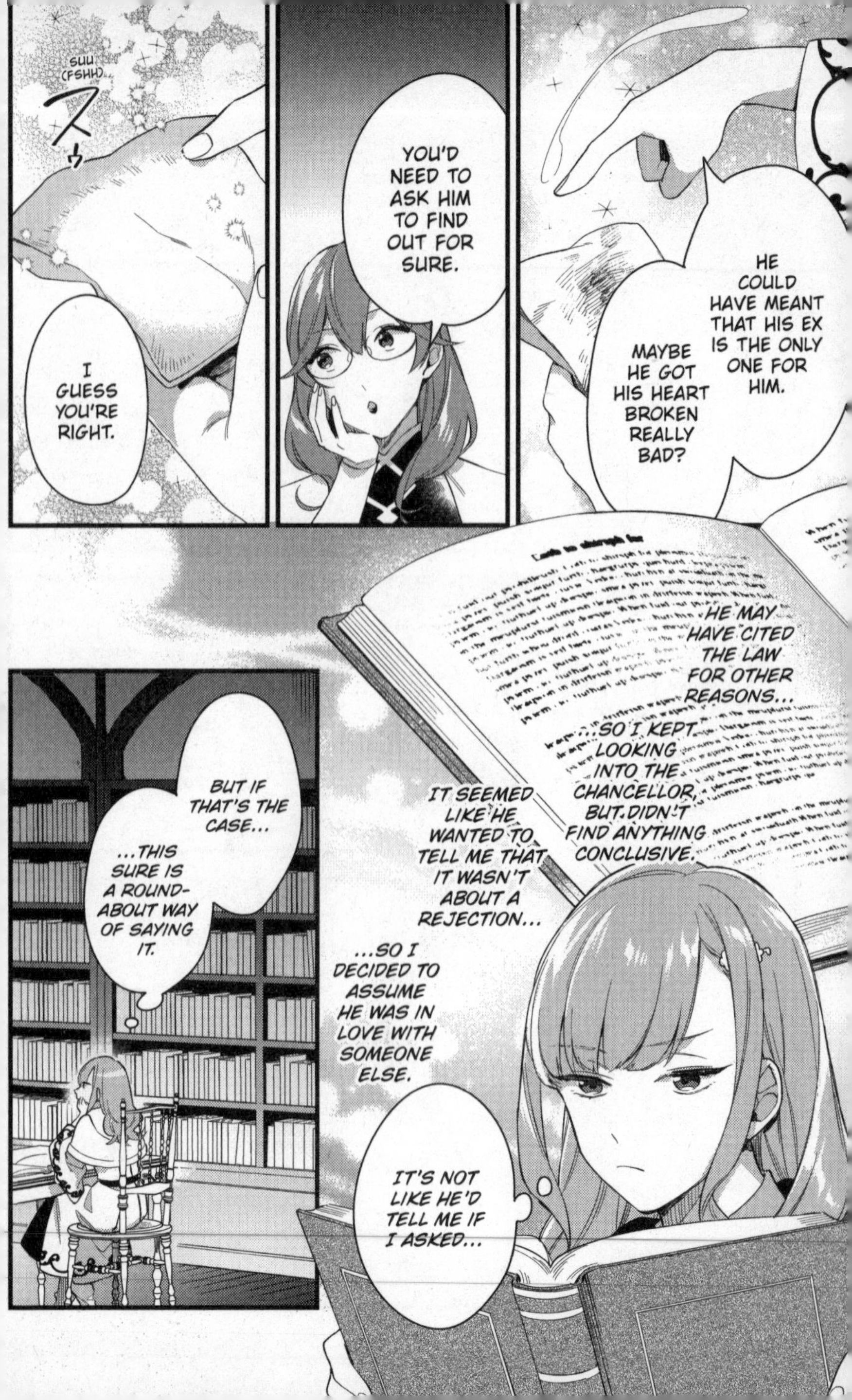
HE COULD HAVE MEANT THAT HIS EX IS THE ONLY ONE FOR HIM.
MAYBE HE GOT HIS HEART BROKEN REALLY BAD?
YOU'D NEED TO ASK HIM TO FIND OUT FOR SURE.
SUU (FSHH)
I GUESS YOU'RE RIGHT.
HE MAY HAVE CITED THE LAW FOR OTHER REASONS...
...SO I KEPT LOOKING INTO THE CHANCELLOR, BUT DIDN'T FIND ANYTHING CONCLUSIVE.
IT SEEMED LIKE HE WANTED TO TELL ME THAT IT WASN'T ABOUT A REJECTION...
...SO I DECIDED TO ASSUME HE WAS IN LOVE WITH SOMEONE ELSE.
IT'S NOT LIKE HE'D TELL ME IF I ASKED...
BUT IF THAT'S THE CASE...
...THIS SURE IS A ROUND-ABOUT WAY OF SAYING IT.

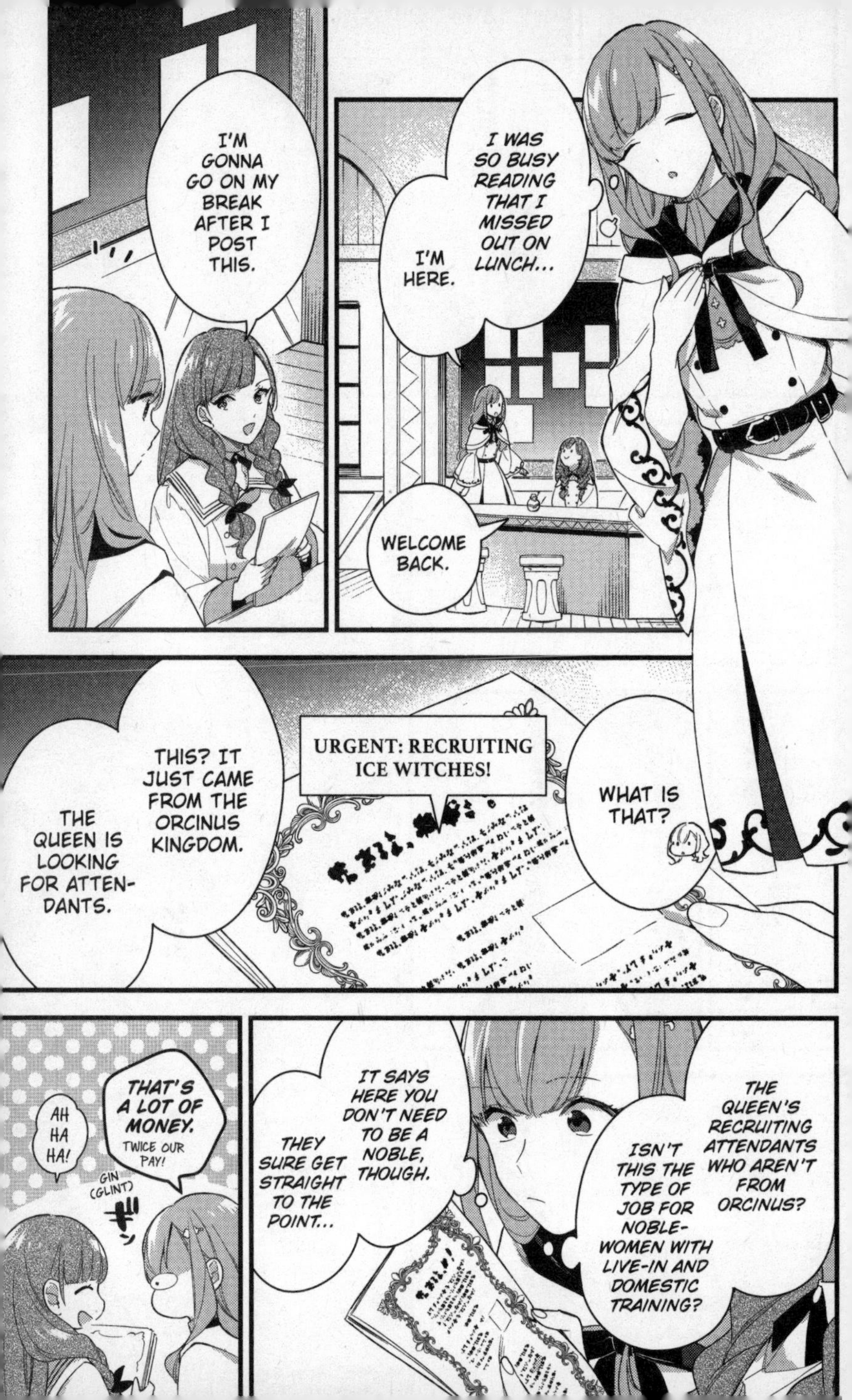
I WAS SO BUSY READING THAT I MISSED OUT ON LUNCH...
I'M HERE.
WELCOME BACK.
I'M GONNA GO ON MY BREAK AFTER I POST THIS.
WHAT IS THAT?
URGENT: RECRUITING ICE WITCHES!
THIS? IT JUST CAME FROM THE ORCINUS KINGDOM.
THE QUEEN IS LOOKING FOR ATTEN-DANTS.
THE QUEEN'S RECRUITING ATTENDANTS WHO AREN'T FROM ORCINUS?
ISN'T THIS THE TYPE OF JOB FOR NOBLE-WOMEN WITH LIVE-IN AND DOMESTIC TRAINING?
IT SAYS HERE YOU DON'T NEED TO BE A NOBLE, THOUGH.
THEY SURE GET STRAIGHT TO THE POINT...
THAT'S A LOT OF MONEY.
TWICE OUR PAY!
AH HA HA!
GIN (GLINT)

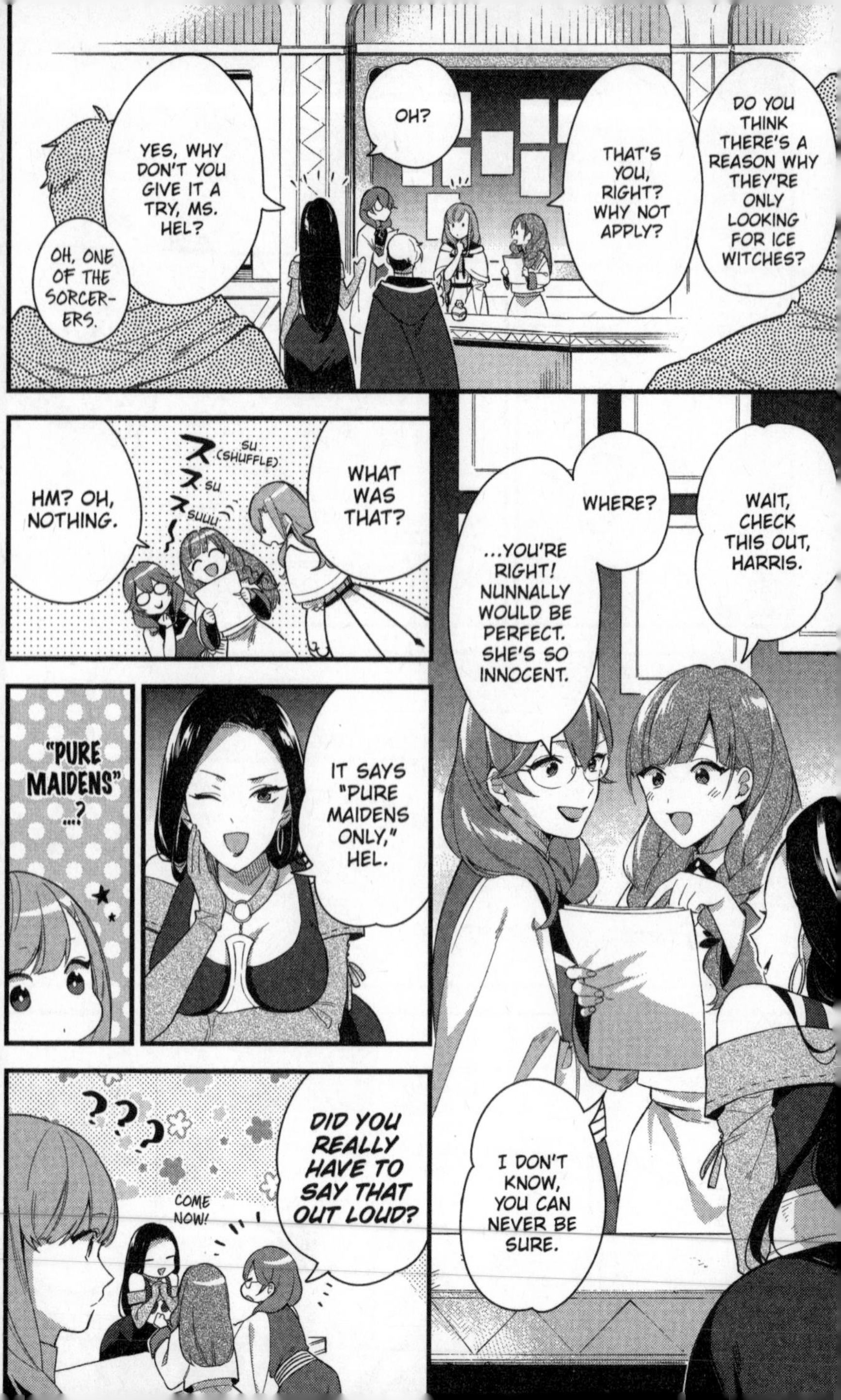
DO YOU THINK THERE'S A REASON WHY THEY'RE ONLY LOOKING FOR ICE WITCHES?
THAT'S YOU, RIGHT? WHY NOT APPLY?
OH?
YES, WHY DON'T YOU GIVE IT A TRY, MS. HEL?
OH, ONE OF THE SORCERERS.
WAIT, CHECK THIS OUT, HARRIS.
WHERE?
...YOU'RE RIGHT! NUNNALLY WOULD BE PERFECT. SHE'S SO INNOCENT.
I DON'T KNOW, YOU CAN NEVER BE SURE.
WHAT WAS THAT?
SU (SHUFFLE)
SU
SUUU
HM? OH, NOTHING.
IT SAYS "PURE MAIDENS ONLY," HEL.
"PURE MAIDENS" ...?
DID YOU REALLY HAVE TO SAY THAT OUT LOUD?
COME NOW!

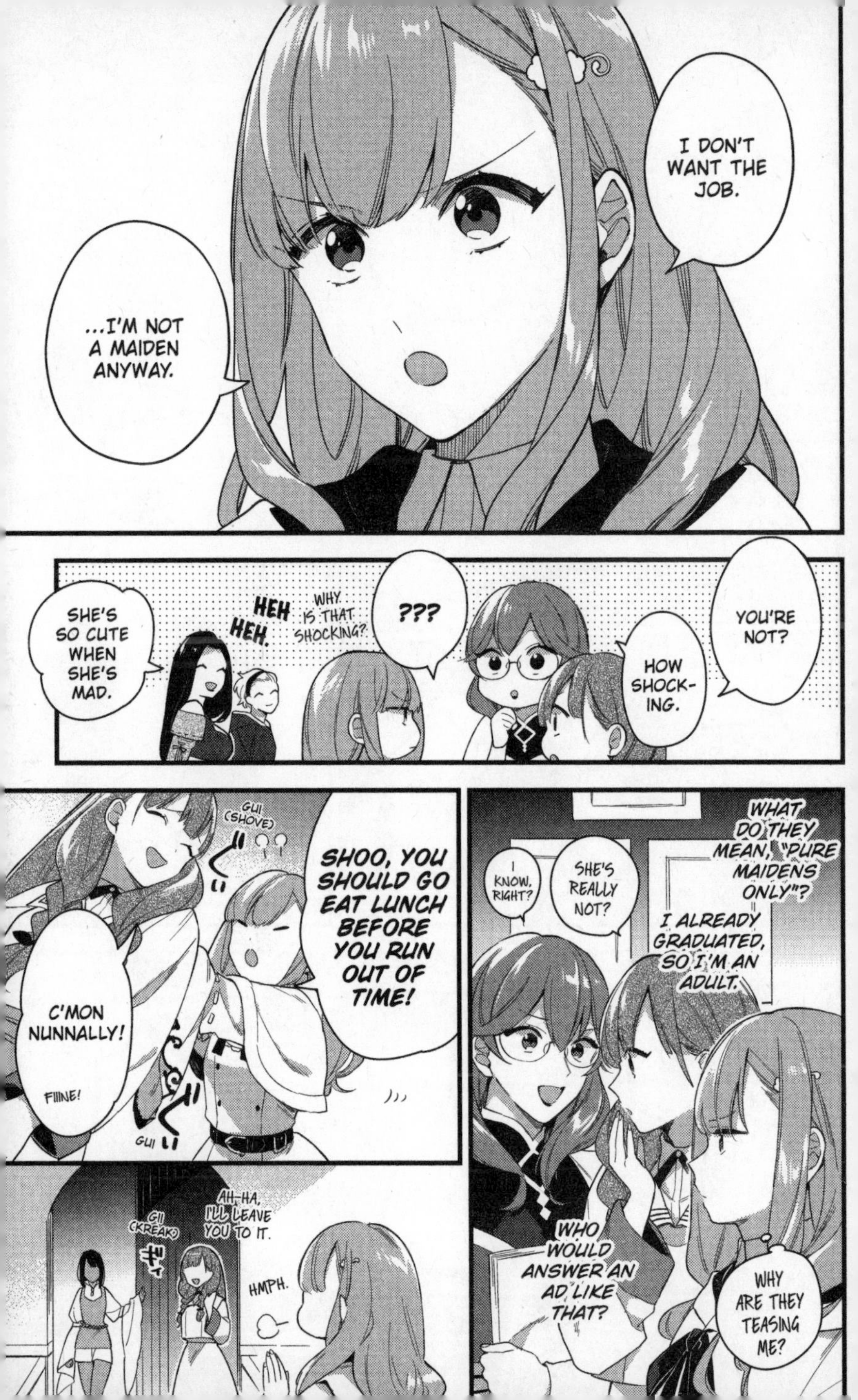
I DON'T WANT THE JOB.
...I'M NOT A MAIDEN ANYWAY.
YOU'RE NOT?
HOW SHOCKING.
???
WHY IS THAT SHOCKING?
HEH HEH.
SHE'S SO CUTE WHEN SHE'S MAD.
WHAT DO THEY MEAN, "PURE MAIDENS ONLY"?
I ALREADY GRADUATED, SO I'M AN ADULT.
SHE'S REALLY NOT?
I KNOW, RIGHT?
WHO WOULD ANSWER AN AD LIKE THAT?
WHY ARE THEY TEASING ME?
GUI (SHOVE)
SHOO, YOU SHOULD GO EAT LUNCH BEFORE YOU RUN OUT OF TIME!
C'MON NUNNALLY!
FIIINE!
GUI
AH-HA, I'LL LEAVE YOU TO IT.
GII (KREAK)
HMPH.

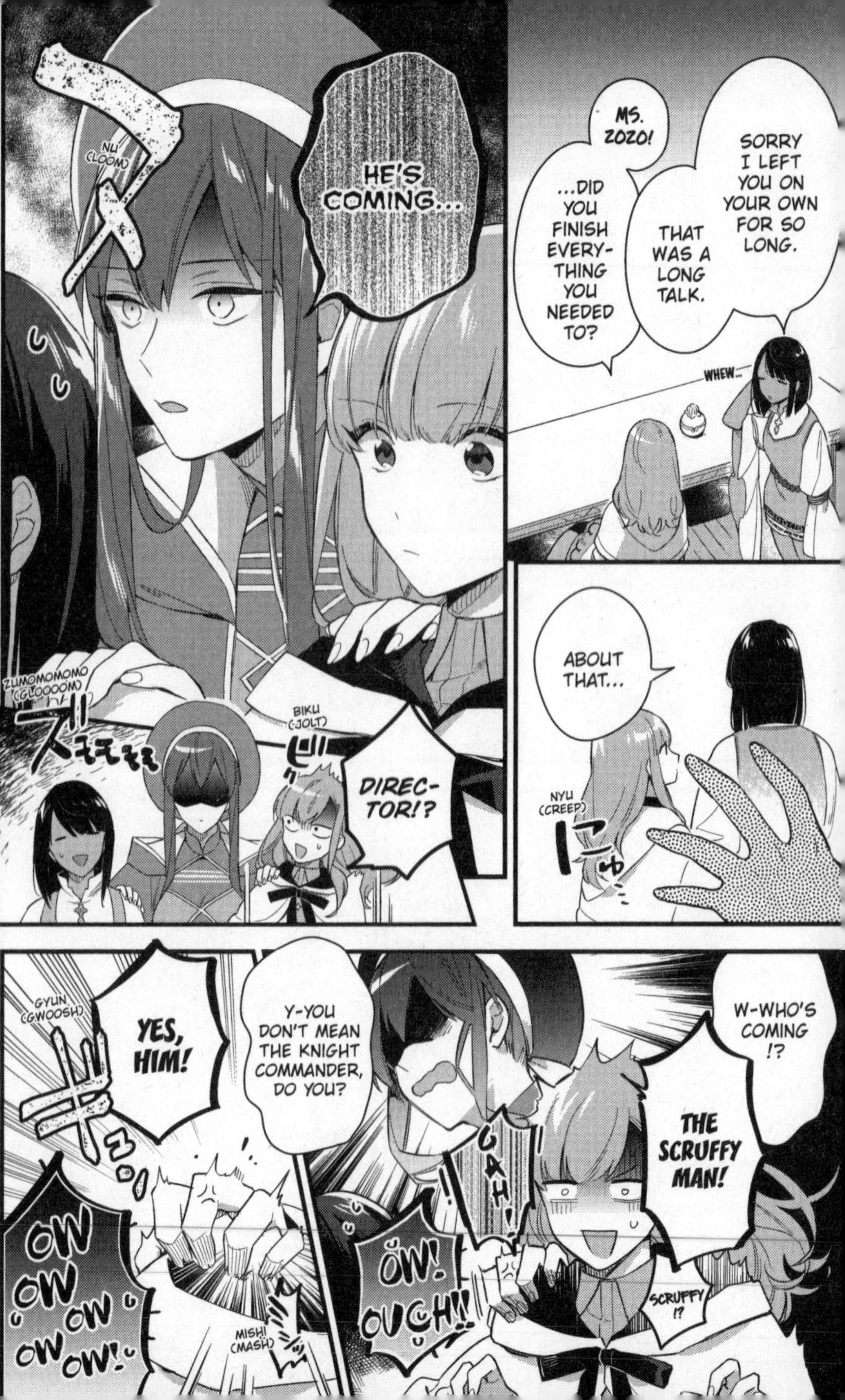
SORRY I LEFT YOU ON YOUR OWN FOR SO LONG.
THAT WAS A LONG TALK.
MS. ZOZO!
...DID YOU FINISH EVERY-THING YOU NEEDED TO?
WHEW...
NU (LOOM)
HE'S COMING...
ABOUT THAT...
NYU (CREEP)
ZUMOMOMOMO (GLOOOOM)
BIKU (-JOLT)
DIREC-TOR!?
W-WHO'S COMING!?
THE SCRUFFY MAN!
SCRUFFY!?
Y-YOU DON'T MEAN THE KNIGHT COMMANDER, DO YOU?
YES, HIM!
GYUN (GWOOSH)
GAH!
OW! OUCH!!
MISHI (MASH)
OW OW OW OW OW OW!

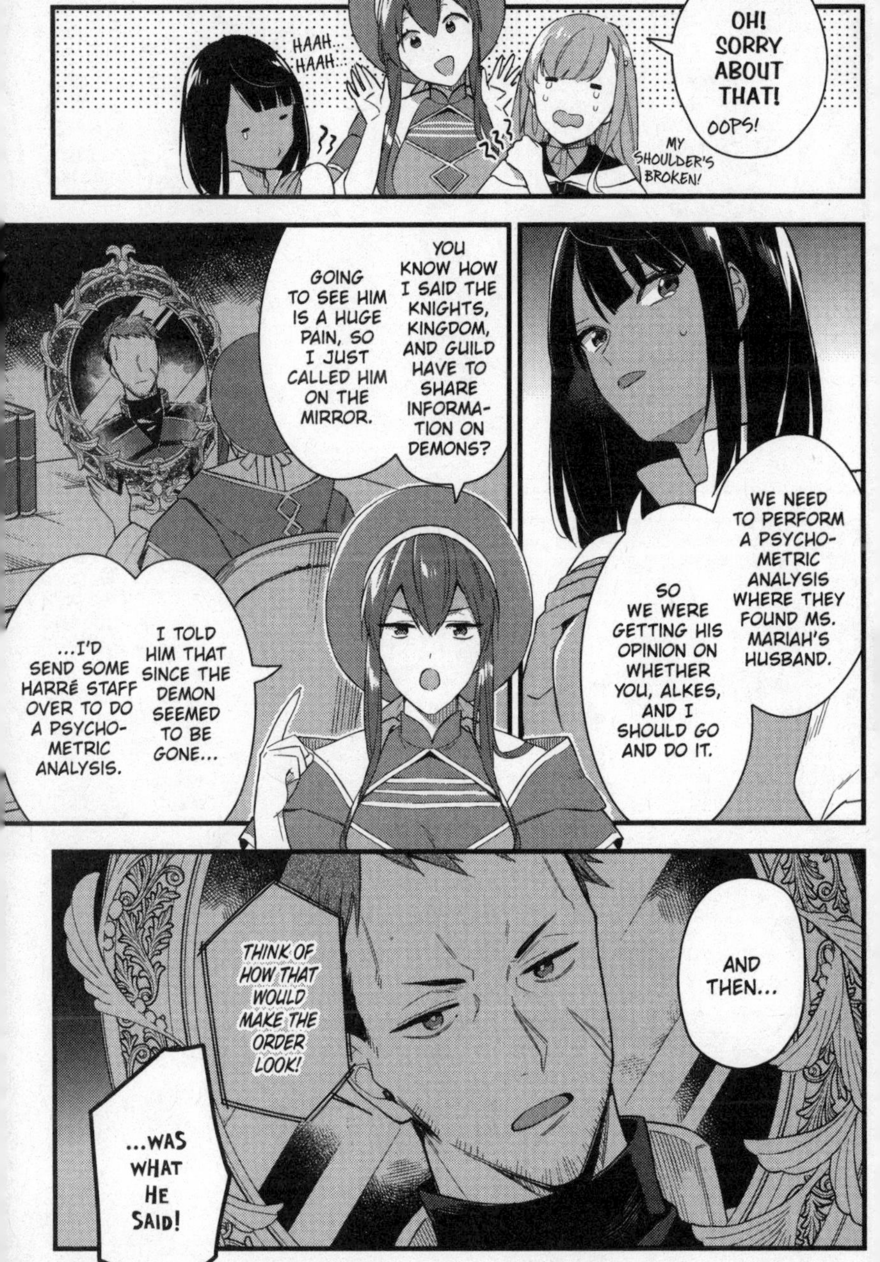
OH! SORRY ABOUT THAT!
OOPS!
MY SHOULDER'S BROKEN!
HAAH... HAAH...
WE NEED TO PERFORM A PSYCHO-METRIC ANALYSIS WHERE THEY FOUND MS. MARIAH'S HUSBAND.
SO WE WERE GETTING HIS OPINION ON WHETHER YOU, ALKES, AND I SHOULD GO AND DO IT.
YOU KNOW HOW I SAID THE KNIGHTS, KINGDOM, AND GUILD HAVE TO SHARE INFORMA-TION ON DEMONS?
GOING TO SEE HIM IS A HUGE PAIN, SO I JUST CALLED HIM ON THE MIRROR.
I TOLD HIM THAT SINCE THE DEMON SEEMED TO BE GONE...
...I'D SEND SOME HARRÉ STAFF OVER TO DO A PSYCHO-METRIC ANALYSIS.
AND THEN...
THINK OF HOW THAT WOULD MAKE THE ORDER LOOK!
...WAS WHAT HE SAID!

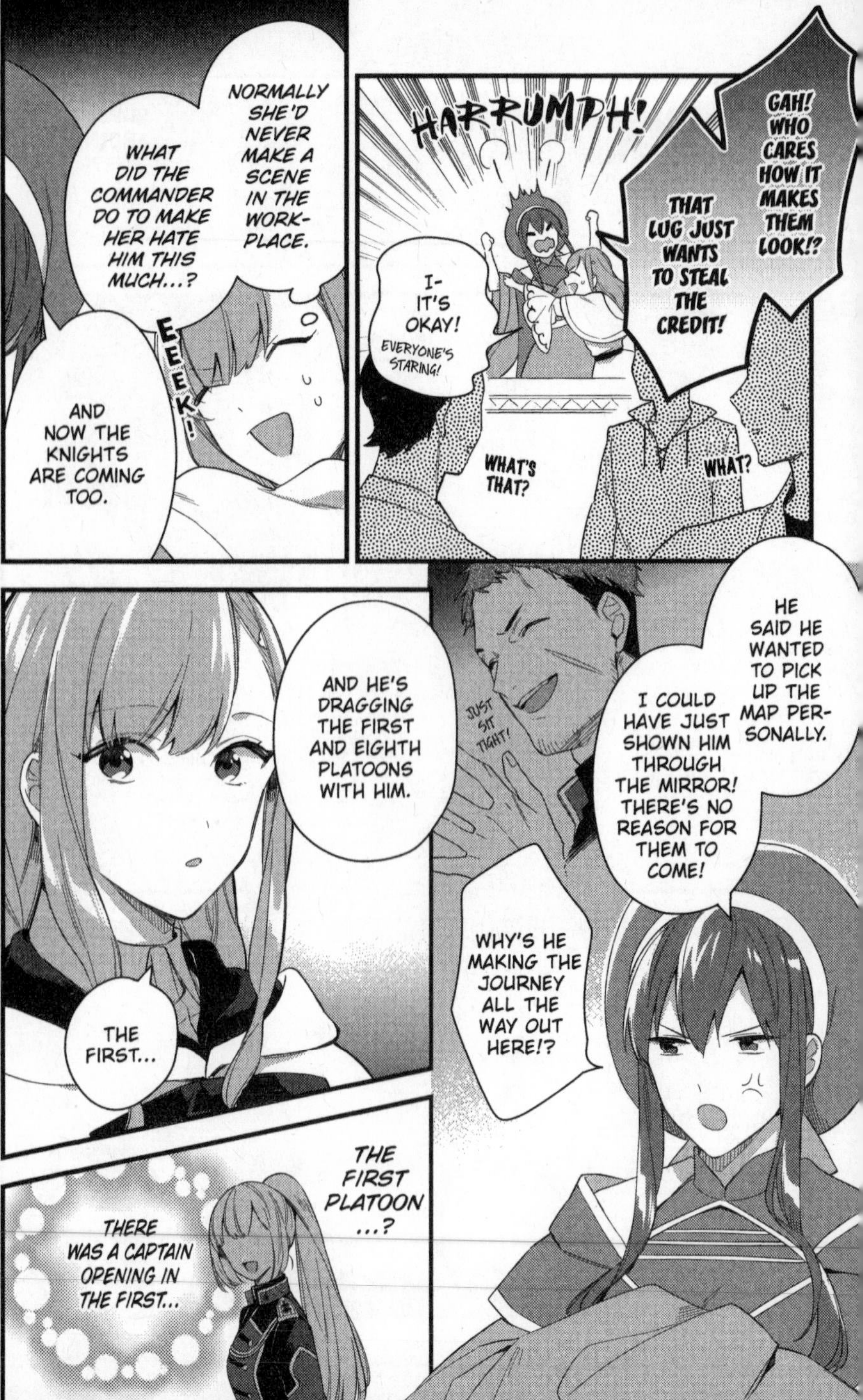
GAH! WHO CARES HOW IT MAKES THEM LOOK!?
THAT LUG JUST WANTS TO STEAL THE CREDIT!
HARRUMPH!
I- IT'S OKAY!
EVERYONE'S STARING!
WHAT?
WHAT'S THAT?
NORMALLY SHE'D NEVER MAKE A SCENE IN THE WORK-PLACE.
WHAT DID THE COMMANDER DO TO MAKE HER HATE HIM THIS MUCH...?
EEEK!
AND NOW THE KNIGHTS ARE COMING TOO.
HE SAID HE WANTED TO PICK UP THE MAP PER-SONALLY.
I COULD HAVE JUST SHOWN HIM THROUGH THE MIRROR! THERE'S NO REASON FOR THEM TO COME!
JUST SIT TIGHT!
WHY'S HE MAKING THE JOURNEY ALL THE WAY OUT HERE!?
AND HE'S DRAGGING THE FIRST AND EIGHTH PLATOONS WITH HIM.
THE FIRST...
THE FIRST PLATOON ...?
THERE WAS A CAPTAIN OPENING IN THE FIRST...

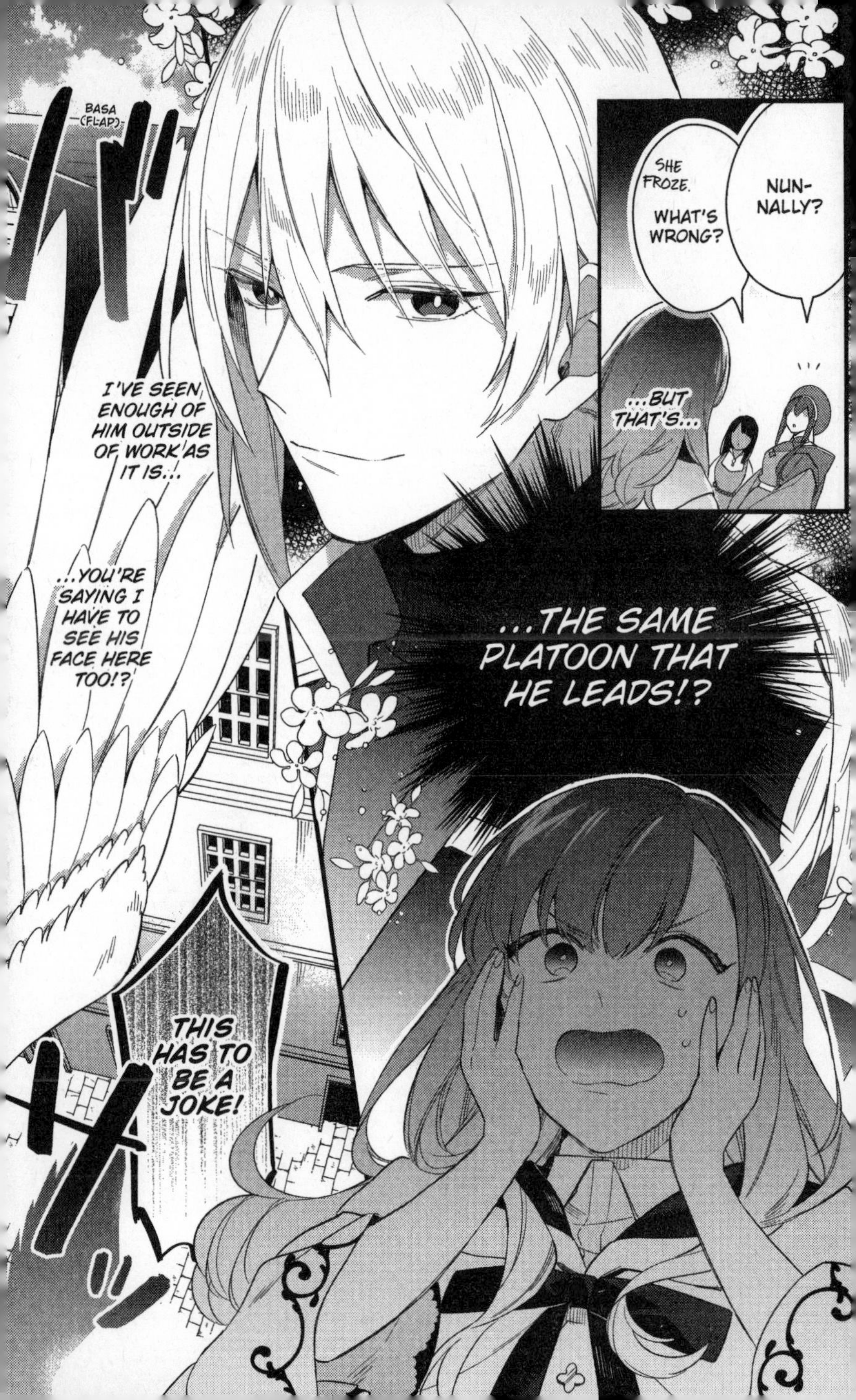
NUN-NALLY?
WHAT'S WRONG?
SHE FROZE.
...BUT THAT'S...
...THE SAME PLATOON THAT HE LEADS!?
BASA (FLAP)
I'VE SEEN ENOUGH OF HIM OUTSIDE OF WORK AS IT IS...
...YOU'RE SAYING I HAVE TO SEE HIS FACE HERE TOO!?
THIS HAS TO BE A JOKE!

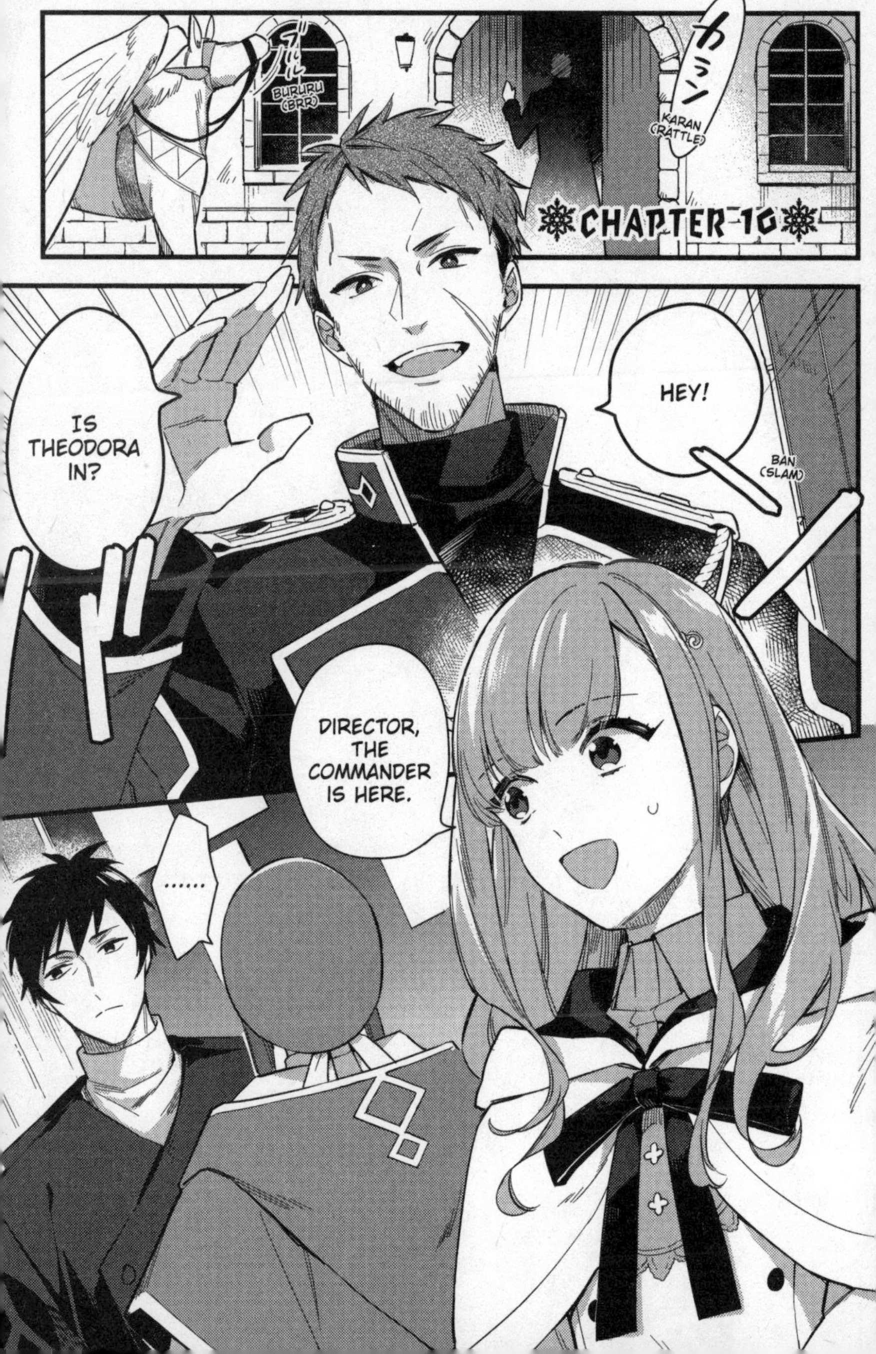
カラン
KARAN (RATTLE)
CHAPTER 10
ブル
BURURU (BRR)
HEY!
BAN (SLAM)
IS THEODORA IN?
DIRECTOR, THE COMMANDER IS HERE.
......

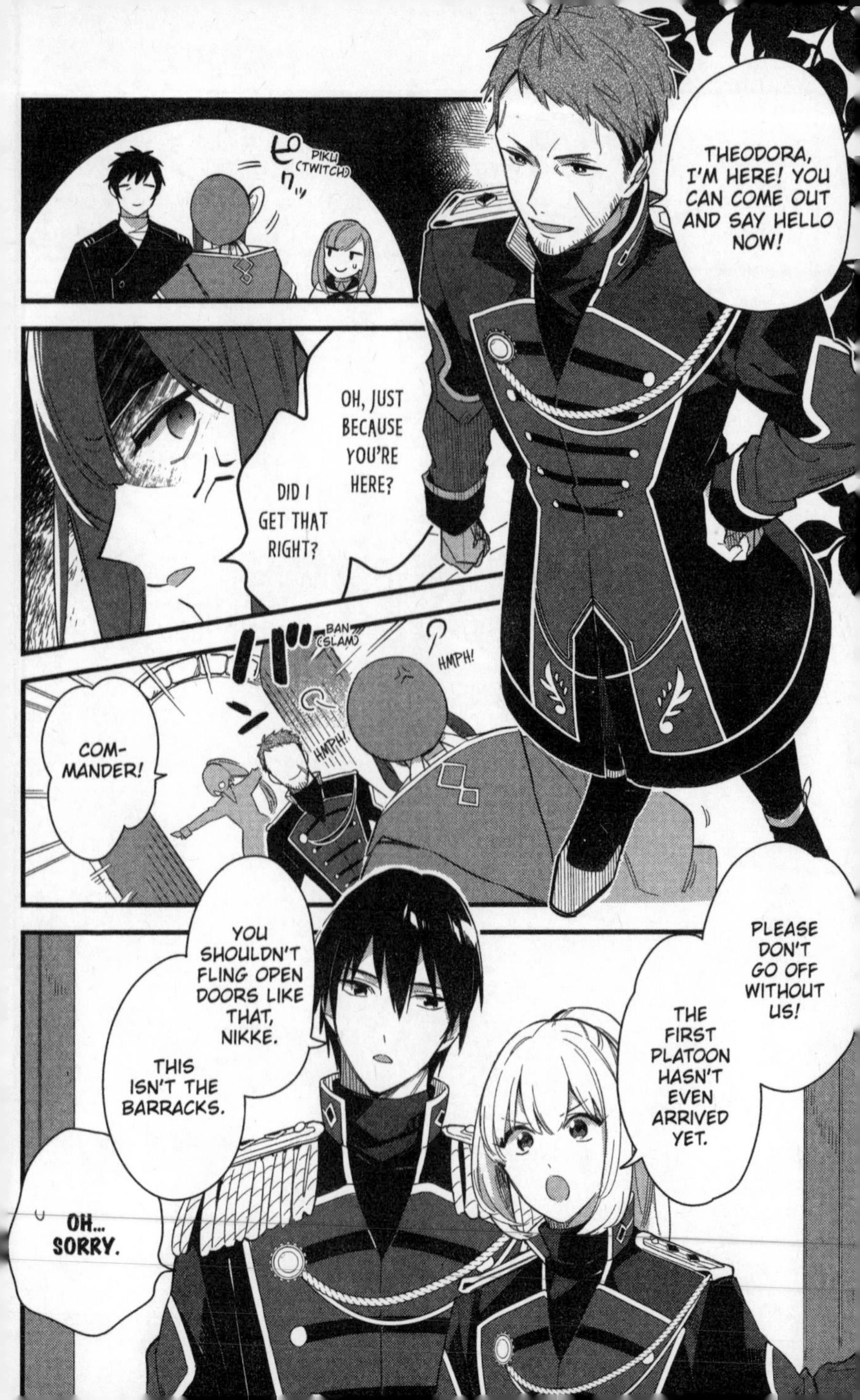
THEODORA, I'M HERE! YOU CAN COME OUT AND SAY HELLO NOW!
PIKU (TWITCH)
OH, JUST BECAUSE YOU'RE HERE?
DID I GET THAT RIGHT?
BAN (SLAM)
HMPH!
HMPH!
COM-MANDER!
PLEASE DON'T GO OFF WITHOUT US!
THE FIRST PLATOON HASN'T EVEN ARRIVED YET.
YOU SHOULDN'T FLING OPEN DOORS LIKE THAT, NIKKE.
THIS ISN'T THE BARRACKS.
OH... SORRY.

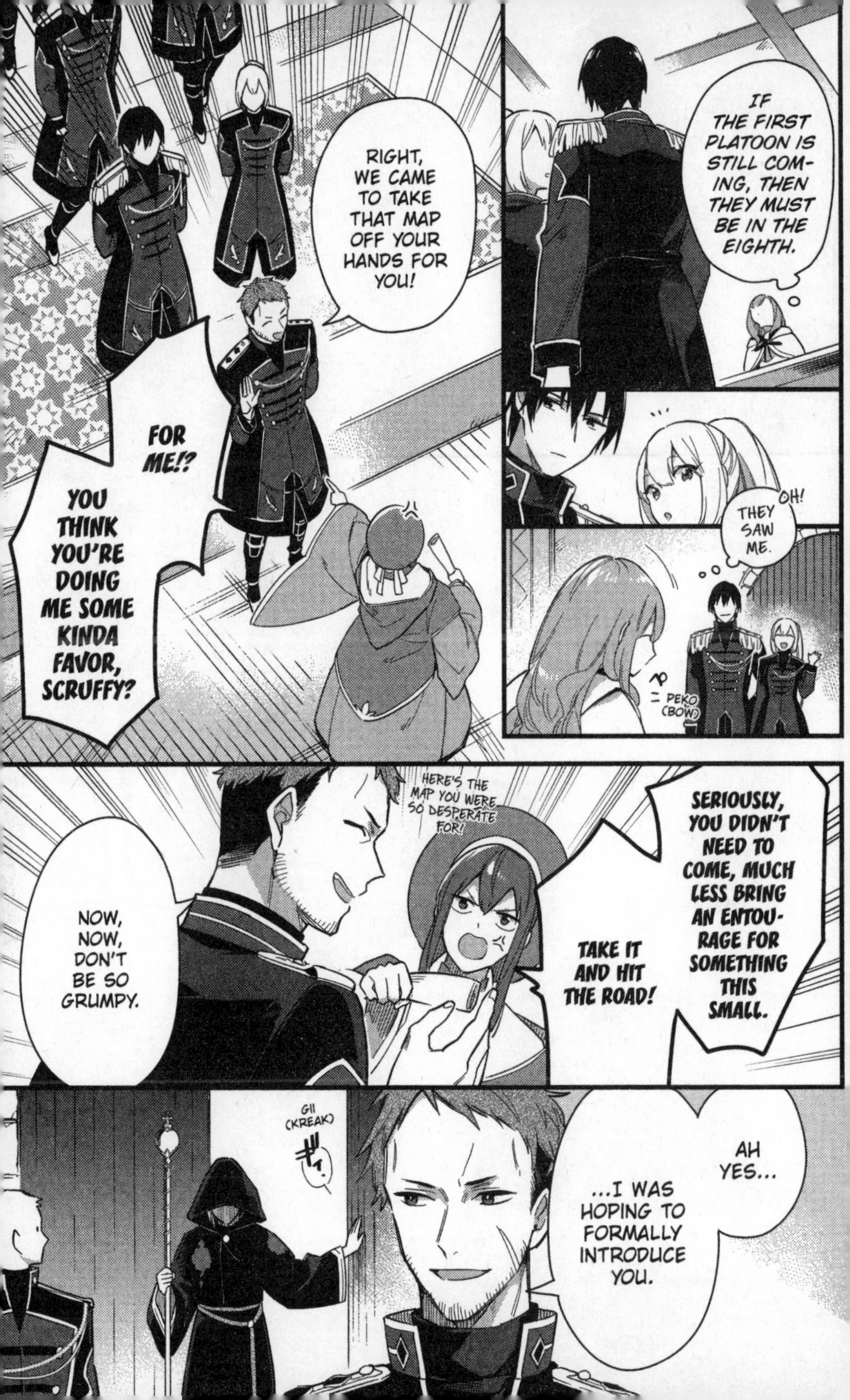
IF THE FIRST PLATOON IS STILL COMING, THEN THEY MUST BE IN THE EIGHTH.
...
OH!
THEY SAW ME.
PEKO (BOW)
RIGHT, WE CAME TO TAKE THAT MAP OFF YOUR HANDS FOR YOU!
FOR ME!?
YOU THINK YOU'RE DOING ME SOME KINDA FAVOR, SCRUFFY?
SERIOUSLY, YOU DIDN'T NEED TO COME, MUCH LESS BRING AN ENTOURAGE FOR SOMETHING THIS SMALL.
TAKE IT AND HIT THE ROAD!
HERE'S THE MAP YOU WERE SO DESPERATE FOR!
NOW, NOW, DON'T BE SO GRUMPY.
AH YES...
...I WAS HOPING TO FORMALLY INTRODUCE YOU.
GII (KREAK)

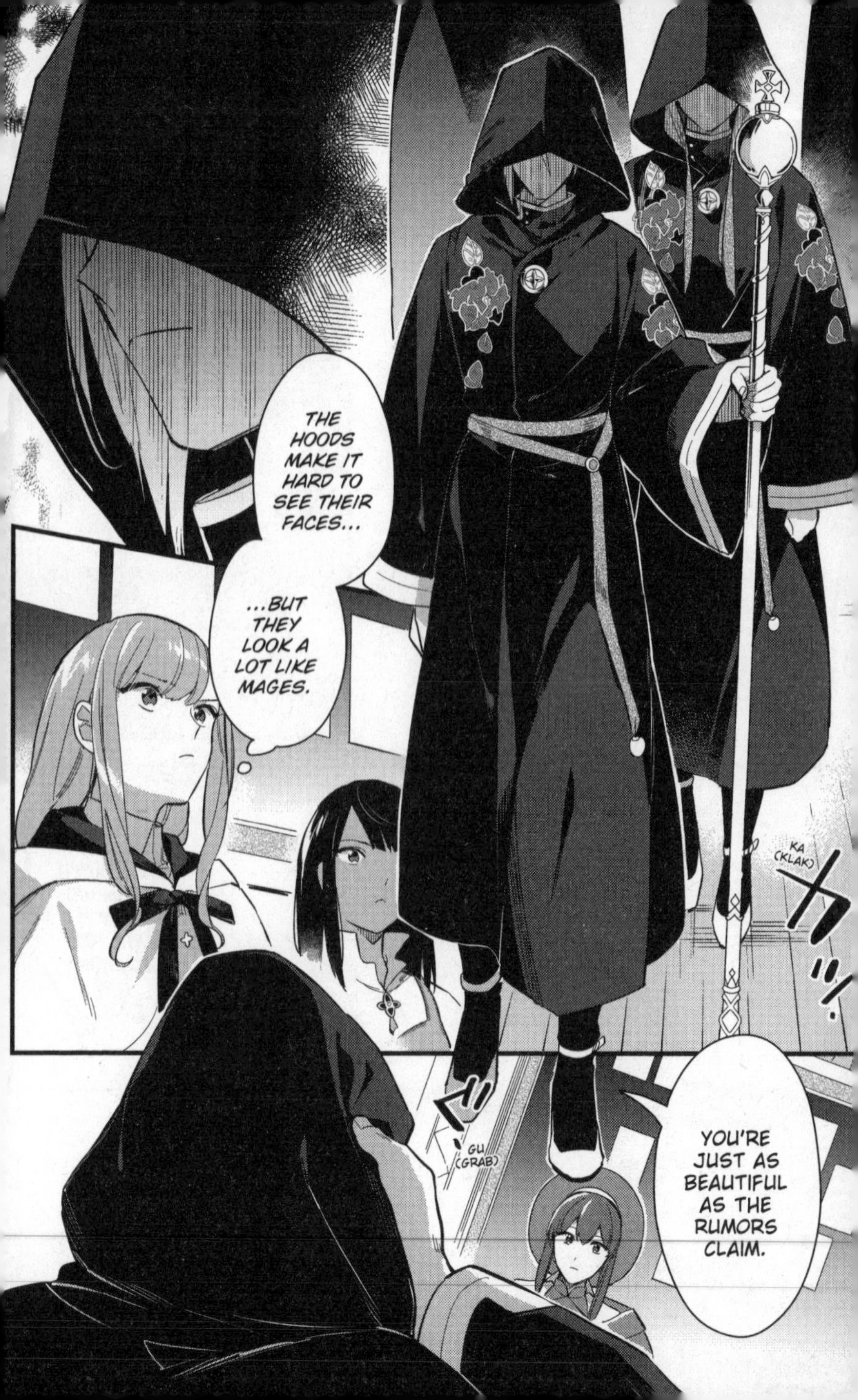
KA (KLAK)
THE HOODS MAKE IT HARD TO SEE THEIR FACES...
...BUT THEY LOOK A LOT LIKE MAGES.
YOU'RE JUST AS BEAUTIFUL AS THE RUMORS CLAIM.
GU (GRAB)

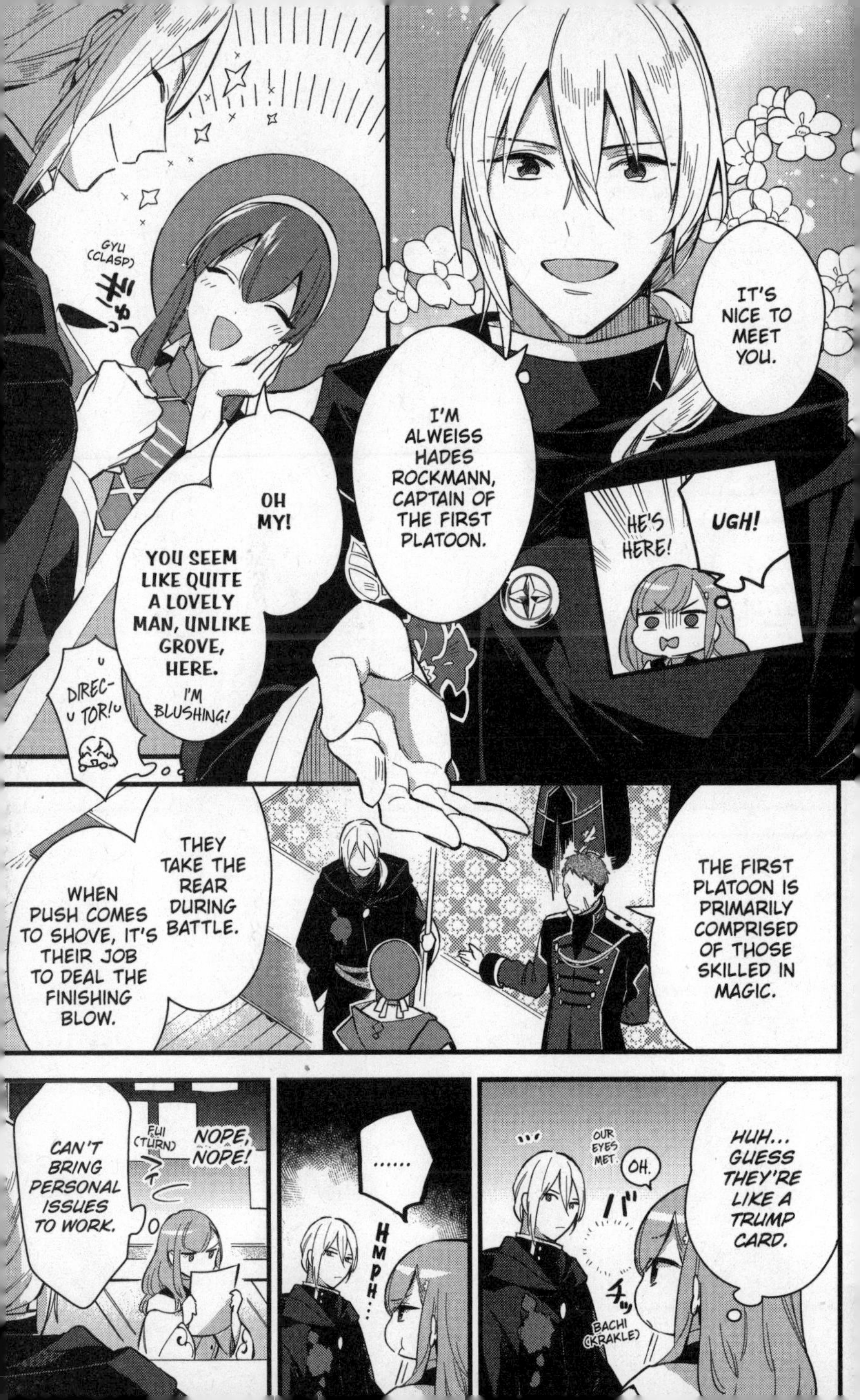
IT'S NICE TO MEET YOU.
I'M ALWEISS HADES ROCKMANN, CAPTAIN OF THE FIRST PLATOON.
UGH!
HE'S HERE!
GYU (CLASP)
OH MY!
YOU SEEM LIKE QUITE A LOVELY MAN, UNLIKE GROVE, HERE.
I'M BLUSHING!
DIREC-TOR!
THE FIRST PLATOON IS PRIMARILY COMPRISED OF THOSE SKILLED IN MAGIC.
THEY TAKE THE REAR DURING BATTLE.
WHEN PUSH COMES TO SHOVE, IT'S THEIR JOB TO DEAL THE FINISHING BLOW.
HUH... GUESS THEY'RE LIKE A TRUMP CARD.
OUR EYES MET.
OH.
BACHI (KRAKLE)
......
HMPH...
NOPE, NOPE!
FUI (TURN)
CAN'T BRING PERSONAL ISSUES TO WORK.

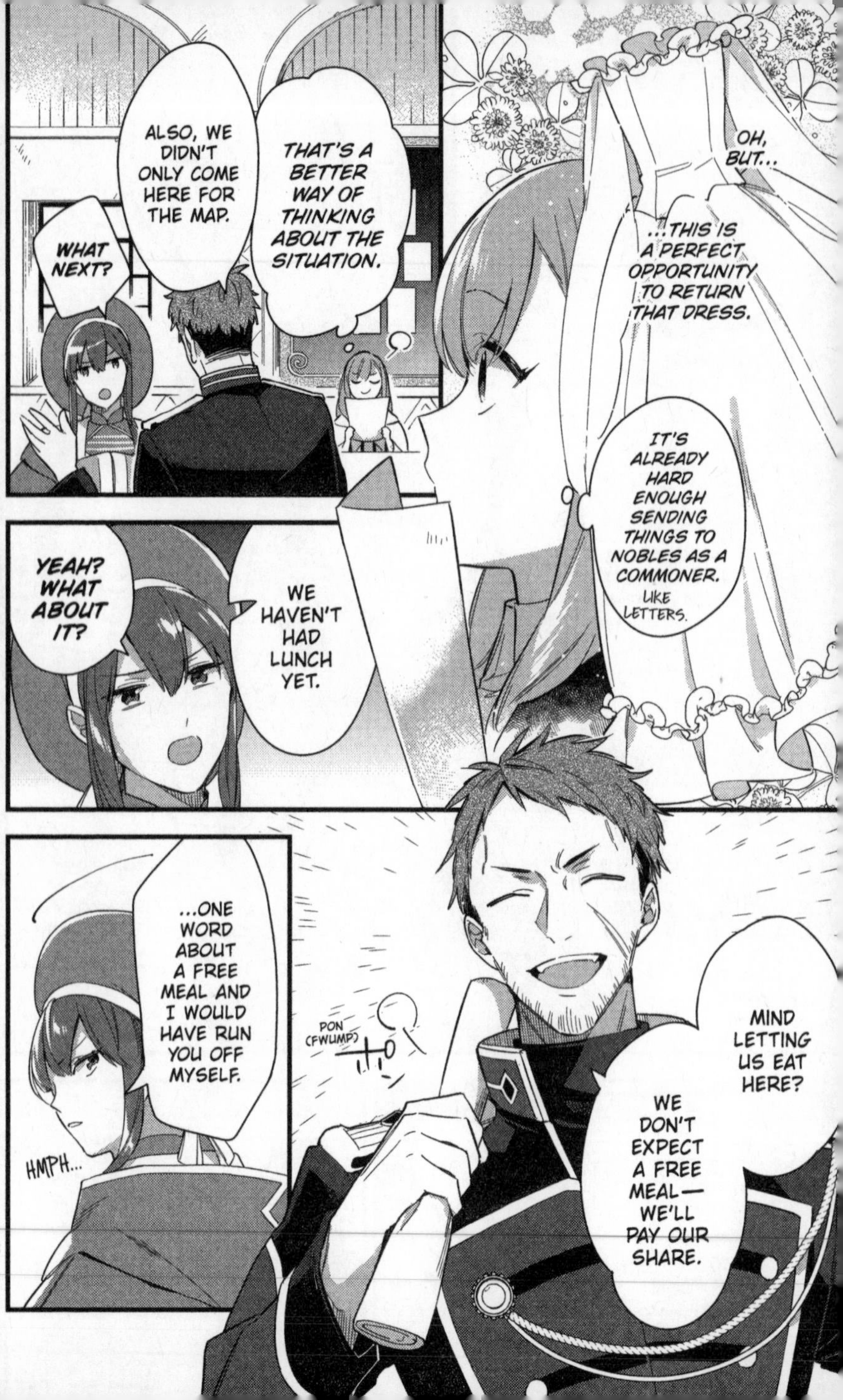
OH, BUT...
...THIS IS A PERFECT OPPORTUNITY TO RETURN THAT DRESS.
IT'S ALREADY HARD ENOUGH SENDING THINGS TO NOBLES AS A COMMONER.
LIKE LETTERS.
THAT'S A BETTER WAY OF THINKING ABOUT THE SITUATION.
ALSO, WE DIDN'T ONLY COME HERE FOR THE MAP.
WHAT NEXT?
WE HAVEN'T HAD LUNCH YET.
YEAH? WHAT ABOUT IT?
MIND LETTING US EAT HERE?
WE DON'T EXPECT A FREE MEAL— WE'LL PAY OUR SHARE.
PON (FWUMP)
...ONE WORD ABOUT A FREE MEAL AND I WOULD HAVE RUN YOU OFF MYSELF.
HMPH...

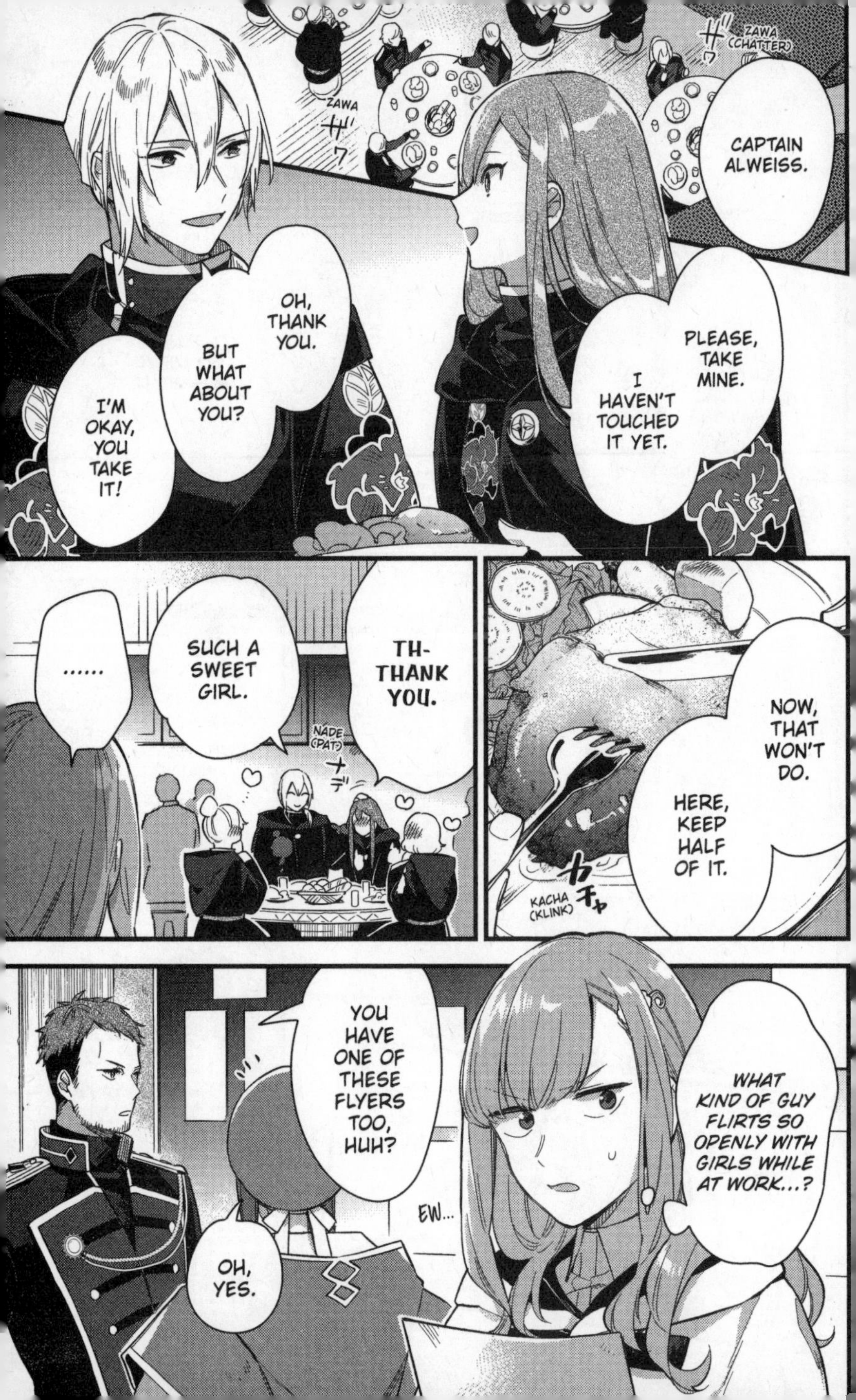
ZAWA (CHATTER)
CAPTAIN ALWEISS.
ZAWA
PLEASE, TAKE MINE.
I HAVEN'T TOUCHED IT YET.
OH, THANK YOU.
BUT WHAT ABOUT YOU?
I'M OKAY, YOU TAKE IT!
NOW, THAT WON'T DO.
HERE, KEEP HALF OF IT.
KACHA (KLINK)
TH-THANK YOU.
NADE (PAT)
SUCH A SWEET GIRL.
......
WHAT KIND OF GUY FLIRTS SO OPENLY WITH GIRLS WHILE AT WORK...?
EW...
YOU HAVE ONE OF THESE FLYERS TOO, HUH?
OH, YES.

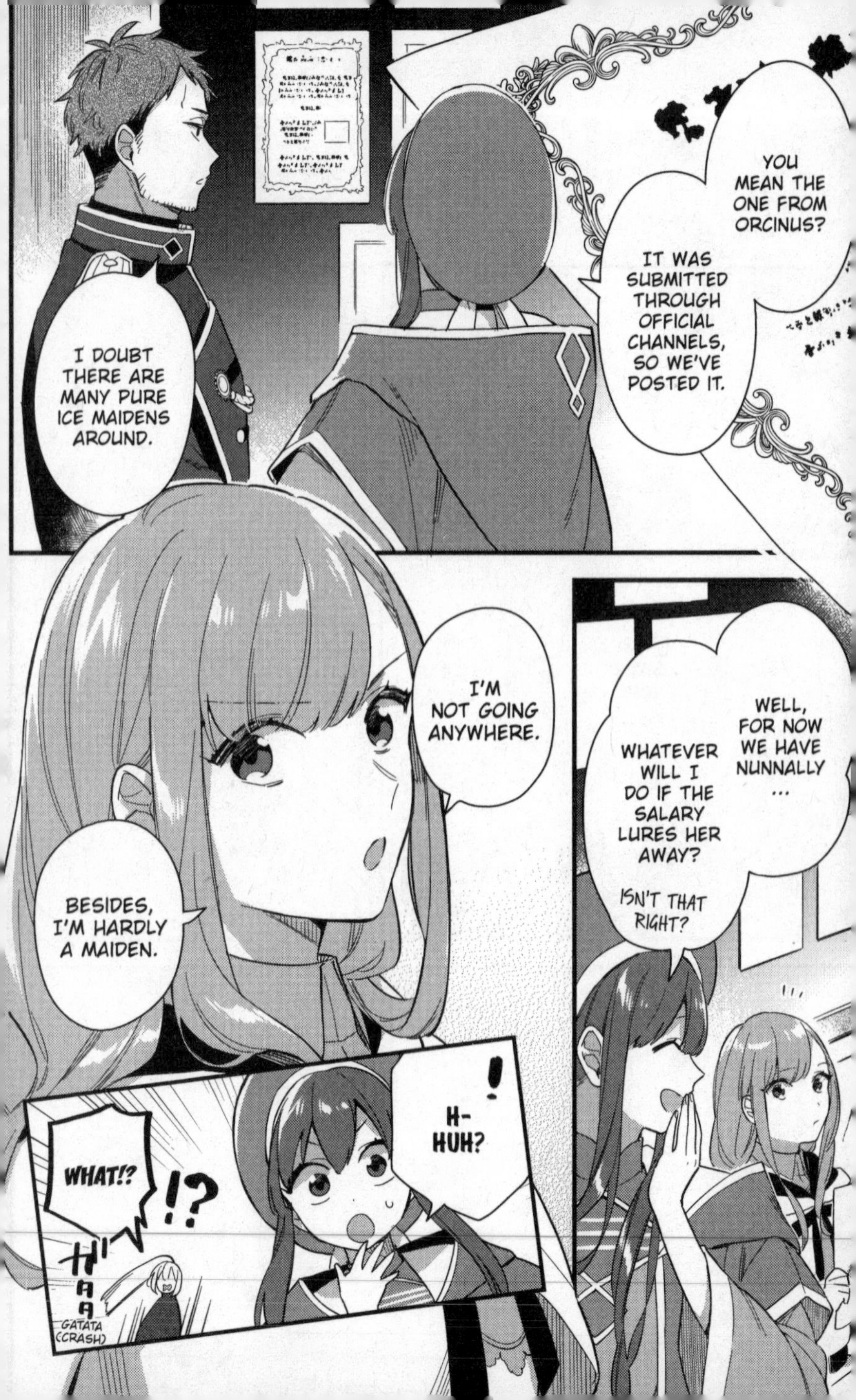
YOU MEAN THE ONE FROM ORCINUS?
IT WAS SUBMITTED THROUGH OFFICIAL CHANNELS, SO WE'VE POSTED IT.
I DOUBT THERE ARE MANY PURE ICE MAIDENS AROUND.
WELL, FOR NOW WE HAVE NUNNALLY ...
WHATEVER WILL I DO IF THE SALARY LURES HER AWAY?
ISN'T THAT RIGHT?
I'M NOT GOING ANYWHERE.
BESIDES, I'M HARDLY A MAIDEN.
!
H-HUH?
WHAT!?
!?
HI
HAA
GATATA (CRASH)

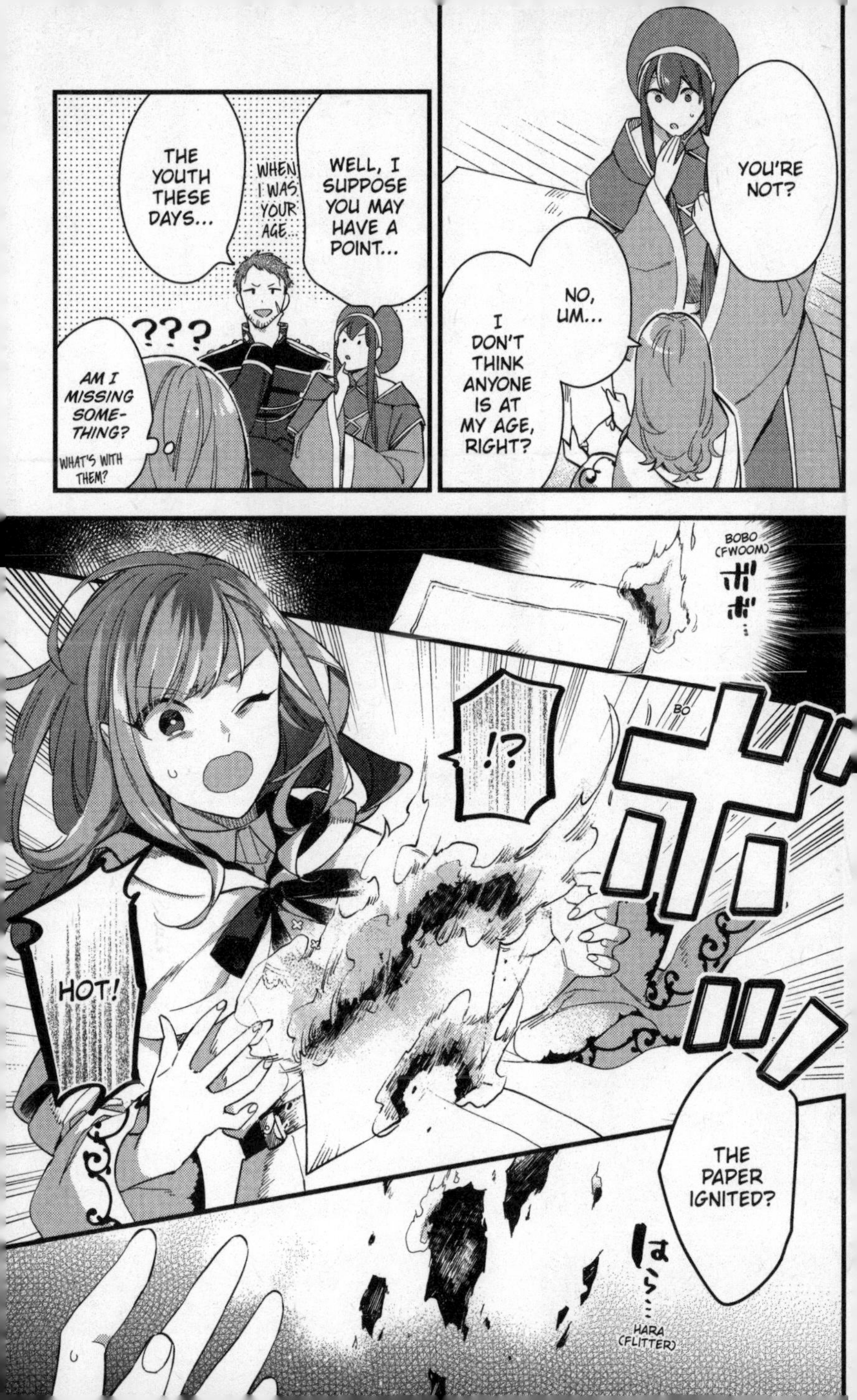
YOU'RE NOT?
NO, UM...
I DON'T THINK ANYONE IS AT MY AGE, RIGHT?
WELL, I SUPPOSE YOU MAY HAVE A POINT...
WHEN I WAS YOUR AGE...
THE YOUTH THESE DAYS...
???
AM I MISSING SOME-THING?
WHAT'S WITH THEM?
BOBO (FWOOM)
ボボ…
BO
!?
HOT!
THE PAPER IGNITED?
はら…
HARA (FLITTER)

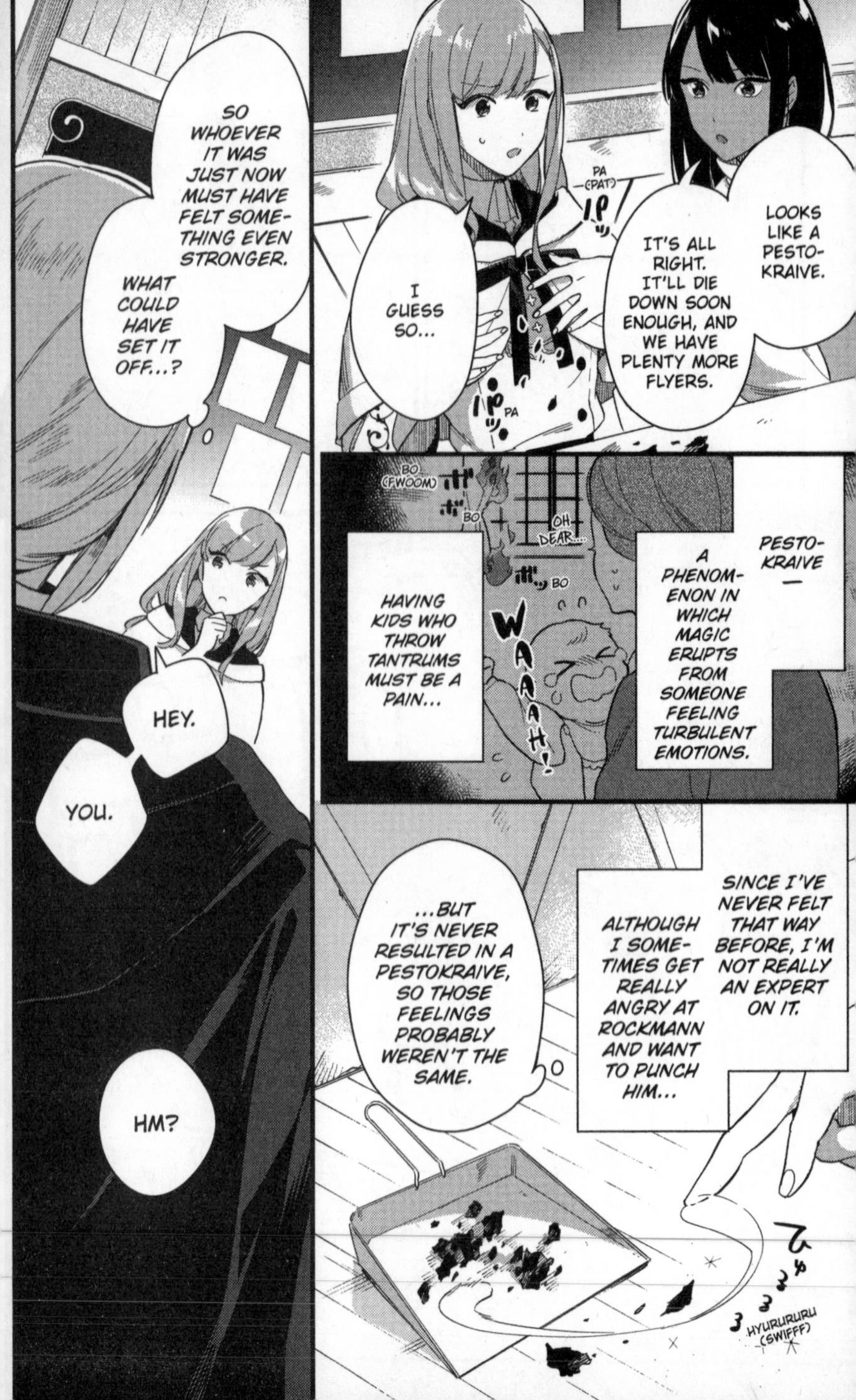
LOOKS LIKE A PESTO-KRAIVE.
IT'S ALL RIGHT. IT'LL DIE DOWN SOON ENOUGH, AND WE HAVE PLENTY MORE FLYERS.
PA (PAT)
I GUESS SO...
PA
PESTO-KRAIVE — A PHENOMENON IN WHICH MAGIC ERUPTS FROM SOMEONE FEELING TURBULENT EMOTIONS.
BO (FWOOM)
BO
OH DEAR...
BO
WAAAH!
HAVING KIDS WHO THROW TANTRUMS MUST BE A PAIN...
SINCE I'VE NEVER FELT THAT WAY BEFORE, I'M NOT REALLY AN EXPERT ON IT.
ALTHOUGH I SOMETIMES GET REALLY ANGRY AT ROCKMANN AND WANT TO PUNCH HIM...
...BUT IT'S NEVER RESULTED IN A PESTOKRAIVE, SO THOSE FEELINGS PROBABLY WEREN'T THE SAME.
HYURURURU (SWIFF)
SO WHOEVER IT WAS JUST NOW MUST HAVE FELT SOMETHING EVEN STRONGER.
WHAT COULD HAVE SET IT OFF...?
HEY.
YOU.
HM?

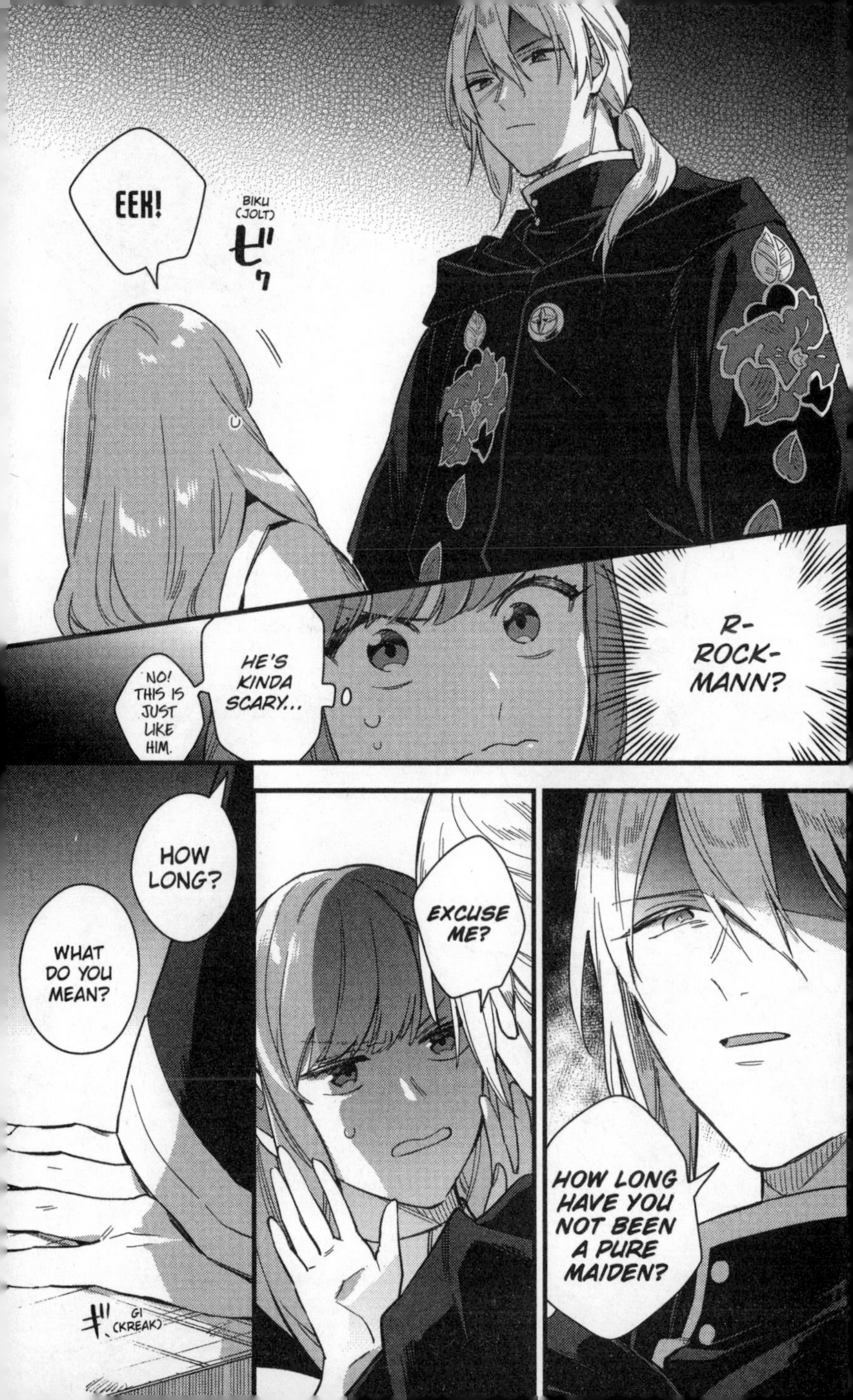
EEK!
BIKU (JOLT)
R-ROCK-MANN?
HE'S KINDA SCARY...
NO! THIS IS JUST LIKE HIM.
HOW LONG HAVE YOU NOT BEEN A PURE MAIDEN?
EXCUSE ME?
HOW LONG?
WHAT DO YOU MEAN?
GI (KREAK)

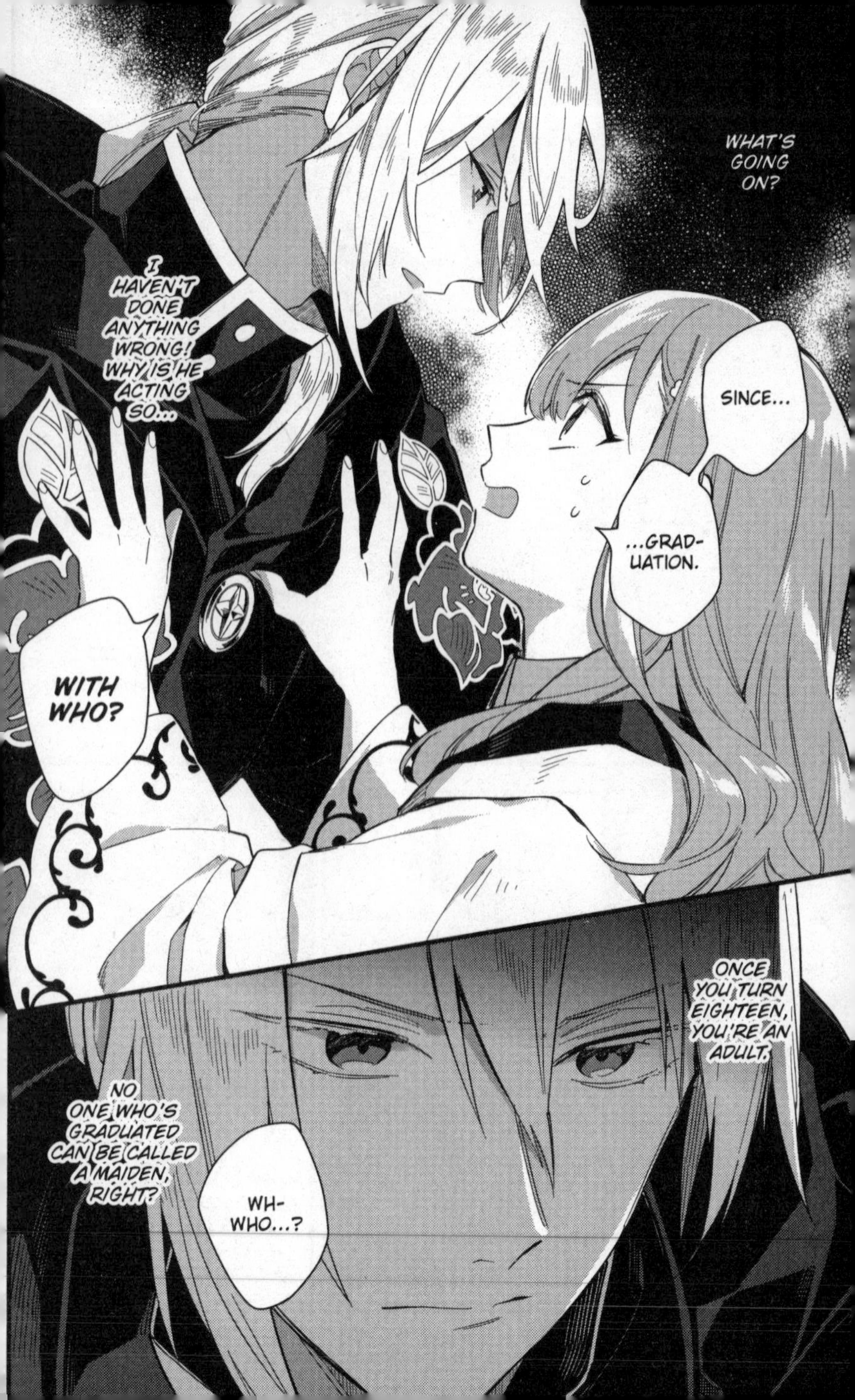
WHAT'S GOING ON?
SINCE...
...GRAD-UATION.
I HAVEN'T DONE ANYTHING WRONG! WHY IS HE ACTING SO...
WITH WHO?
ONCE YOU TURN EIGHTEEN, YOU'RE AN ADULT.
NO ONE WHO'S GRADUATED CAN BE CALLED A MAIDEN, RIGHT?
WH-WHO...?

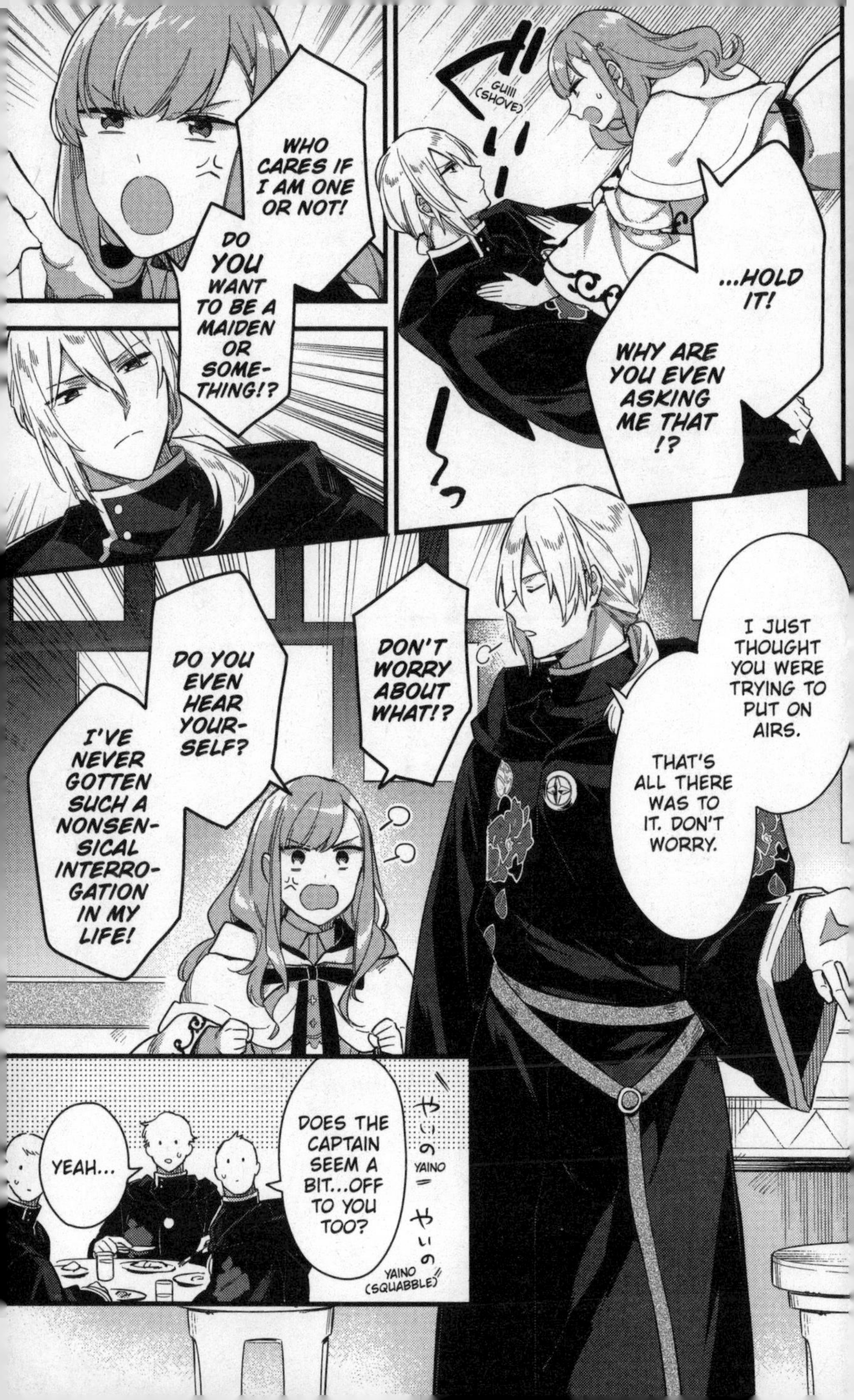
GUIII (SHOVE)
...HOLD IT!
WHY ARE YOU EVEN ASKING ME THAT!?
WHO CARES IF I AM ONE OR NOT!
DO YOU WANT TO BE A MAIDEN OR SOME-THING!?
I JUST THOUGHT YOU WERE TRYING TO PUT ON AIRS.
THAT'S ALL THERE WAS TO IT. DON'T WORRY.
DON'T WORRY ABOUT WHAT!?
DO YOU EVEN HEAR YOUR-SELF?
I'VE NEVER GOTTEN SUCH A NONSEN-SICAL INTERRO-GATION IN MY LIFE!
やいの YAINO
やいの YAINO (SQUABBLE)
DOES THE CAPTAIN SEEM A BIT...OFF TO YOU TOO?
YEAH...

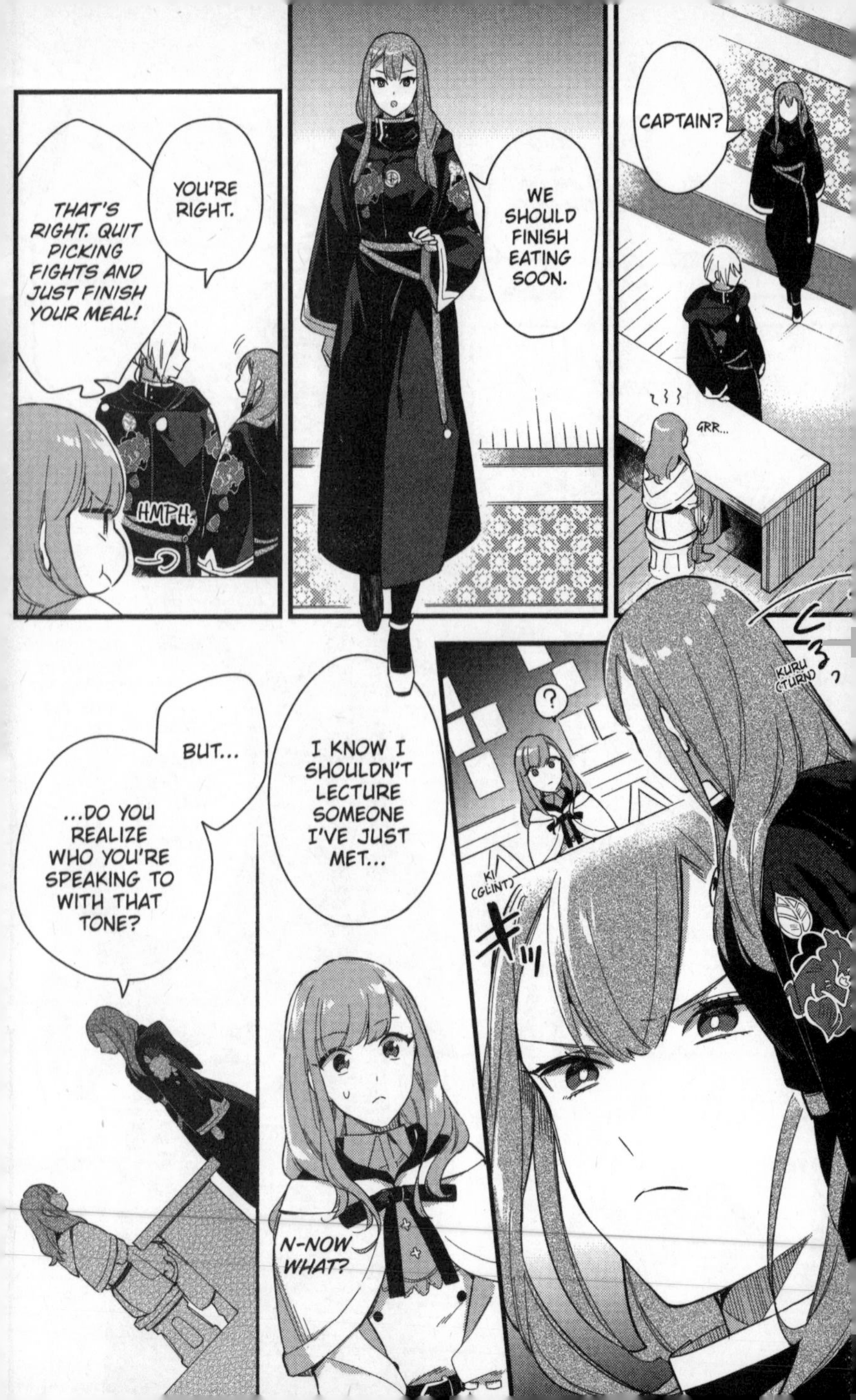
CAPTAIN?
GRR...
WE SHOULD FINISH EATING SOON.
YOU'RE RIGHT.
THAT'S RIGHT. QUIT PICKING FIGHTS AND JUST FINISH YOUR MEAL!
HMPH.
KURU (TURN)
?
KI (GLINT)
I KNOW I SHOULDN'T LECTURE SOMEONE I'VE JUST MET...
BUT...
...DO YOU REALIZE WHO YOU'RE SPEAKING TO WITH THAT TONE?
N-NOW WHAT?

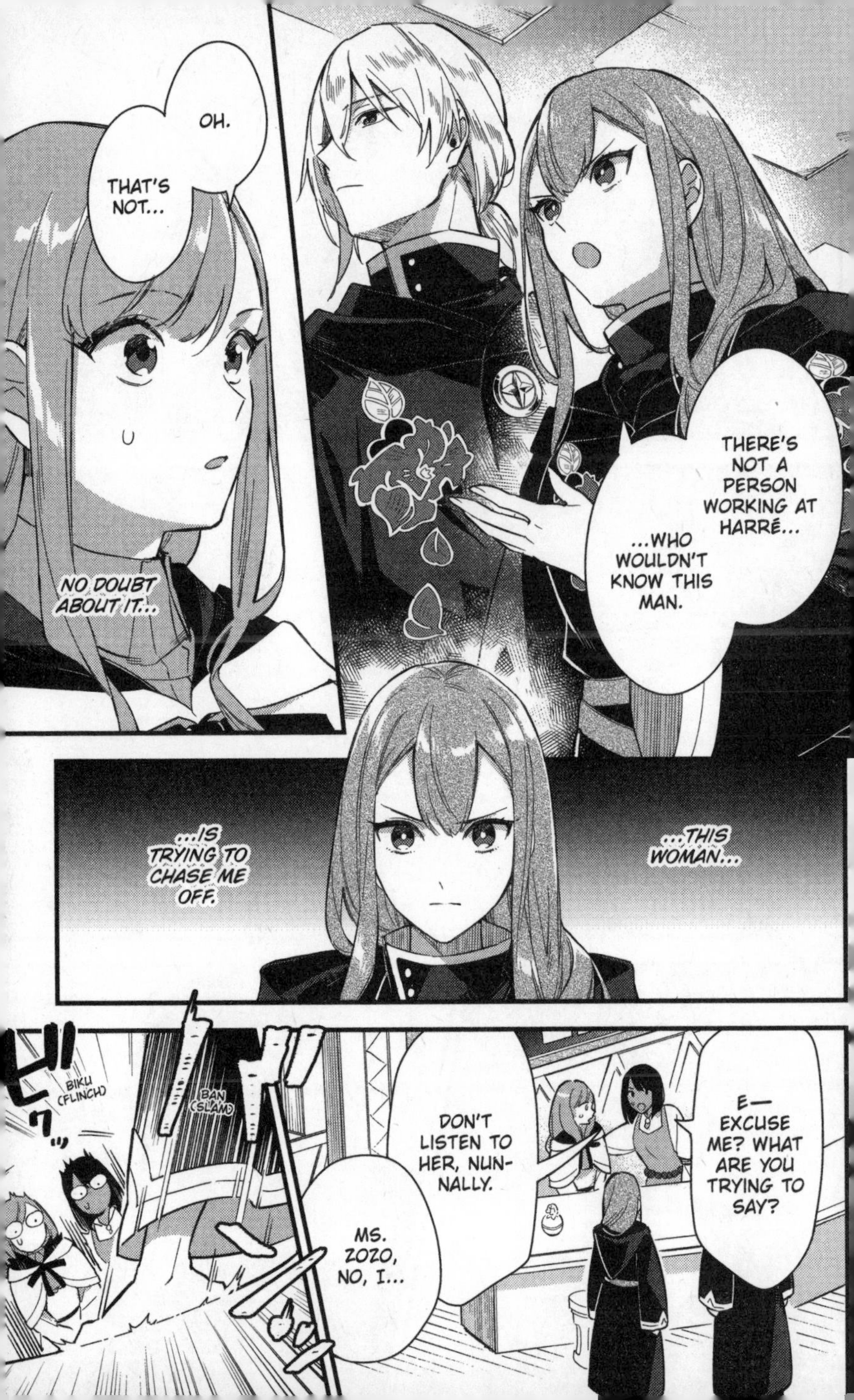
THERE'S NOT A PERSON WORKING AT HARRÉ...
...WHO WOULDN'T KNOW THIS MAN.
OH.
THAT'S NOT...
NO DOUBT ABOUT IT...
...THIS WOMAN...
...IS TRYING TO CHASE ME OFF.
E— EXCUSE ME? WHAT ARE YOU TRYING TO SAY?
DON'T LISTEN TO HER, NUN-NALLY.
MS. ZOZO, NO, I...
BAN (SLAM)
BIKU (FLINCH)

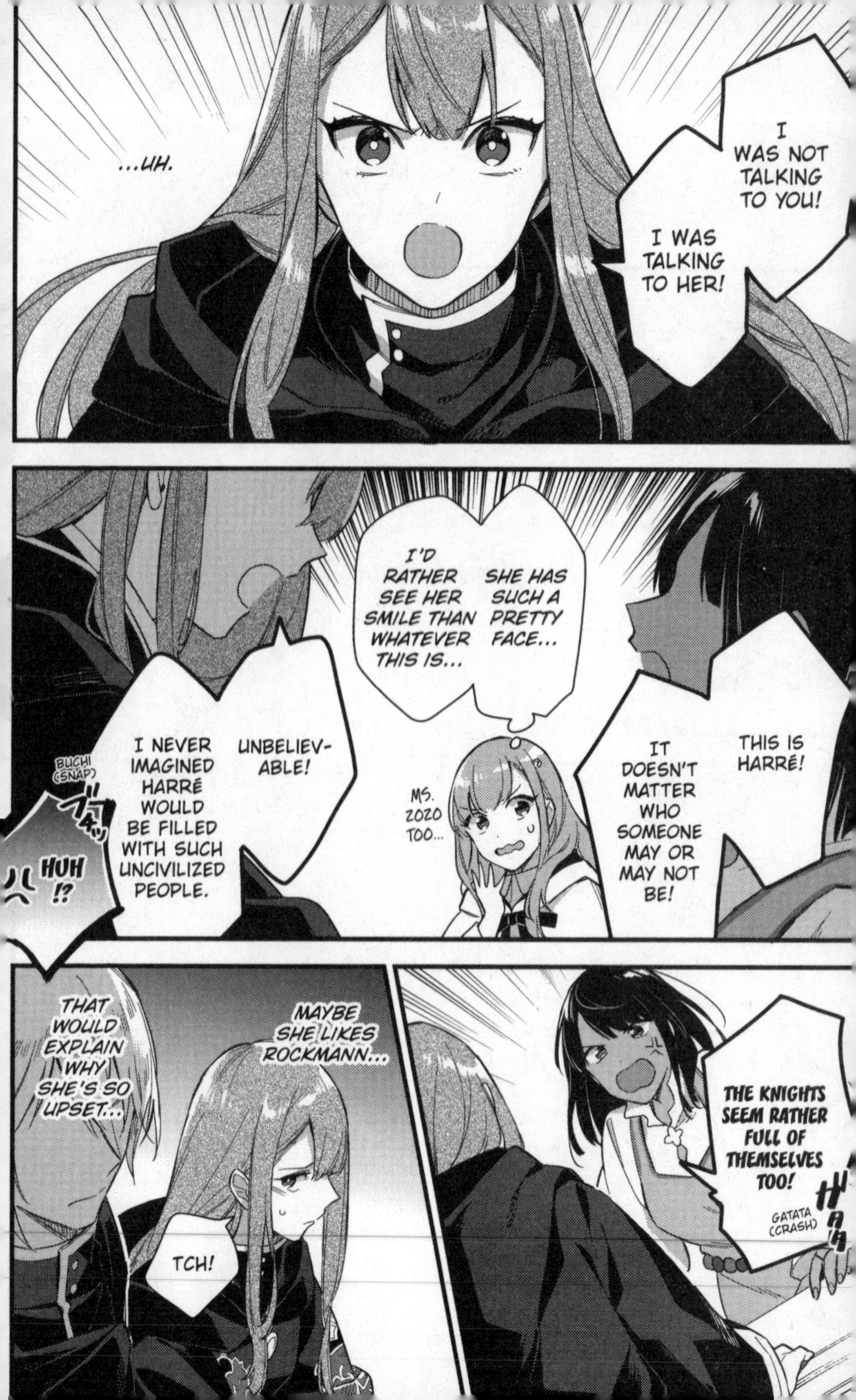
I WAS NOT TALKING TO YOU!
I WAS TALKING TO HER!
...UH.
THIS IS HARRÉ!
IT DOESN'T MATTER WHO SOMEONE MAY OR MAY NOT BE!
I'D RATHER SEE HER SMILE THAN WHATEVER THIS IS...
SHE HAS SUCH A PRETTY FACE...
MS. ZOZO TOO...
UNBELIEVABLE!
I NEVER IMAGINED HARRÉ WOULD BE FILLED WITH SUCH UNCIVILIZED PEOPLE.
BUCHI (SNAP)
HUH!?
THE KNIGHTS SEEM RATHER FULL OF THEMSELVES TOO!
GATATA (CRASH)
MAYBE SHE LIKES ROCKMANN...
THAT WOULD EXPLAIN WHY SHE'S SO UPSET...
TCH!

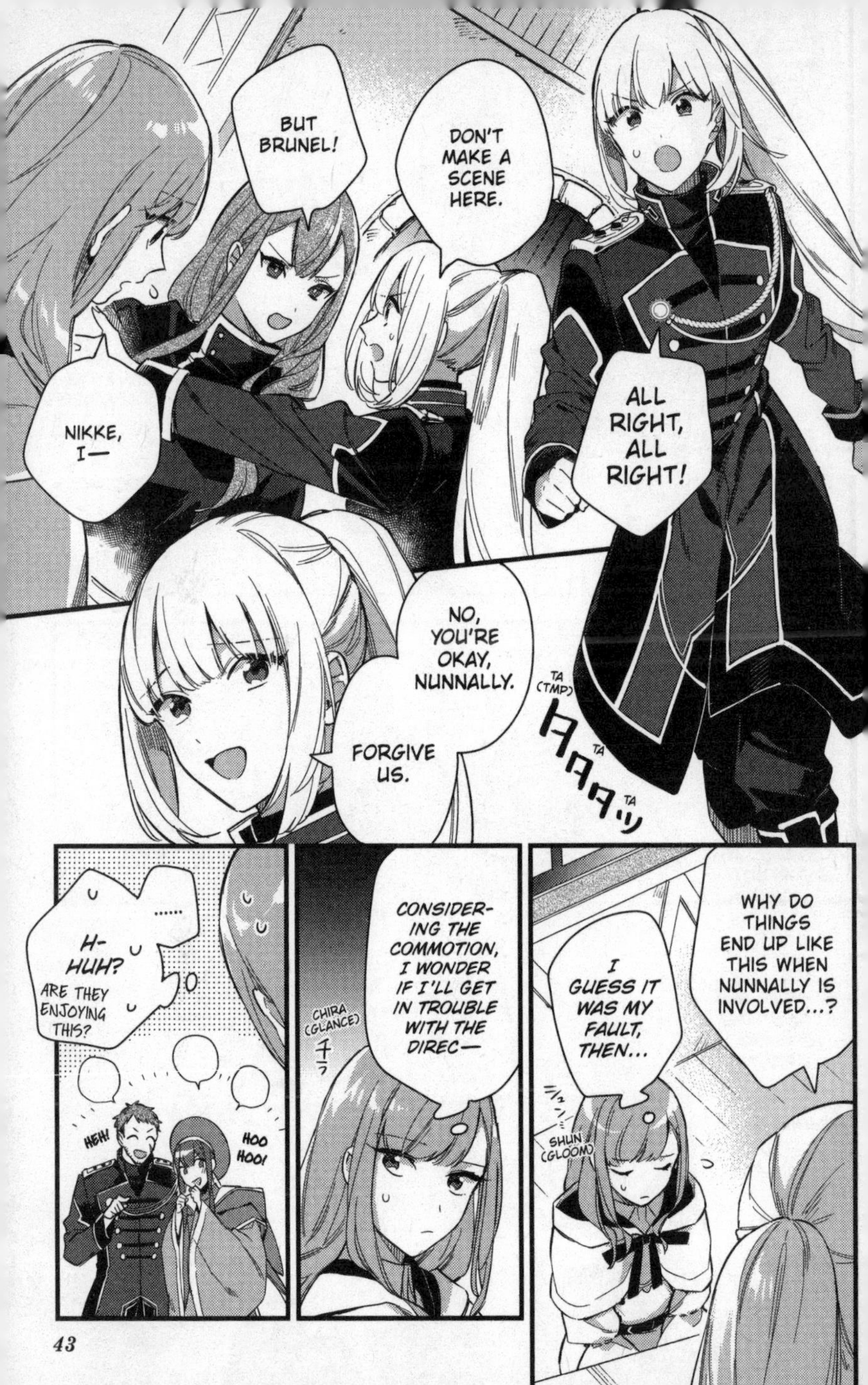
ALL RIGHT, ALL RIGHT!
DON'T MAKE A SCENE HERE.
BUT BRUNEL!
NIKKE, I—
TA (TMP) TA TA
NO, YOU'RE OKAY, NUNNALLY.
FORGIVE US.
WHY DO THINGS END UP LIKE THIS WHEN NUNNALLY IS INVOLVED...?
I GUESS IT WAS MY FAULT, THEN...
SHUN (GLOOM)
CONSIDERING THE COMMOTION, I WONDER IF I'LL GET IN TROUBLE WITH THE DIREC—
CHIRA (GLANCE)
...... H-HUH? ARE THEY ENJOYING THIS?
HEH!
HOO HOO!

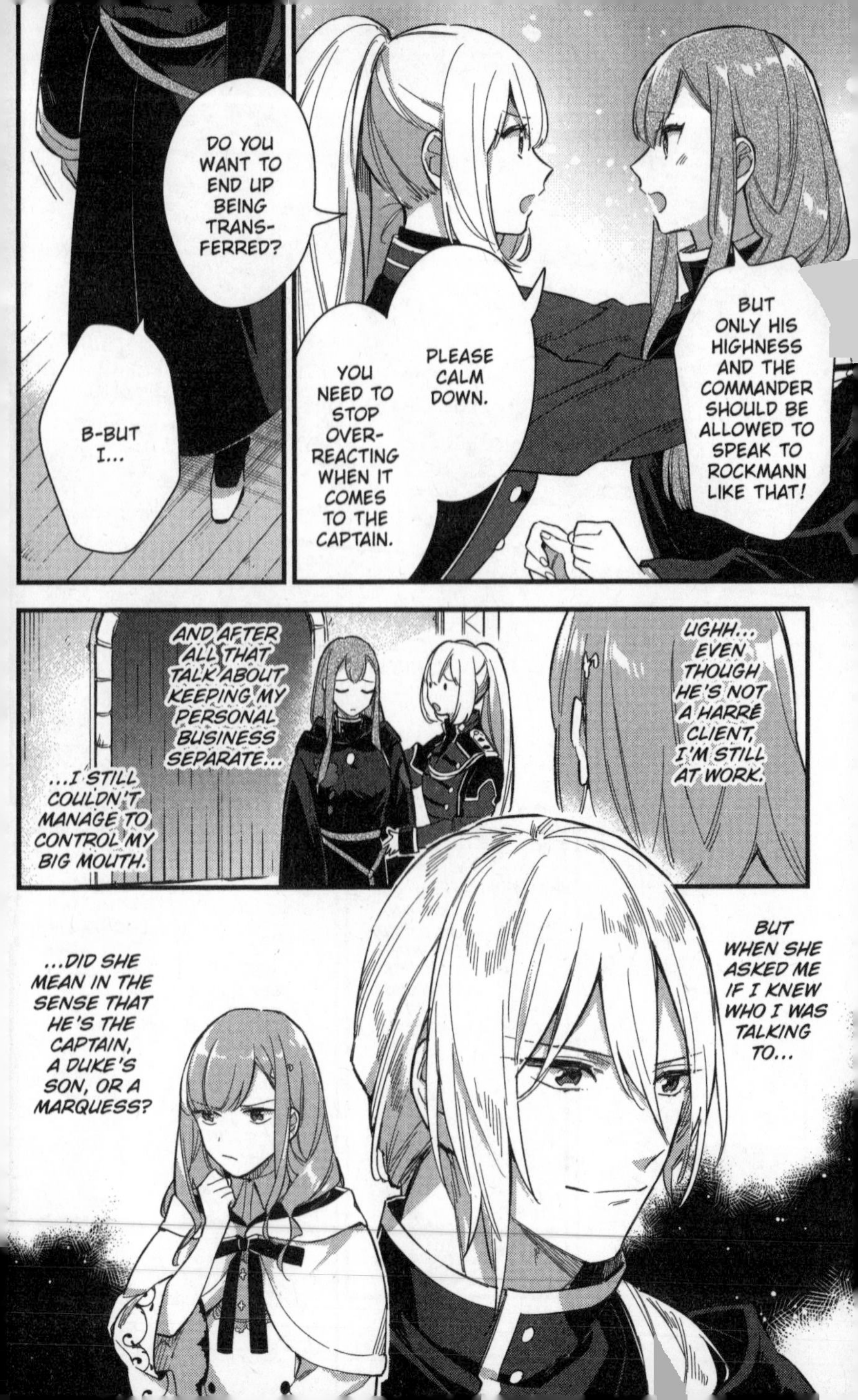
BUT ONLY HIS HIGHNESS AND THE COMMANDER SHOULD BE ALLOWED TO SPEAK TO ROCKMANN LIKE THAT!
PLEASE CALM DOWN.
YOU NEED TO STOP OVER-REACTING WHEN IT COMES TO THE CAPTAIN.
DO YOU WANT TO END UP BEING TRANS-FERRED?
B-BUT I...
UGHH... EVEN THOUGH HE'S NOT A HARRÉ CLIENT, I'M STILL AT WORK.
AND AFTER ALL THAT TALK ABOUT KEEPING MY PERSONAL BUSINESS SEPARATE...
...I STILL COULDN'T MANAGE TO CONTROL MY BIG MOUTH.
BUT WHEN SHE ASKED ME IF I KNEW WHO I WAS TALKING TO...
...DID SHE MEAN IN THE SENSE THAT HE'S THE CAPTAIN, A DUKE'S SON, OR A MARQUESS?

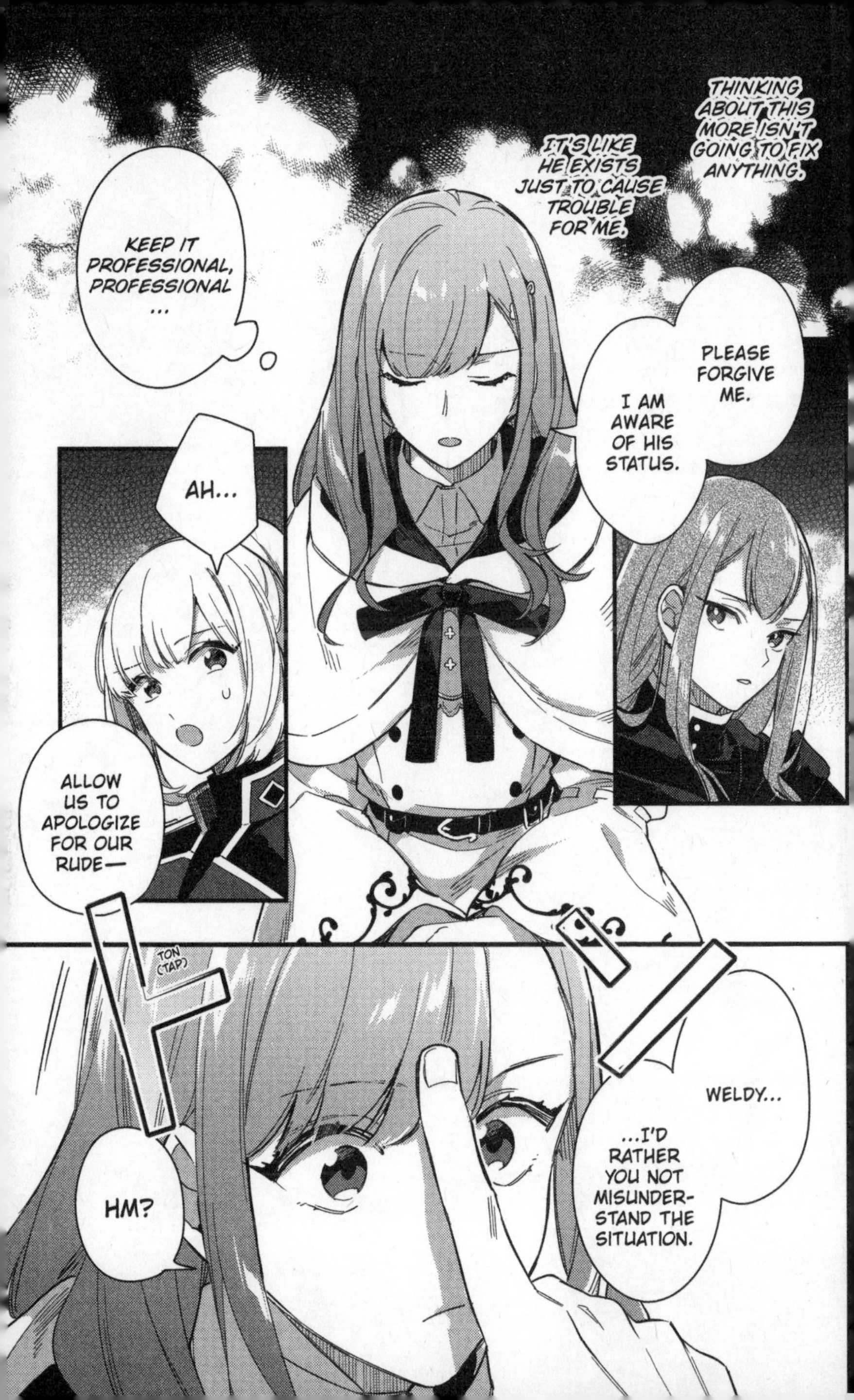
THINKING ABOUT THIS MORE ISN'T GOING TO FIX ANYTHING.
IT'S LIKE HE EXISTS JUST TO CAUSE TROUBLE FOR ME.
KEEP IT PROFESSIONAL, PROFESSIONAL ...
PLEASE FORGIVE ME.
I AM AWARE OF HIS STATUS.
AH...
ALLOW US TO APOLOGIZE FOR OUR RUDE—
WELDY...
...I'D RATHER YOU NOT MISUNDER-STAND THE SITUATION.
TON (TAP)
HM?

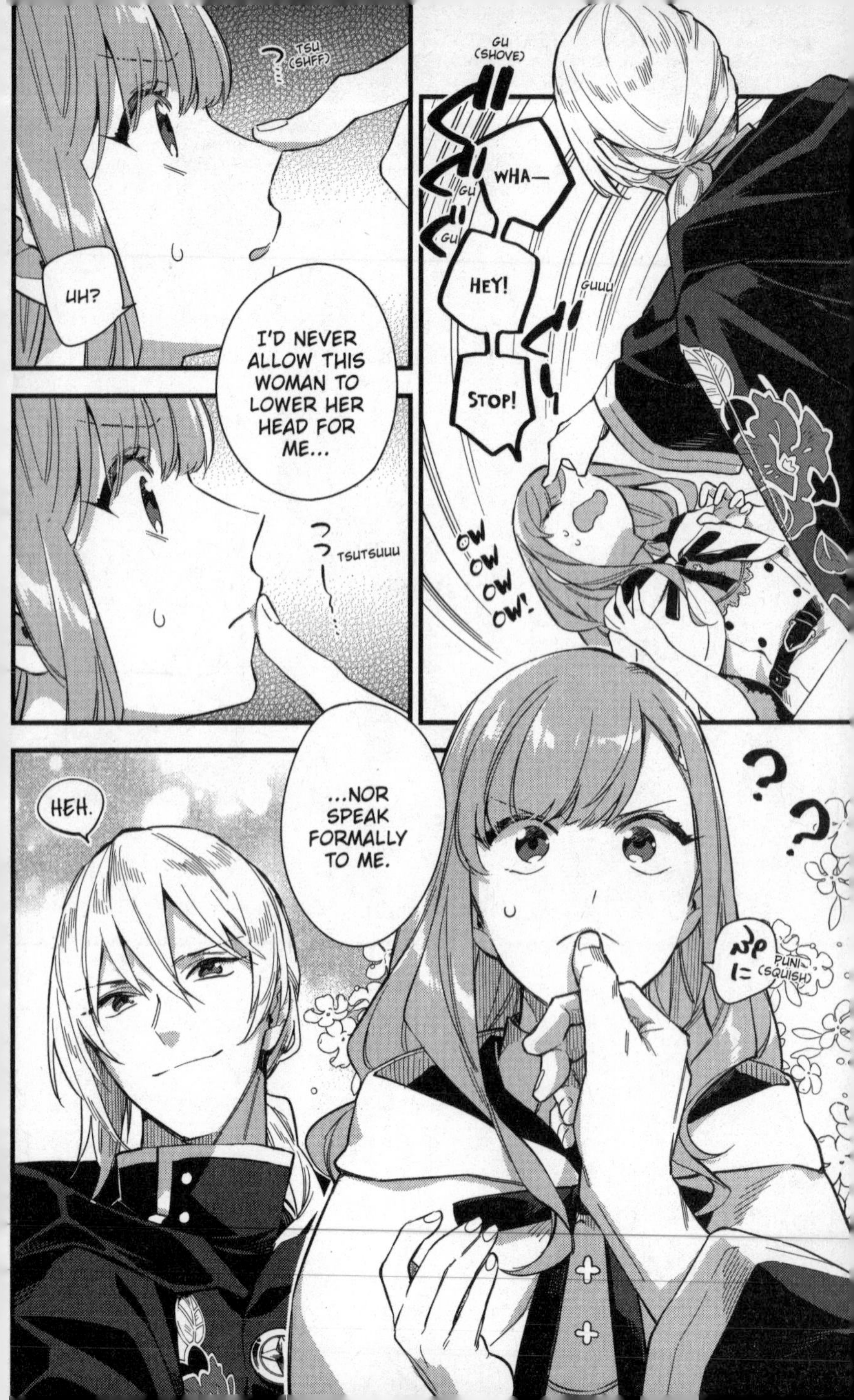
GU (SHOVE)
WHA—
GU
GU
HEY!
GUUU
STOP!
OW OW OW OW!
TSU (SHFF)
...
UH?
I'D NEVER ALLOW THIS WOMAN TO LOWER HER HEAD FOR ME...
TSUTSUUU
...NOR SPEAK FORMALLY TO ME.
?
?
PUNI (SQUISH)
HEH.

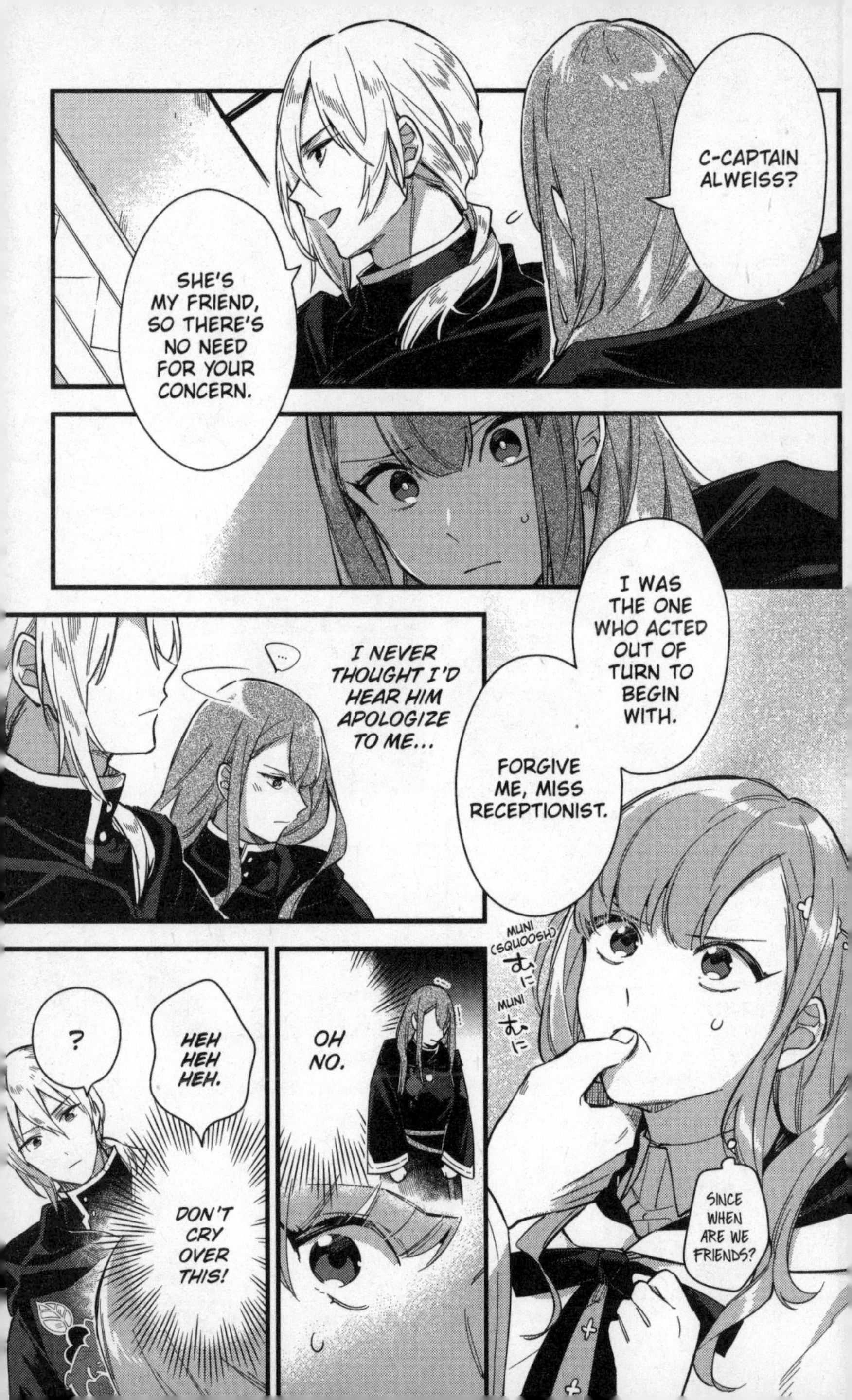
C-CAPTAIN ALWEISS?
SHE'S MY FRIEND, SO THERE'S NO NEED FOR YOUR CONCERN.
I WAS THE ONE WHO ACTED OUT OF TURN TO BEGIN WITH.
FORGIVE ME, MISS RECEPTIONIST.
I NEVER THOUGHT I'D HEAR HIM APOLOGIZE TO ME...
...
MUNI (SQUOOSH)
むに
MUNI
むに
SINCE WHEN ARE WE FRIENDS?
OH NO.
HEH HEH HEH.
?
DON'T CRY OVER THIS!

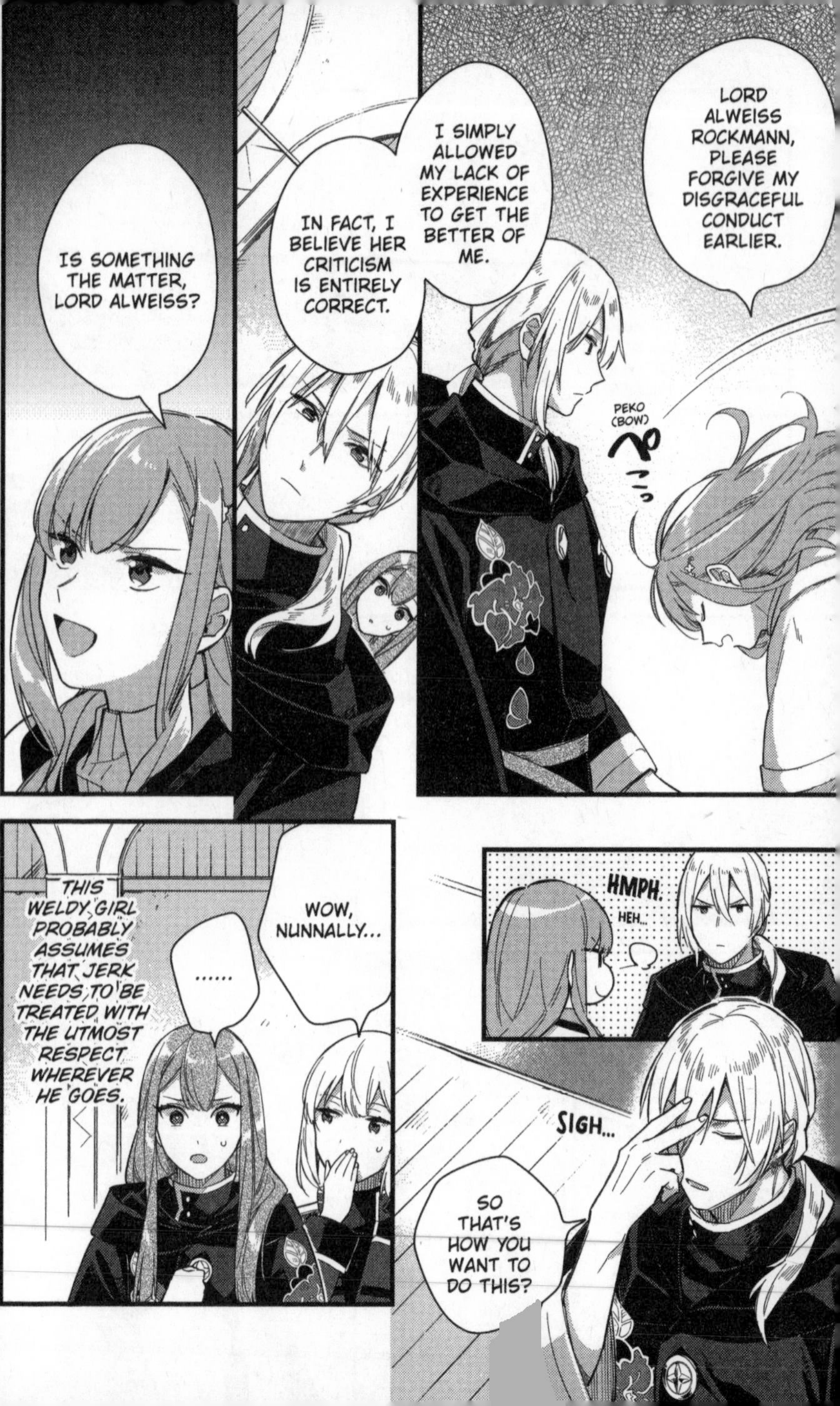
LORD ALWEISS ROCKMANN, PLEASE FORGIVE MY DISGRACEFUL CONDUCT EARLIER.
PEKO (BOW)
I SIMPLY ALLOWED MY LACK OF EXPERIENCE TO GET THE BETTER OF ME.
IN FACT, I BELIEVE HER CRITICISM IS ENTIRELY CORRECT.
IS SOMETHING THE MATTER, LORD ALWEISS?
HMPH.
HEH...
SIGH...
SO THAT'S HOW YOU WANT TO DO THIS?
WOW, NUNNALLY...
......
THIS WELDY GIRL PROBABLY ASSUMES THAT JERK NEEDS TO BE TREATED WITH THE UTMOST RESPECT WHEREVER HE GOES.

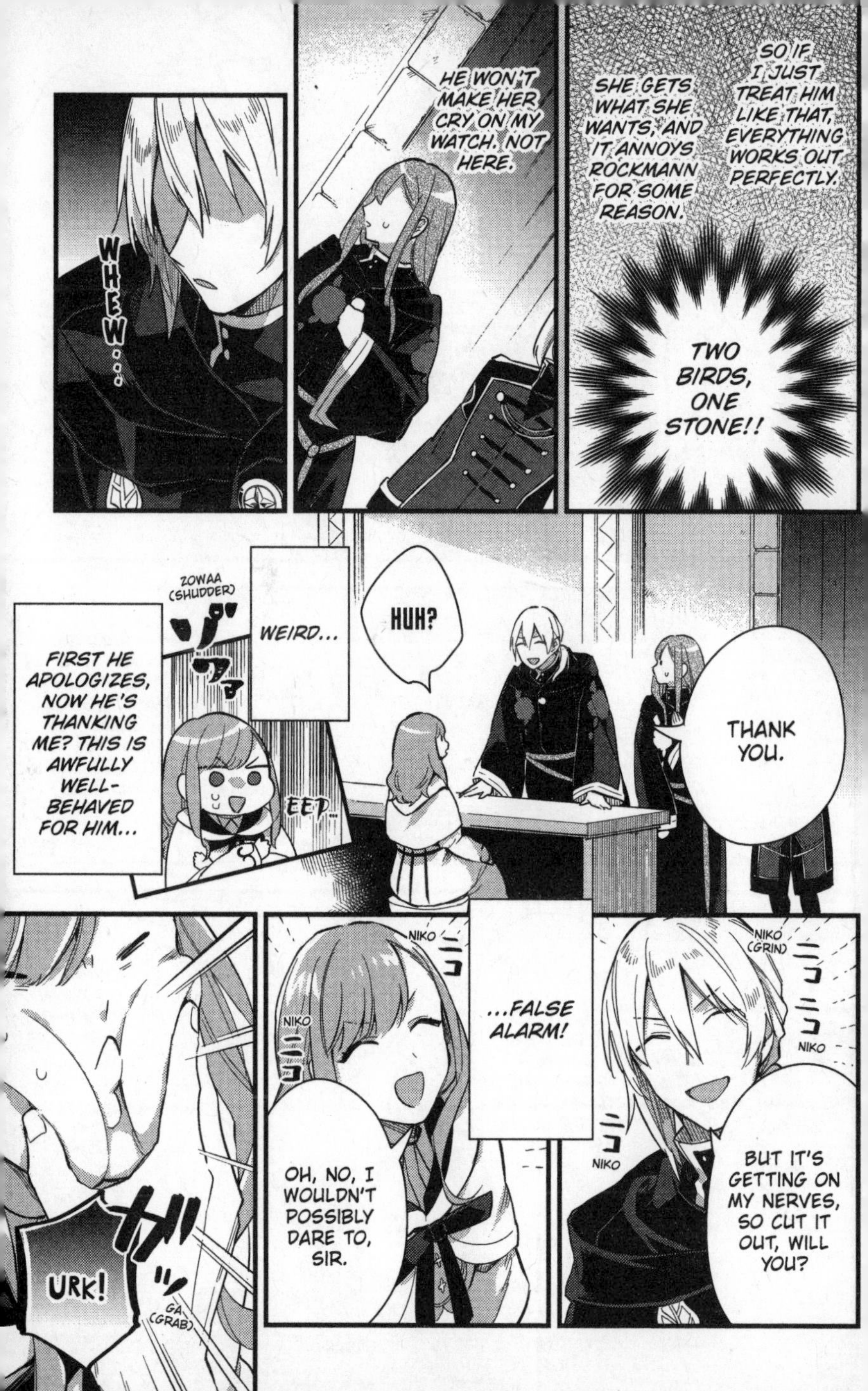
SO IF I JUST TREAT HIM LIKE THAT, EVERYTHING WORKS OUT PERFECTLY.
SHE GETS WHAT SHE WANTS, AND IT ANNOYS ROCKMANN FOR SOME REASON.
TWO BIRDS, ONE STONE!!
HE WON'T MAKE HER CRY ON MY WATCH. NOT HERE.
WHEW...
THANK YOU.
HUH?
WEIRD...
ZOWAA (SHUDDER)
FIRST HE APOLOGIZES, NOW HE'S THANKING ME? THIS IS AWFULLY WELL-BEHAVED FOR HIM...
EEP...
NIKO (GRIN)
NIKO
NIKO
BUT IT'S GETTING ON MY NERVES, SO CUT IT OUT, WILL YOU?
...FALSE ALARM!
NIKO
NIKO
OH, NO, I WOULDN'T POSSIBLY DARE TO, SIR.
URK!
GA (GRAB)

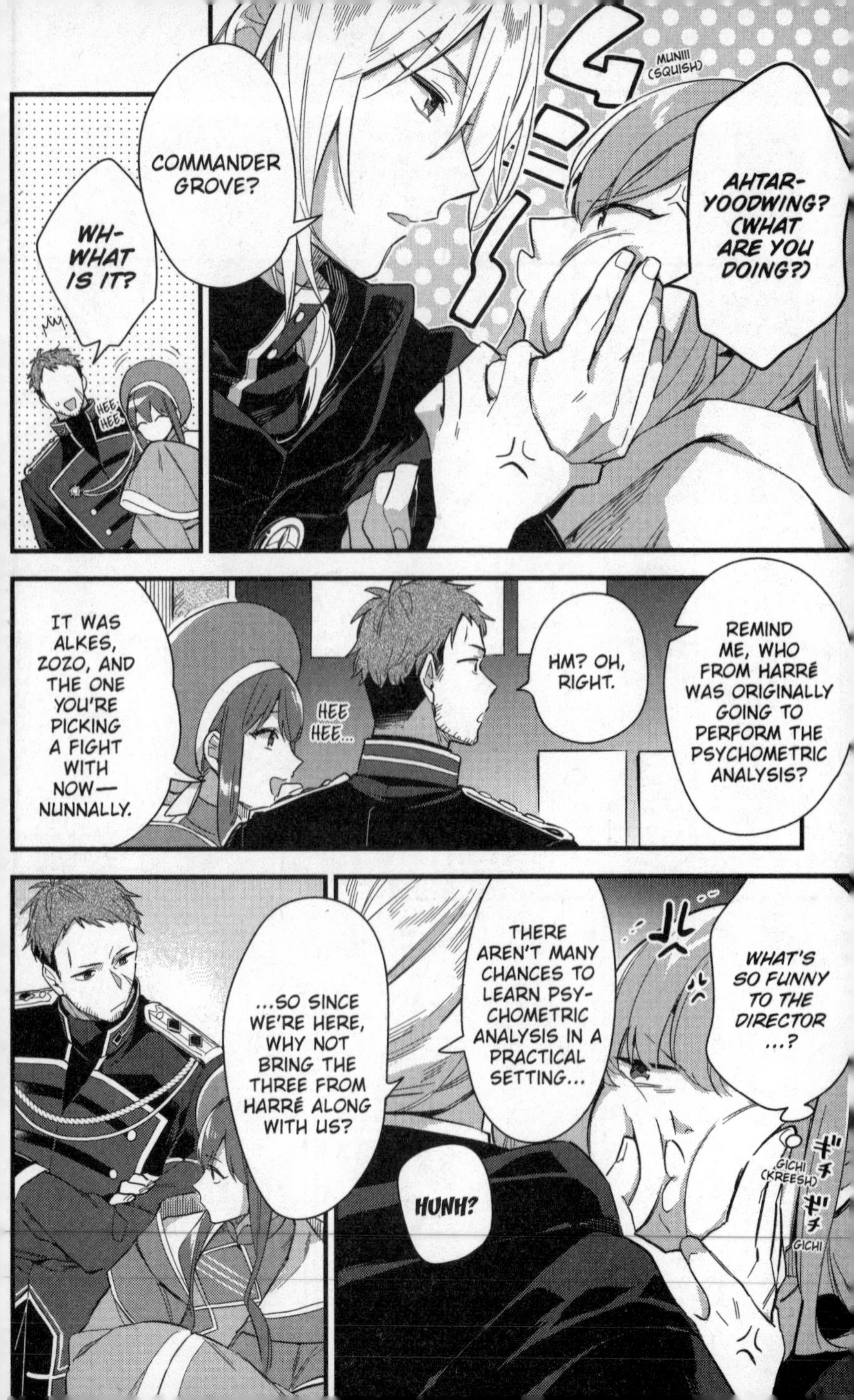
MUNIII (SQUISH)
AHTAR-YOODWING? (WHAT ARE YOU DOING?)
COMMANDER GROVE?
WH-WHAT IS IT?
HEE HEE.
REMIND ME, WHO FROM HARRÉ WAS ORIGINALLY GOING TO PERFORM THE PSYCHOMETRIC ANALYSIS?
HM? OH, RIGHT.
HEE HEE...
IT WAS ALKES, ZOZO, AND THE ONE YOU'RE PICKING A FIGHT WITH NOW—NUNNALLY.
WHAT'S SO FUNNY TO THE DIRECTOR ...?
GICHI (KREESH)
GICHI
THERE AREN'T MANY CHANCES TO LEARN PSY-CHOMETRIC ANALYSIS IN A PRACTICAL SETTING...
...SO SINCE WE'RE HERE, WHY NOT BRING THE THREE FROM HARRÉ ALONG WITH US?
HUNH?

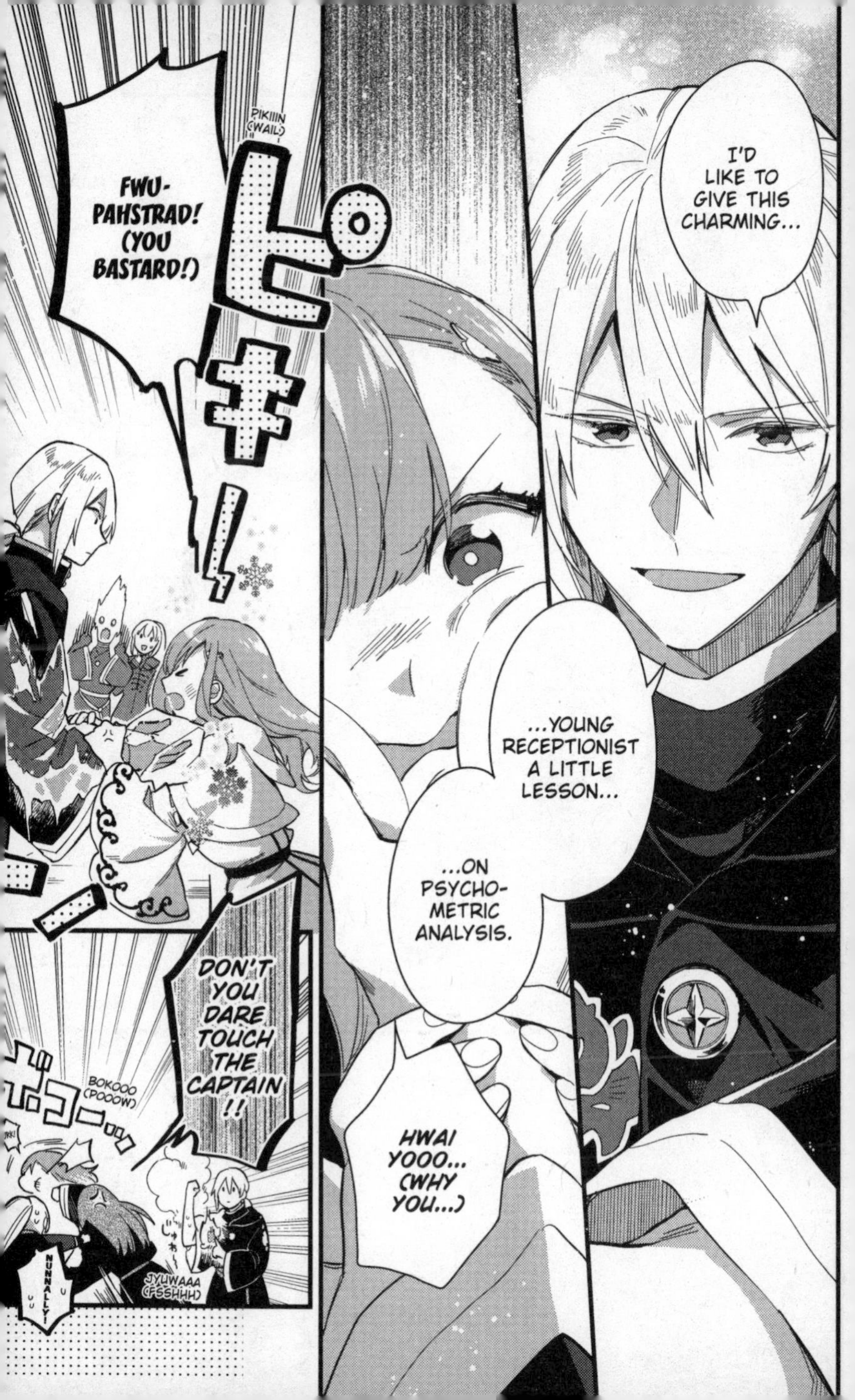
I'D LIKE TO GIVE THIS CHARMING...
...YOUNG RECEPTIONIST A LITTLE LESSON...
...ON PSYCHO-METRIC ANALYSIS.
HWAI YOOO... (WHY YOU...)
PIKIIIN (WAIL)
FWU-PAHSTRAD! (YOU BASTARD!)
DON'T YOU DARE TOUCH THE CAPTAIN!!
BOKOOO (POOOW)
JYUWAAA (FSSHHH)
NUNNALLY!

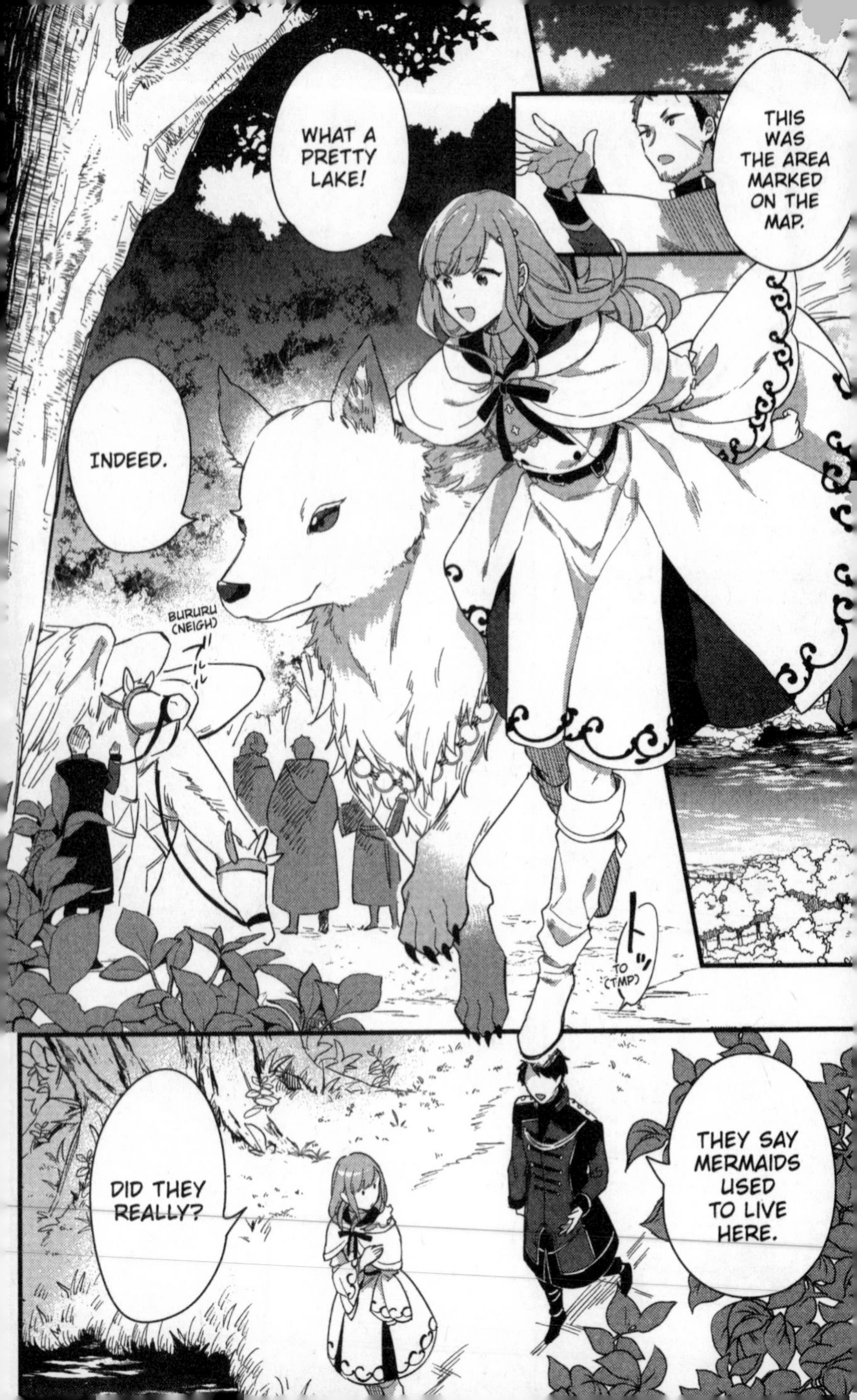
THIS WAS THE AREA MARKED ON THE MAP.
WHAT A PRETTY LAKE!
INDEED.
BURURU (NEIGH)
TO (TMP)
THEY SAY MERMAIDS USED TO LIVE HERE.
DID THEY REALLY?

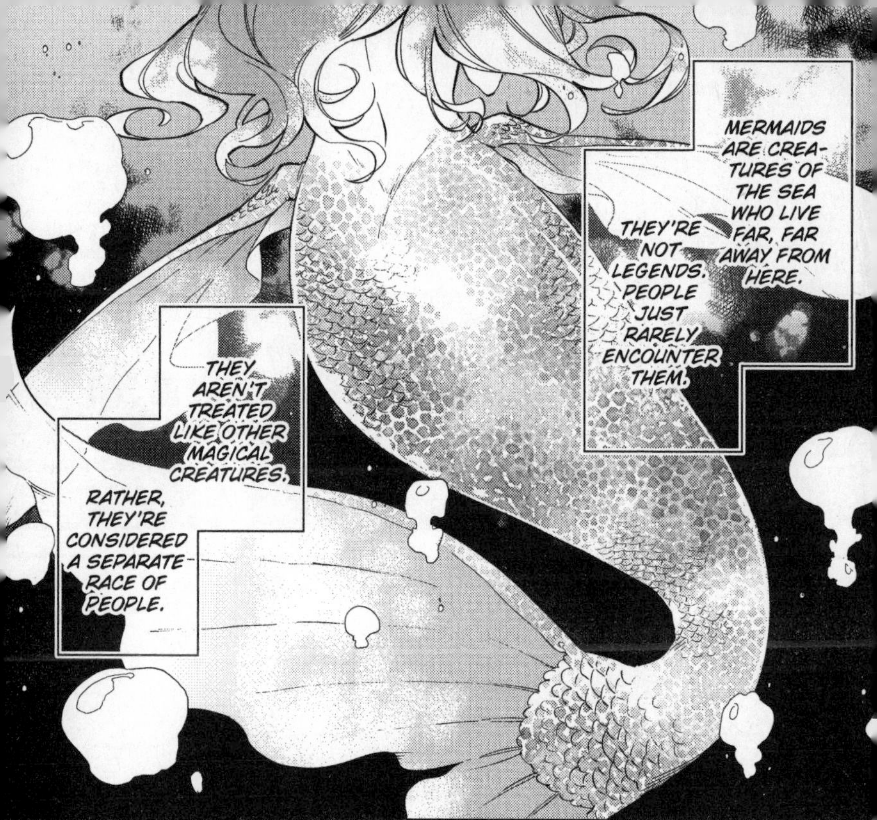
MERMAIDS ARE CREATURES OF THE SEA WHO LIVE FAR, FAR AWAY FROM HERE.
THEY'RE NOT LEGENDS. PEOPLE JUST RARELY ENCOUNTER THEM.
THEY AREN'T TREATED LIKE OTHER MAGICAL CREATURES.
RATHER, THEY'RE CONSIDERED A SEPARATE RACE OF PEOPLE.
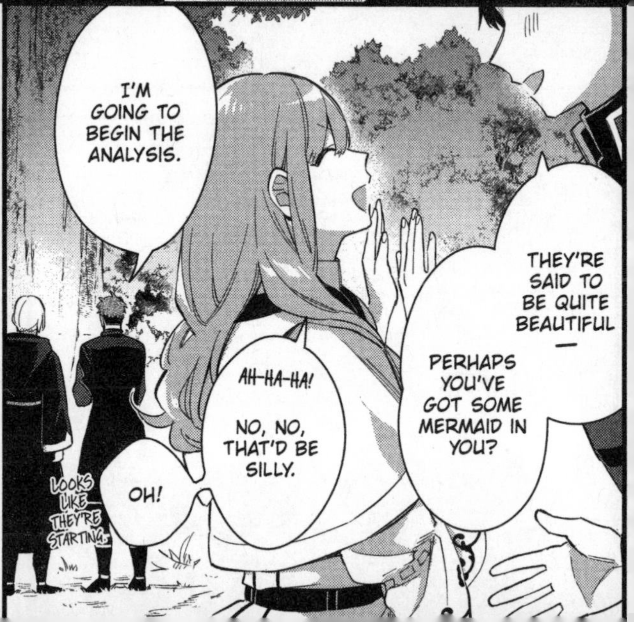
THEY'RE SAID TO BE QUITE BEAUTIFUL —
PERHAPS YOU'VE GOT SOME MERMAID IN YOU?
AH-HA-HA!
NO, NO, THAT'D BE SILLY.
OH!
LOOKS LIKE THEY'RE STARTING.
I'M GOING TO BEGIN THE ANALYSIS.
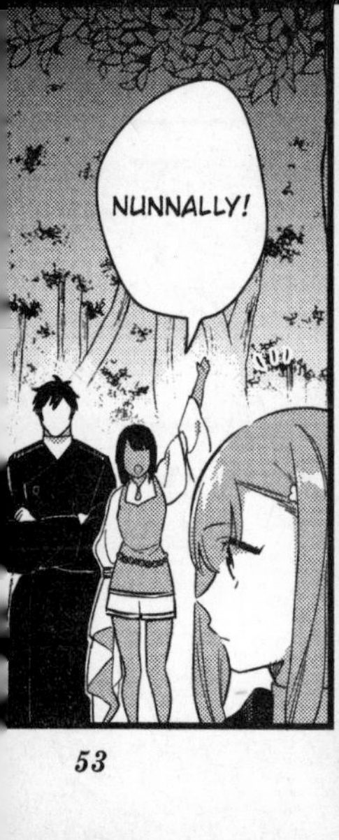
NUNNALLY!

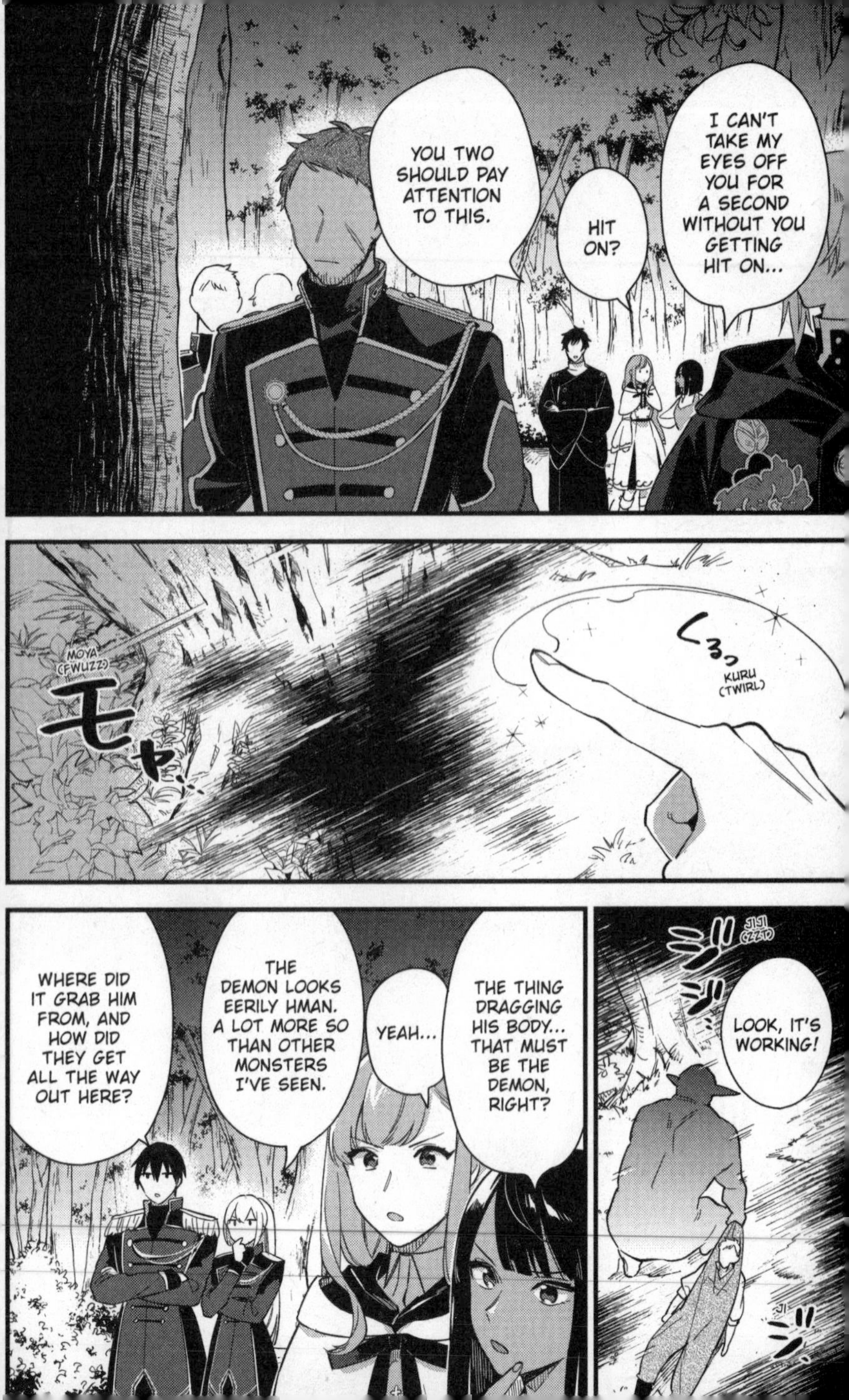
I CAN'T TAKE MY EYES OFF YOU FOR A SECOND WITHOUT YOU GETTING HIT ON...
HIT ON?
YOU TWO SHOULD PAY ATTENTION TO THIS.
くるっ
KURU (TWIRL)
モヤ
MOYA (FWUZZ)
JIJI (ZZZT)
LOOK, IT'S WORKING!
JI
THE THING DRAGGING HIS BODY... THAT MUST BE THE DEMON, RIGHT?
YEAH...
THE DEMON LOOKS EERILY HMAN. A LOT MORE SO THAN OTHER MONSTERS I'VE SEEN.
WHERE DID IT GRAB HIM FROM, AND HOW DID THEY GET ALL THE WAY OUT HERE?

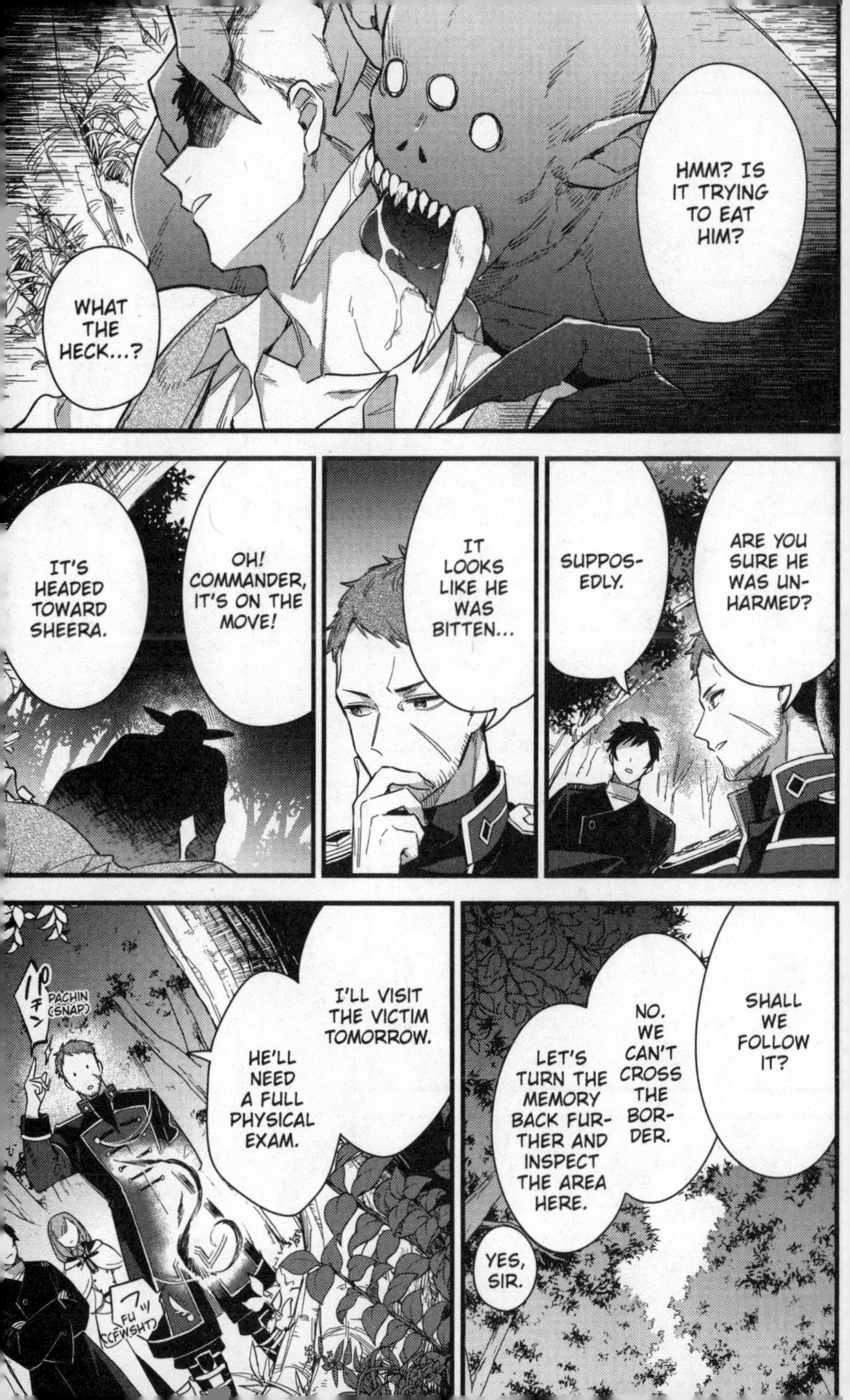
HMM? IS IT TRYING TO EAT HIM?
WHAT THE HECK...?
ARE YOU SURE HE WAS UN-HARMED?
SUPPOS-EDLY.
IT LOOKS LIKE HE WAS BITTEN...
OH! COMMANDER, IT'S ON THE MOVE!
IT'S HEADED TOWARD SHEERA.
SHALL WE FOLLOW IT?
NO. WE CAN'T CROSS THE BOR-DER.
LET'S TURN THE MEMORY BACK FUR-THER AND INSPECT THE AREA HERE.
YES, SIR.
I'LL VISIT THE VICTIM TOMORROW.
HE'LL NEED A FULL PHYSICAL EXAM.
PACHIN (SNAP)
FU (FWSHT)

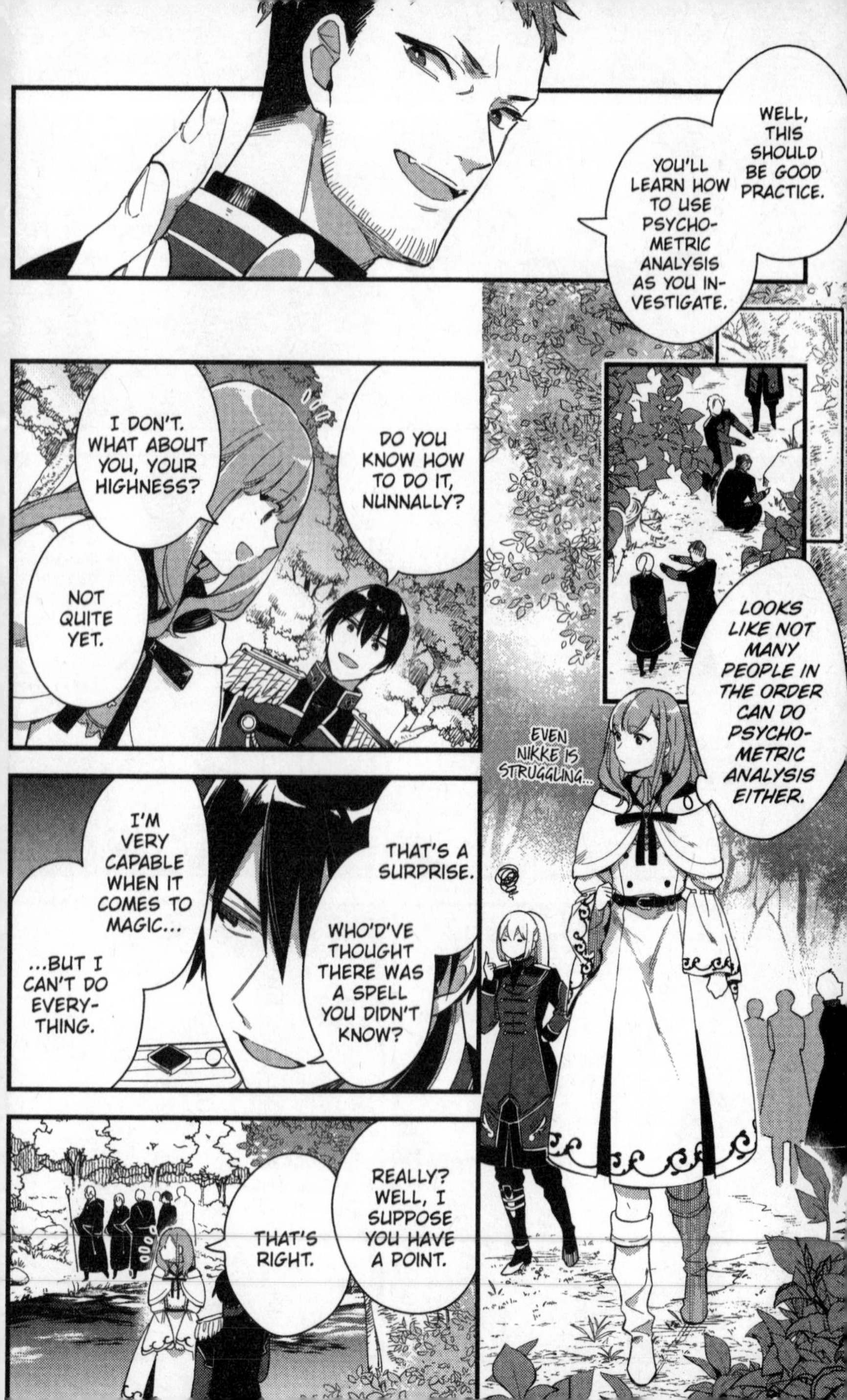
WELL, THIS SHOULD BE GOOD PRACTICE.
YOU'LL LEARN HOW TO USE PSYCHO-METRIC ANALYSIS AS YOU IN-VESTIGATE.
LOOKS LIKE NOT MANY PEOPLE IN THE ORDER CAN DO PSYCHO-METRIC ANALYSIS EITHER.
EVEN NIKKE IS STRUGGLING...
DO YOU KNOW HOW TO DO IT, NUNNALLY?
I DON'T. WHAT ABOUT YOU, YOUR HIGHNESS?
NOT QUITE YET.
THAT'S A SURPRISE.
WHO'D'VE THOUGHT THERE WAS A SPELL YOU DIDN'T KNOW?
I'M VERY CAPABLE WHEN IT COMES TO MAGIC...
...BUT I CAN'T DO EVERY-THING.
REALLY? WELL, I SUPPOSE YOU HAVE A POINT.
THAT'S RIGHT.

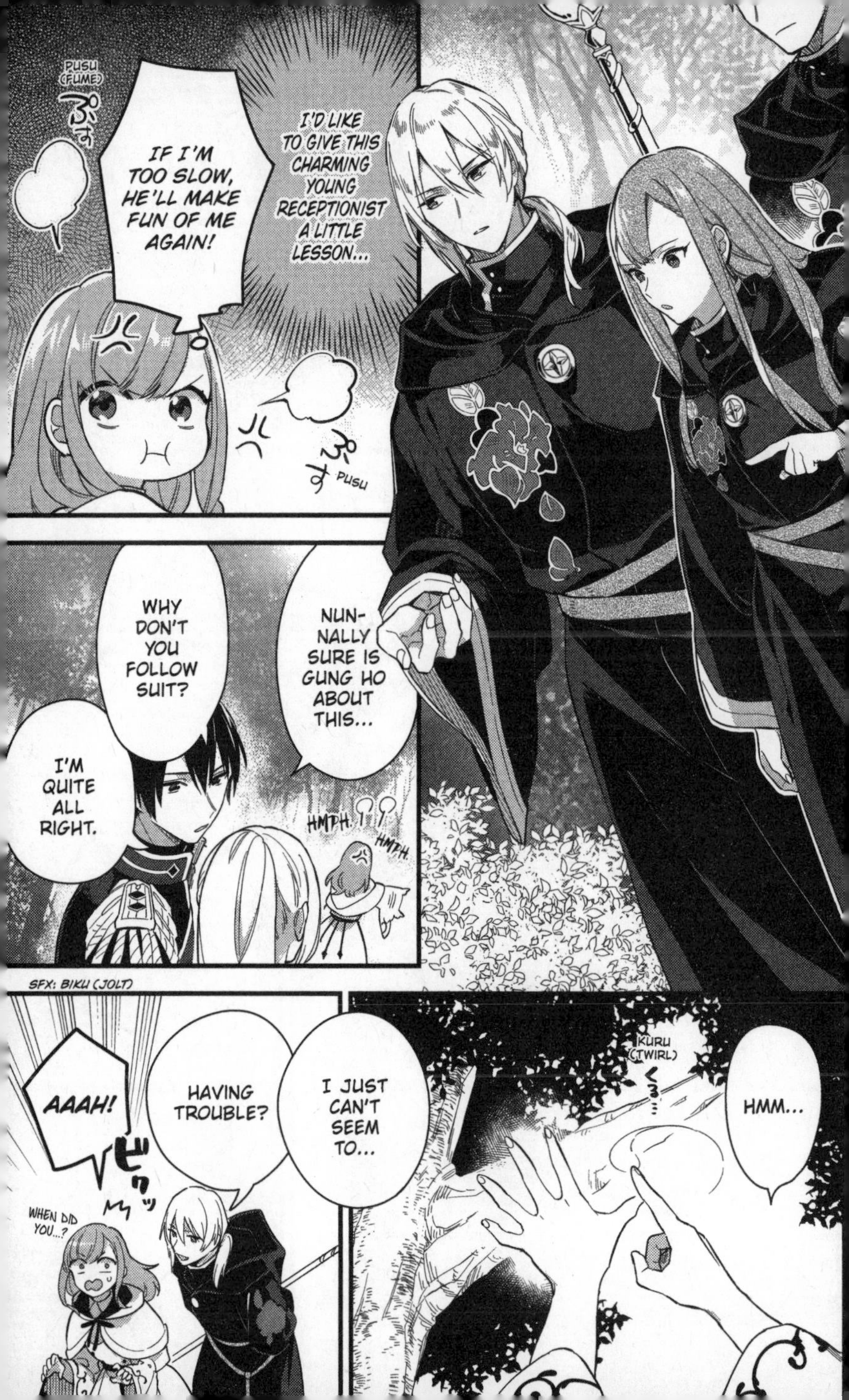
I'D LIKE TO GIVE THIS CHARMING YOUNG RECEPTIONIST A LITTLE LESSON...
IF I'M TOO SLOW, HE'LL MAKE FUN OF ME AGAIN!
ぷす
PUSU (FUME)
ぷす
PUSU
NUN-NALLY SURE IS GUNG HO ABOUT THIS...
WHY DON'T YOU FOLLOW SUIT?
I'M QUITE ALL RIGHT.
HMPH.
HMPH.
SFX: BIKU (JOLT)
HMM...
KURU (TWIRL)
I JUST CAN'T SEEM TO...
HAVING TROUBLE?
AAAH!
ビクッ
WHEN DID YOU...?

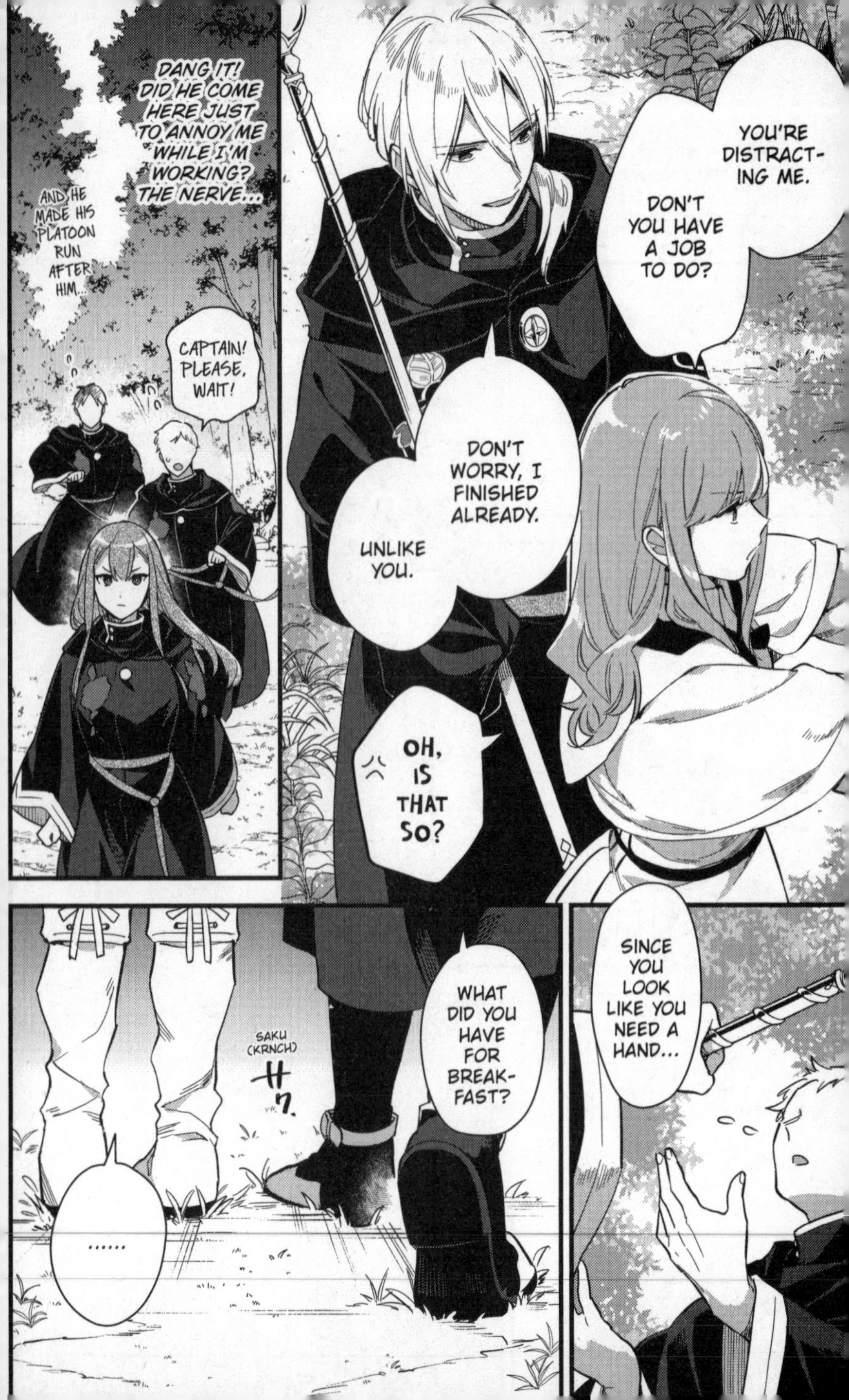
YOU'RE DISTRACTING ME.
DON'T YOU HAVE A JOB TO DO?
DON'T WORRY, I FINISHED ALREADY.
UNLIKE YOU.
OH, IS THAT SO?
DANG IT! DID HE COME HERE JUST TO ANNOY ME WHILE I'M WORKING? THE NERVE...
AND HE MADE HIS PLATOON RUN AFTER HIM...
CAPTAIN! PLEASE, WAIT!
SINCE YOU LOOK LIKE YOU NEED A HAND...
WHAT DID YOU HAVE FOR BREAKFAST?
SAKU (KRNCH)
......

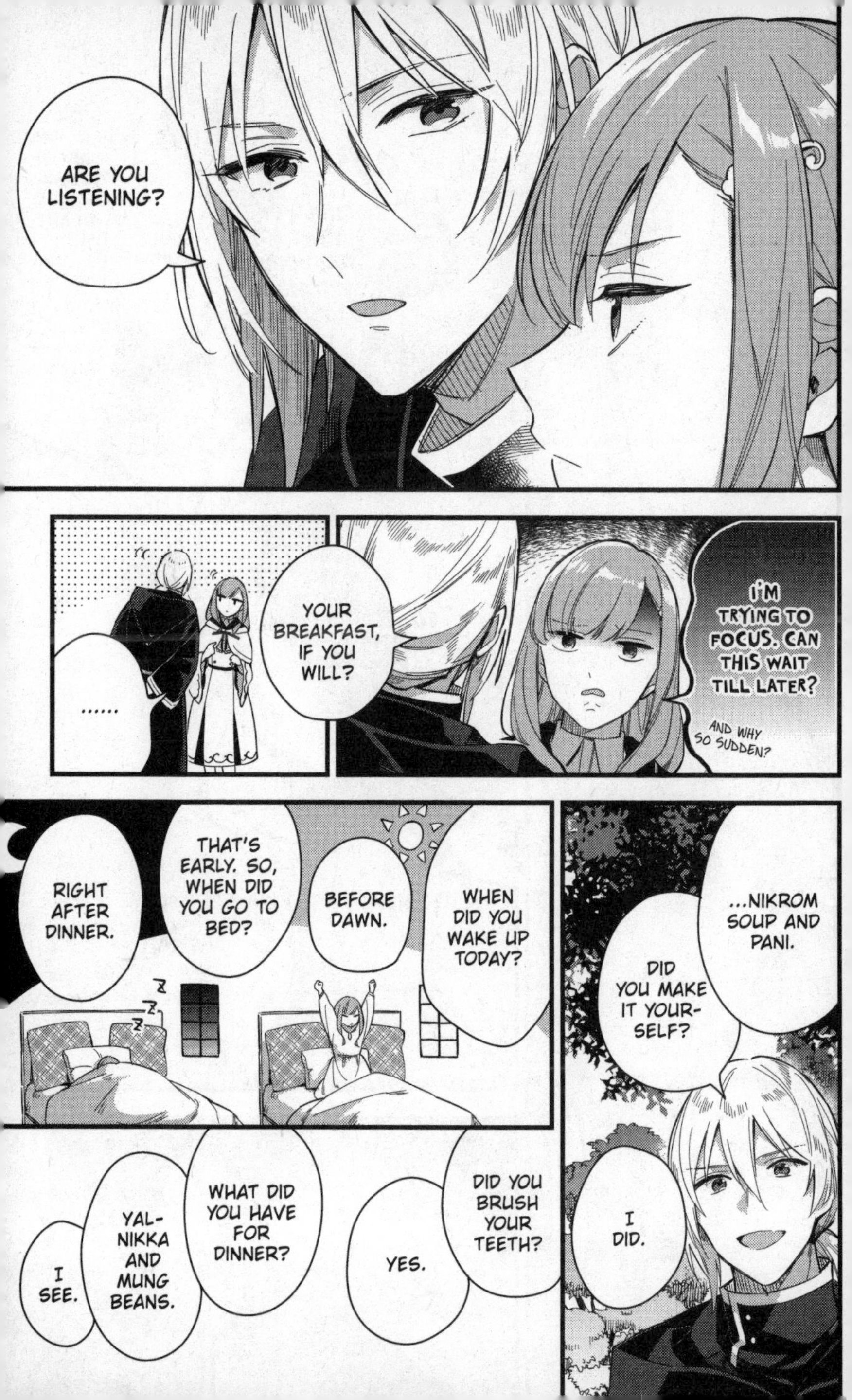
ARE YOU LISTENING?
I'M TRYING TO FOCUS. CAN THIS WAIT TILL LATER?
AND WHY SO SUDDEN?
YOUR BREAKFAST, IF YOU WILL?
......
...NIKROM SOUP AND PANI.
DID YOU MAKE IT YOUR-SELF?
I DID.
WHEN DID YOU WAKE UP TODAY?
BEFORE DAWN.
THAT'S EARLY. SO, WHEN DID YOU GO TO BED?
RIGHT AFTER DINNER.
Z
Z
Z
DID YOU BRUSH YOUR TEETH?
YES.
WHAT DID YOU HAVE FOR DINNER?
YAL-NIKKA AND MUNG BEANS.
I SEE.

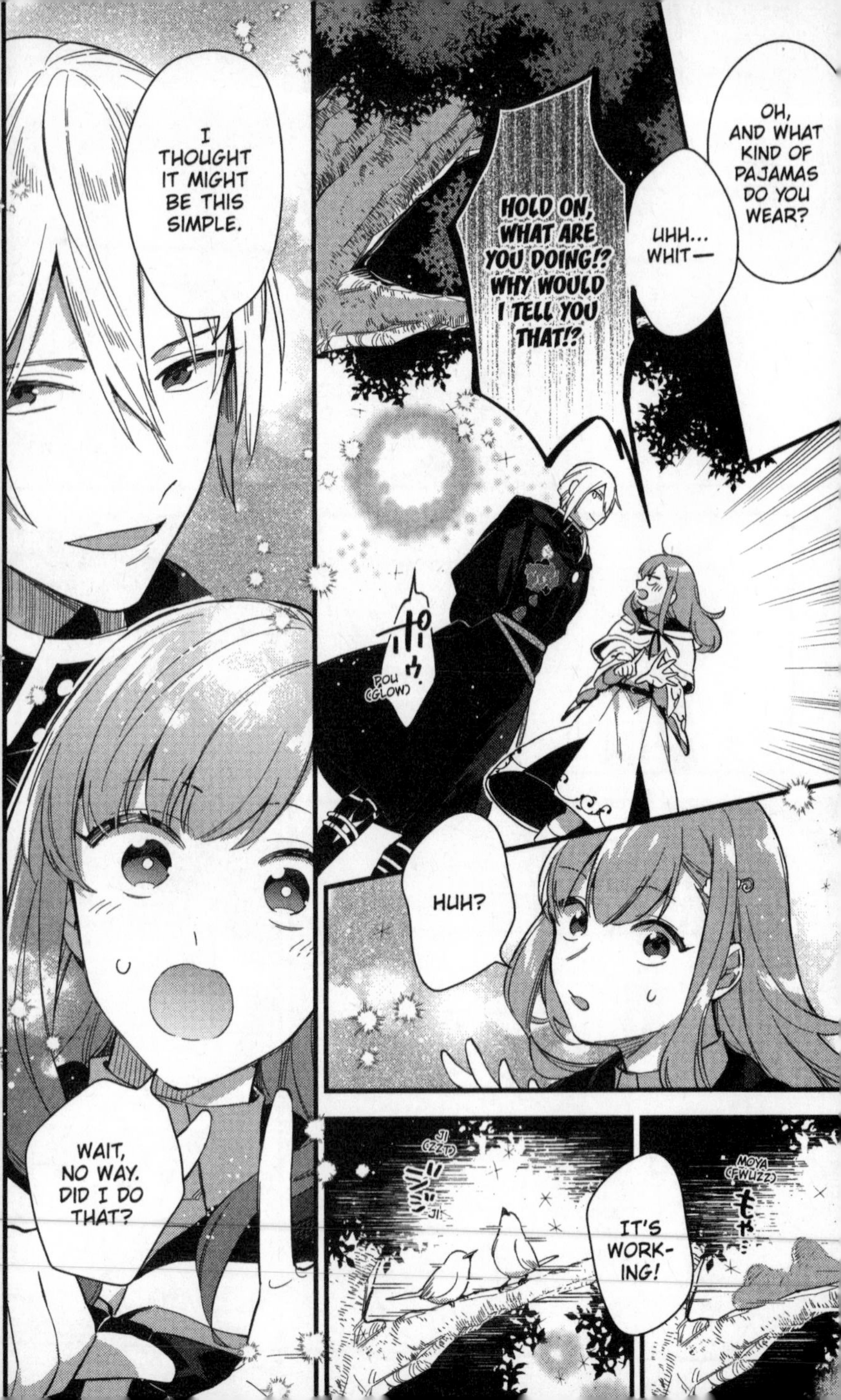
OH, AND WHAT KIND OF PAJAMAS DO YOU WEAR?
UHH... WHIT—
HOLD ON, WHAT ARE YOU DOING!? WHY WOULD I TELL YOU THAT!?
POU (GLOW)
HUH?
MOYA (FWUZZ)
IT'S WORK-ING!
JI (ZZT)
JI
I THOUGHT IT MIGHT BE THIS SIMPLE.
WAIT, NO WAY. DID I DO THAT?

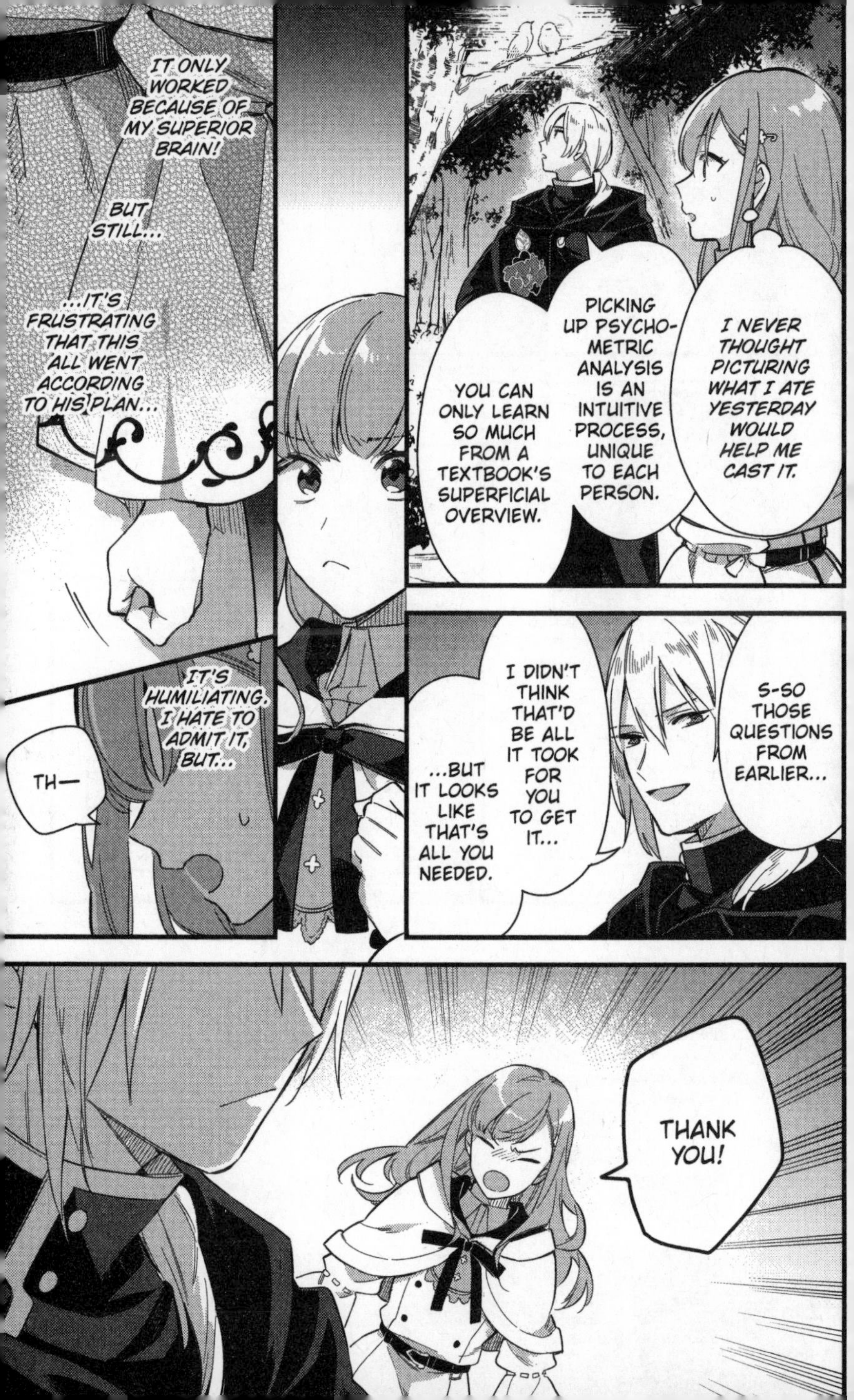
I NEVER THOUGHT PICTURING WHAT I ATE YESTERDAY WOULD HELP ME CAST IT.
PICKING UP PSYCHO-METRIC ANALYSIS IS AN INTUITIVE PROCESS, UNIQUE TO EACH PERSON.
YOU CAN ONLY LEARN SO MUCH FROM A TEXTBOOK'S SUPERFICIAL OVERVIEW.
S-SO THOSE QUESTIONS FROM EARLIER...
I DIDN'T THINK THAT'D BE ALL IT TOOK FOR YOU TO GET IT...
...BUT IT LOOKS LIKE THAT'S ALL YOU NEEDED.
IT ONLY WORKED BECAUSE OF MY SUPERIOR BRAIN!
BUT STILL...
...IT'S FRUSTRATING THAT THIS ALL WENT ACCORDING TO HIS PLAN...
IT'S HUMILIATING. I HATE TO ADMIT IT, BUT...
TH—
THANK YOU!

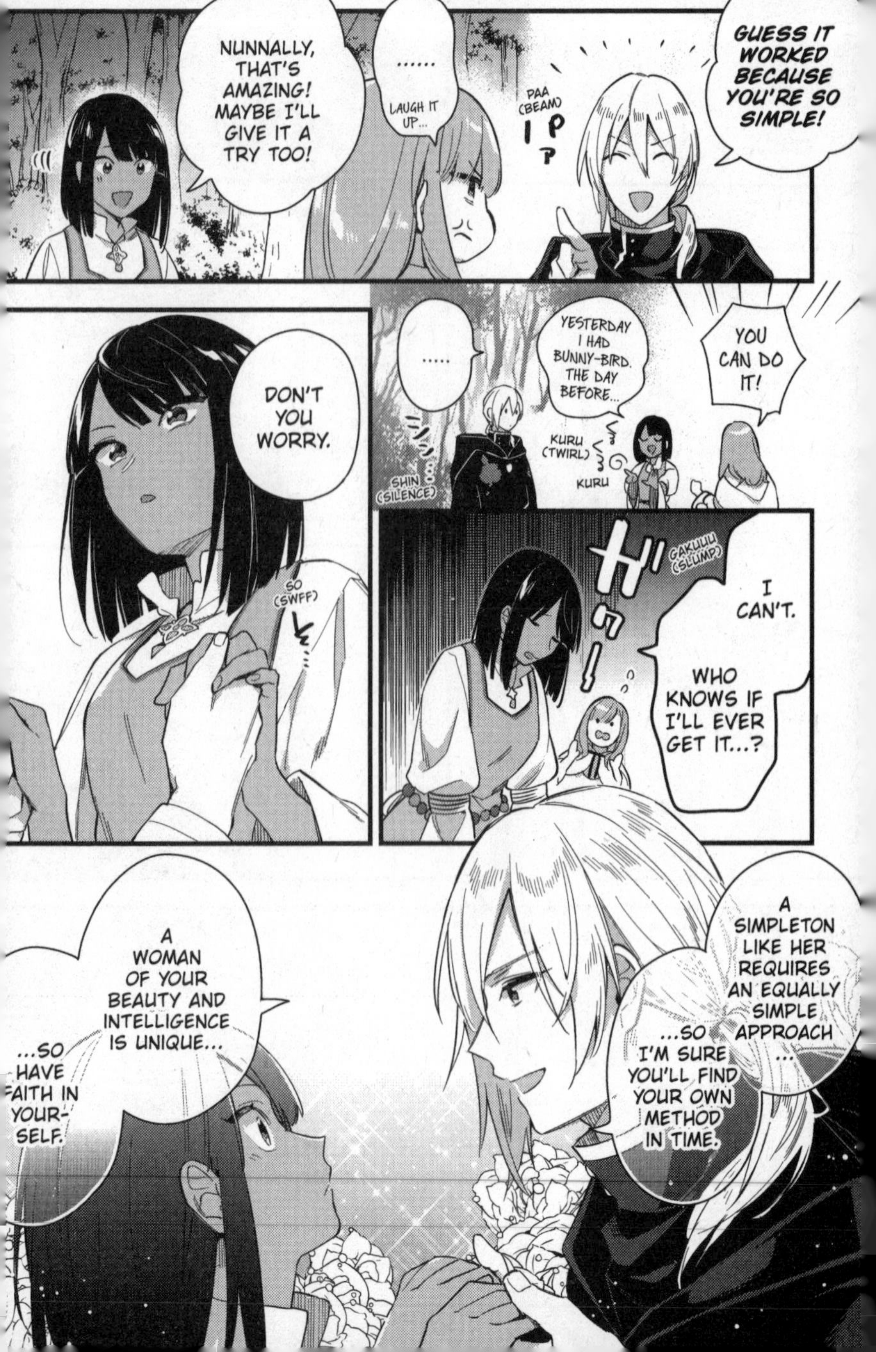
GUESS IT WORKED BECAUSE YOU'RE SO SIMPLE!
PAA (BEAM)
......
LAUGH IT UP...
NUNNALLY, THAT'S AMAZING! MAYBE I'LL GIVE IT A TRY TOO!
YOU CAN DO IT!
YESTERDAY I HAD BUNNY-BIRD. THE DAY BEFORE...
KURU (TWIRL)
KURU
.....
SHIN (SILENCE)
DON'T YOU WORRY.
GAKUUU (SLUMP)
I CAN'T.
WHO KNOWS IF I'LL EVER GET IT...?
SO (SWFF)
A SIMPLETON LIKE HER REQUIRES AN EQUALLY SIMPLE APPROACH...
...SO I'M SURE YOU'LL FIND YOUR OWN METHOD IN TIME.
A WOMAN OF YOUR BEAUTY AND INTELLIGENCE IS UNIQUE...
...SO HAVE FAITH IN YOUR-SELF.

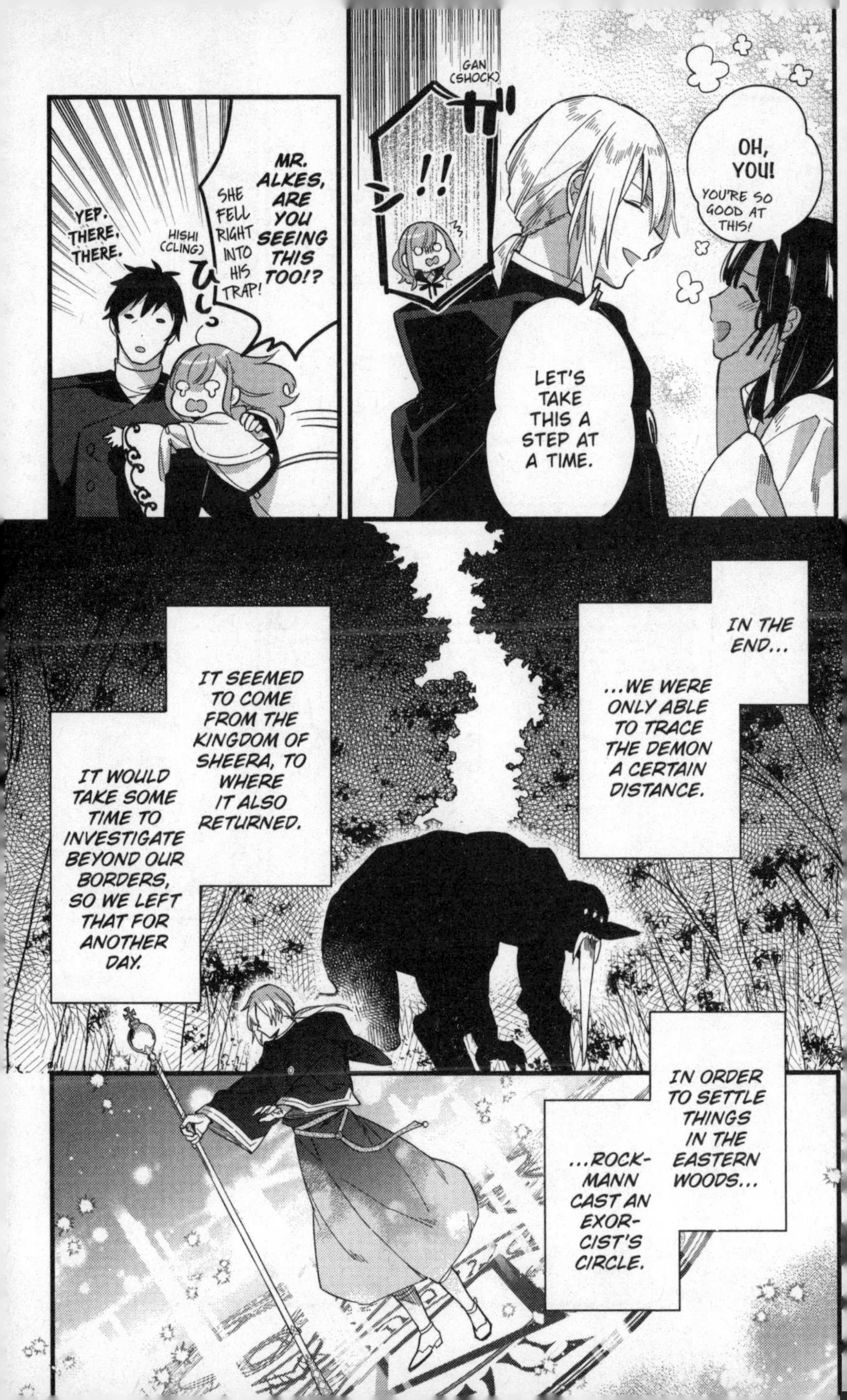
OH, YOU!
YOU'RE SO GOOD AT THIS!
LET'S TAKE THIS A STEP AT A TIME.
GAN (SHOCK)
!!
MR. ALKES, ARE YOU SEEING THIS TOO!?
SHE FELL RIGHT INTO HIS TRAP!
HISHI (CLING)
YEP. THERE, THERE.
IN THE END...
...WE WERE ONLY ABLE TO TRACE THE DEMON A CERTAIN DISTANCE.
IT SEEMED TO COME FROM THE KINGDOM OF SHEERA, TO WHERE IT ALSO RETURNED.
IT WOULD TAKE SOME TIME TO INVESTIGATE BEYOND OUR BORDERS, SO WE LEFT THAT FOR ANOTHER DAY.
IN ORDER TO SETTLE THINGS IN THE EASTERN WOODS...
...ROCK-MANN CAST AN EXOR-CIST'S CIRCLE.

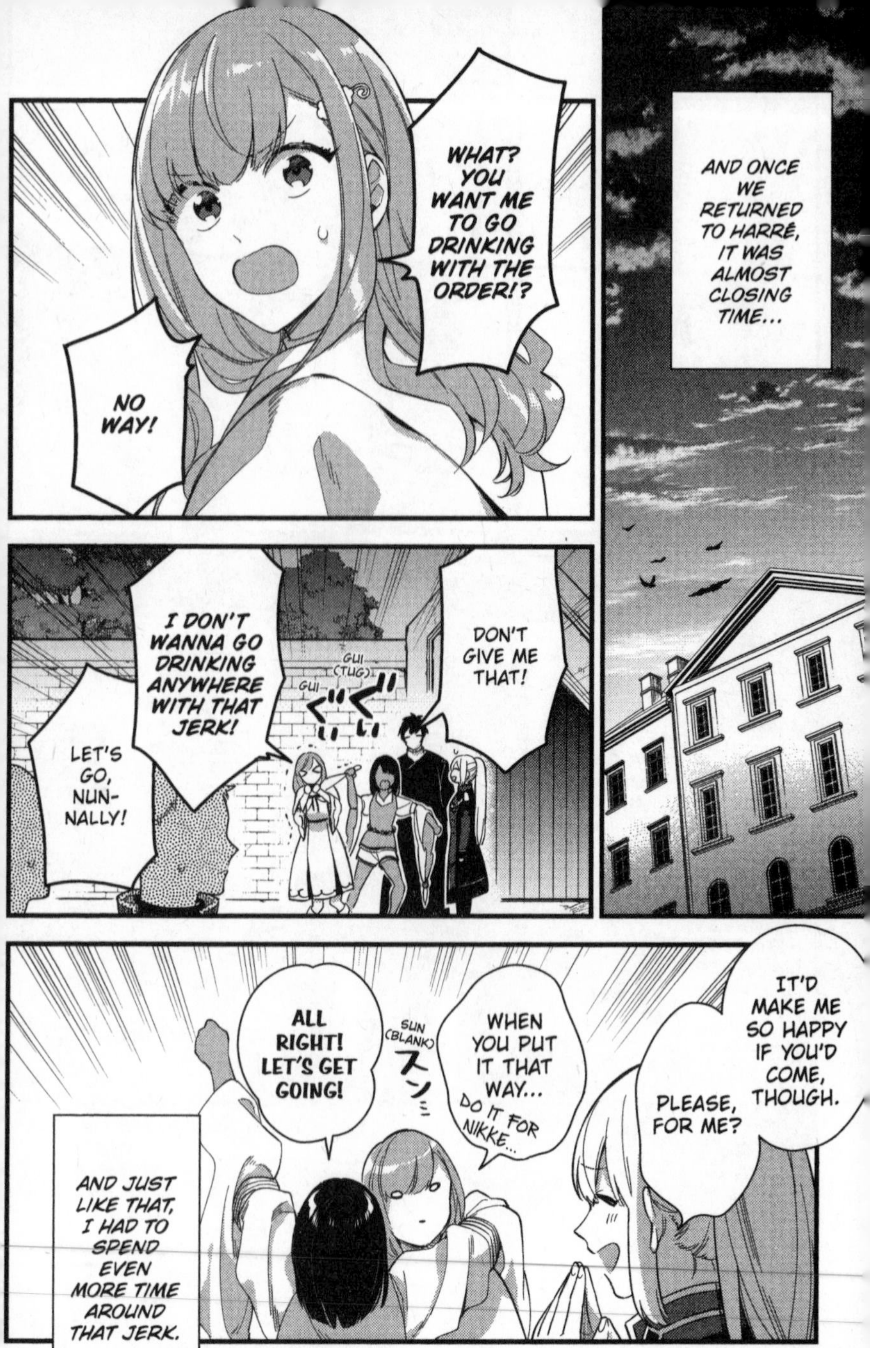
AND ONCE WE RETURNED TO HARRÉ, IT WAS ALMOST CLOSING TIME...
WHAT? YOU WANT ME TO GO DRINKING WITH THE ORDER!?
NO WAY!
DON'T GIVE ME THAT!
GUI (TUG) GUI
I DON'T WANNA GO DRINKING ANYWHERE WITH THAT JERK!
LET'S GO, NUN-NALLY!
IT'D MAKE ME SO HAPPY IF YOU'D COME, THOUGH.
PLEASE, FOR ME?
WHEN YOU PUT IT THAT WAY...
DO IT FOR NIKKE...
SUN (BLANK)
ALL RIGHT! LET'S GET GOING!
AND JUST LIKE THAT, I HAD TO SPEND EVEN MORE TIME AROUND THAT JERK.

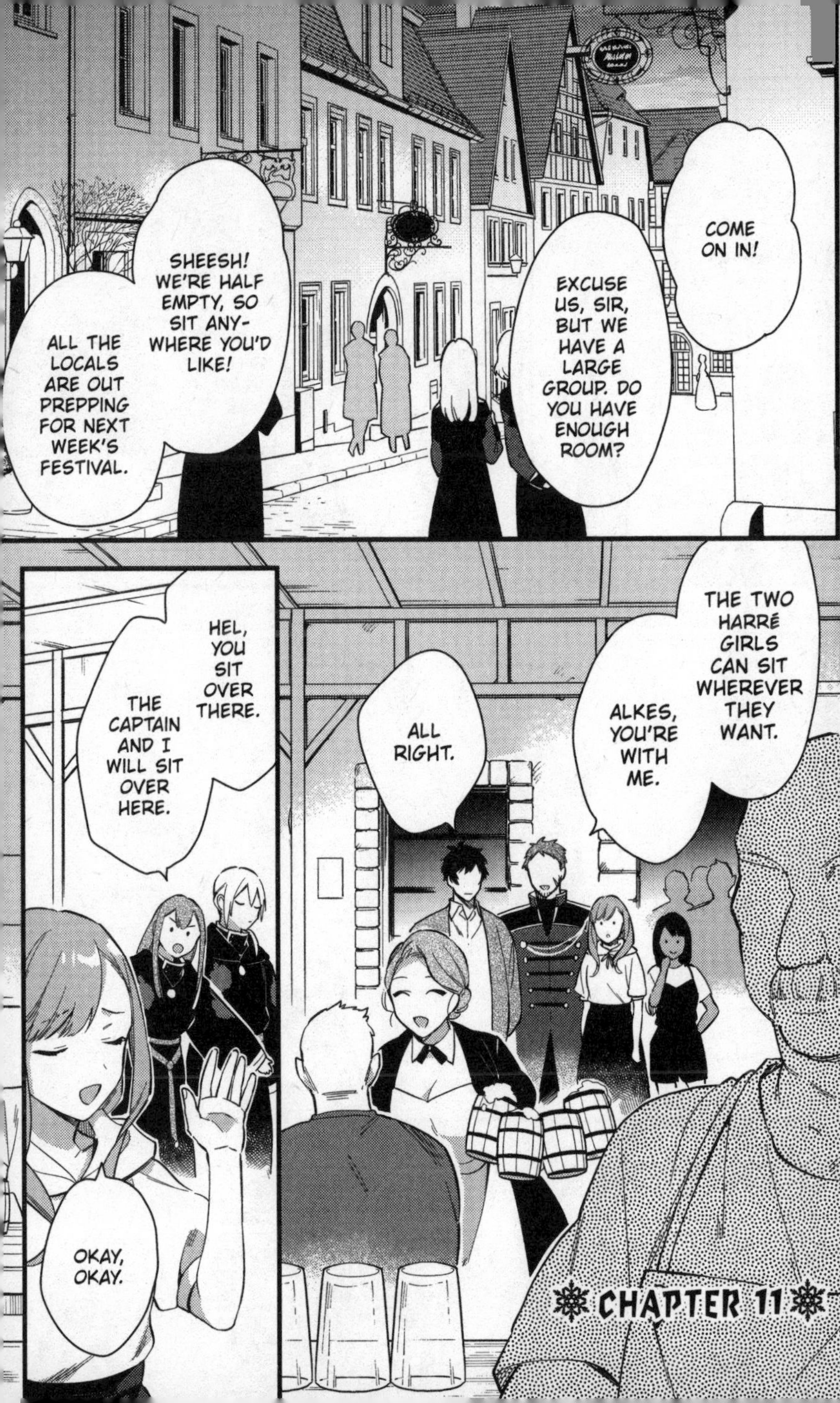
COME ON IN!
EXCUSE US, SIR, BUT WE HAVE A LARGE GROUP. DO YOU HAVE ENOUGH ROOM?
SHEESH! WE'RE HALF EMPTY, SO SIT ANY-WHERE YOU'D LIKE!
ALL THE LOCALS ARE OUT PREPPING FOR NEXT WEEK'S FESTIVAL.
CHAPTER 11
THE TWO HARRÉ GIRLS CAN SIT WHEREVER THEY WANT.
ALKES, YOU'RE WITH ME.
ALL RIGHT.
HEL, YOU SIT OVER THERE.
THE CAPTAIN AND I WILL SIT OVER HERE.
OKAY, OKAY.

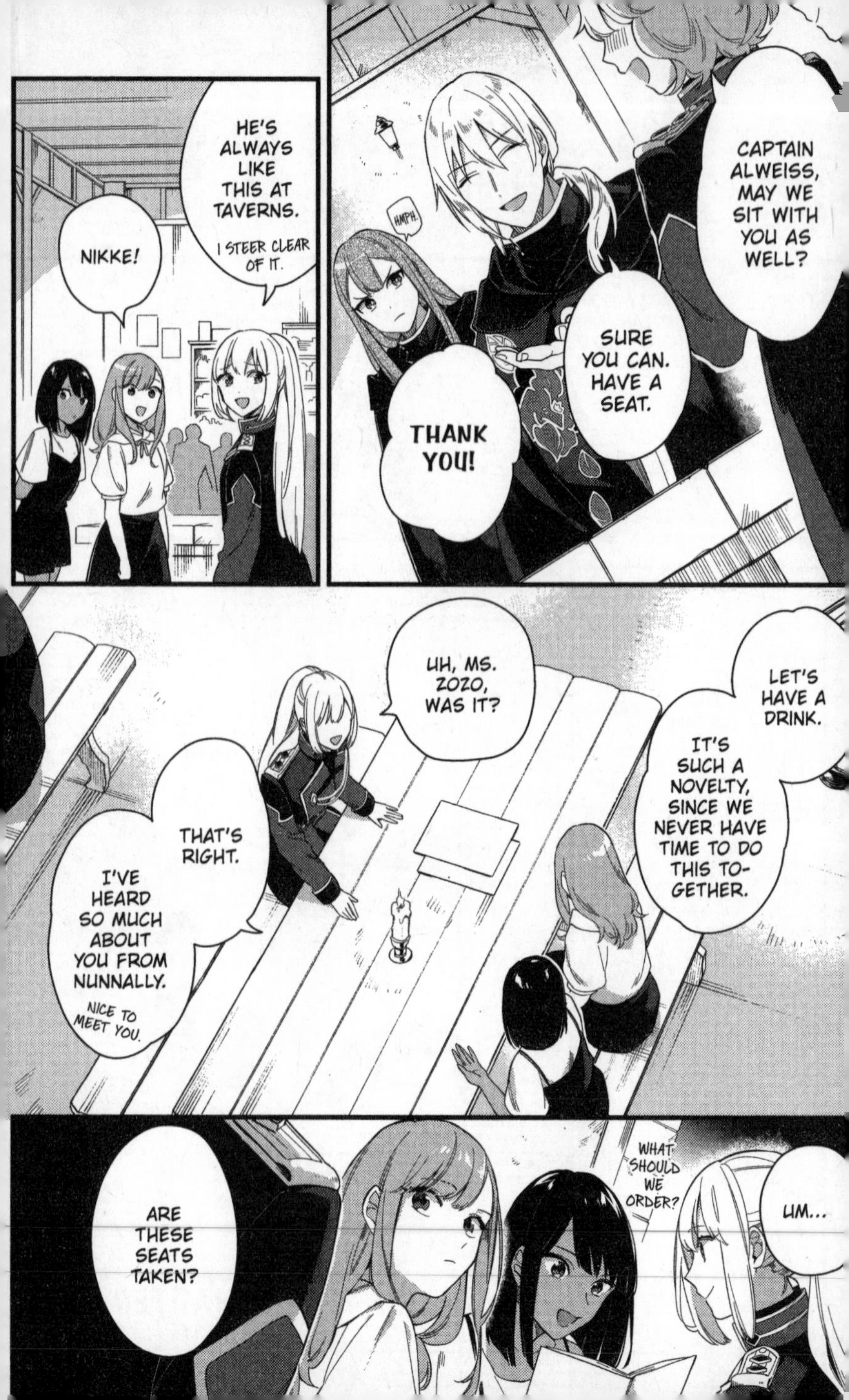
CAPTAIN ALWEISS, MAY WE SIT WITH YOU AS WELL?
HMPH.
SURE YOU CAN. HAVE A SEAT.
THANK YOU!
HE'S ALWAYS LIKE THIS AT TAVERNS.
I STEER CLEAR OF IT.
NIKKE!
LET'S HAVE A DRINK.
IT'S SUCH A NOVELTY, SINCE WE NEVER HAVE TIME TO DO THIS TO-GETHER.
UH, MS. ZOZO, WAS IT?
THAT'S RIGHT.
I'VE HEARD SO MUCH ABOUT YOU FROM NUNNALLY.
NICE TO MEET YOU.
UM...
WHAT SHOULD WE ORDER?
ARE THESE SEATS TAKEN?

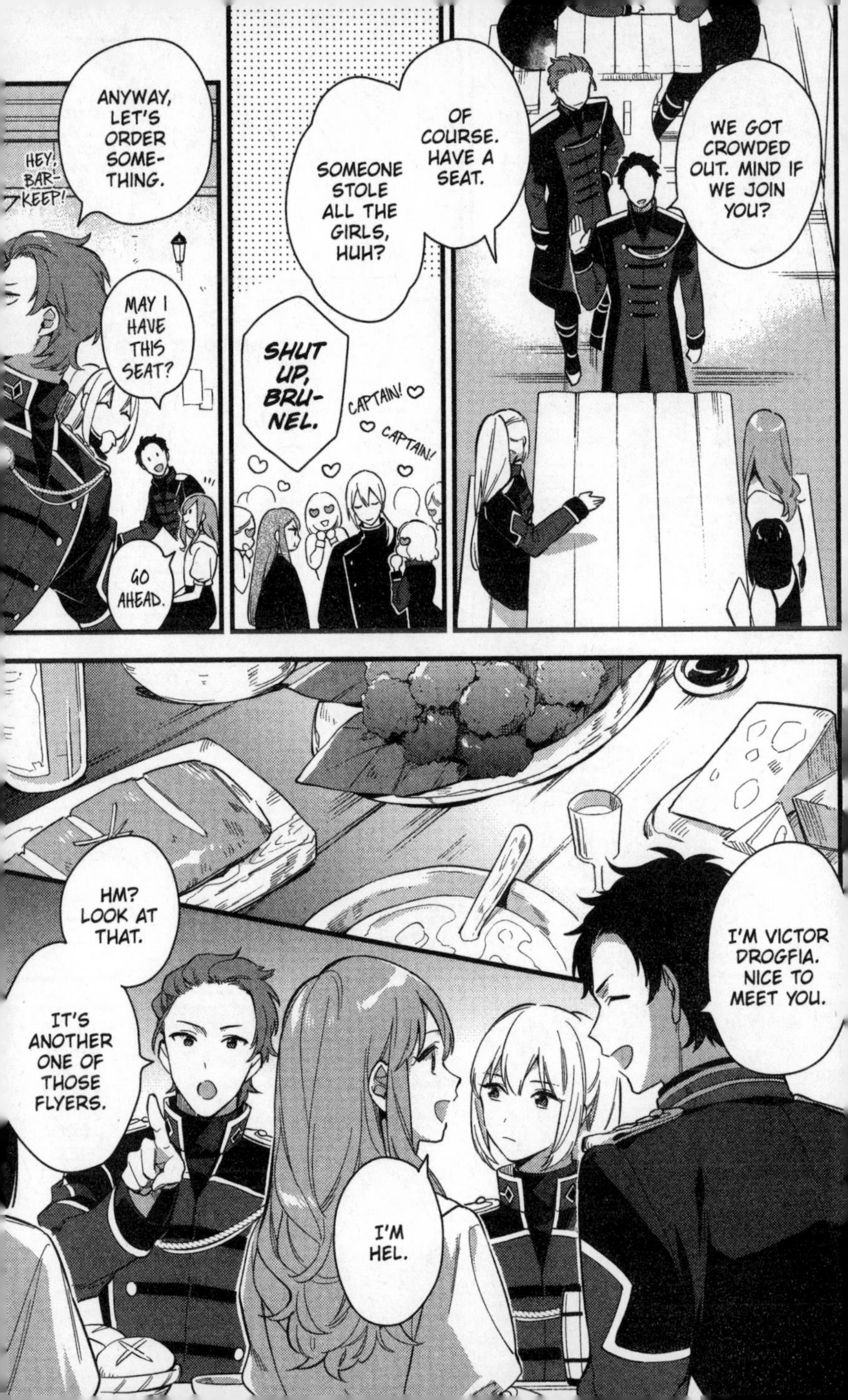
WE GOT CROWDED OUT. MIND IF WE JOIN YOU?
OF COURSE. HAVE A SEAT.
SOMEONE STOLE ALL THE GIRLS, HUH?
SHUT UP, BRU-NEL.
CAPTAIN!
CAPTAIN!
ANYWAY, LET'S ORDER SOME-THING.
HEY, BAR-KEEP!
MAY I HAVE THIS SEAT?
GO AHEAD.
I'M VICTOR DROGFIA. NICE TO MEET YOU.
I'M HEL.
HM? LOOK AT THAT.
IT'S ANOTHER ONE OF THOSE FLYERS.

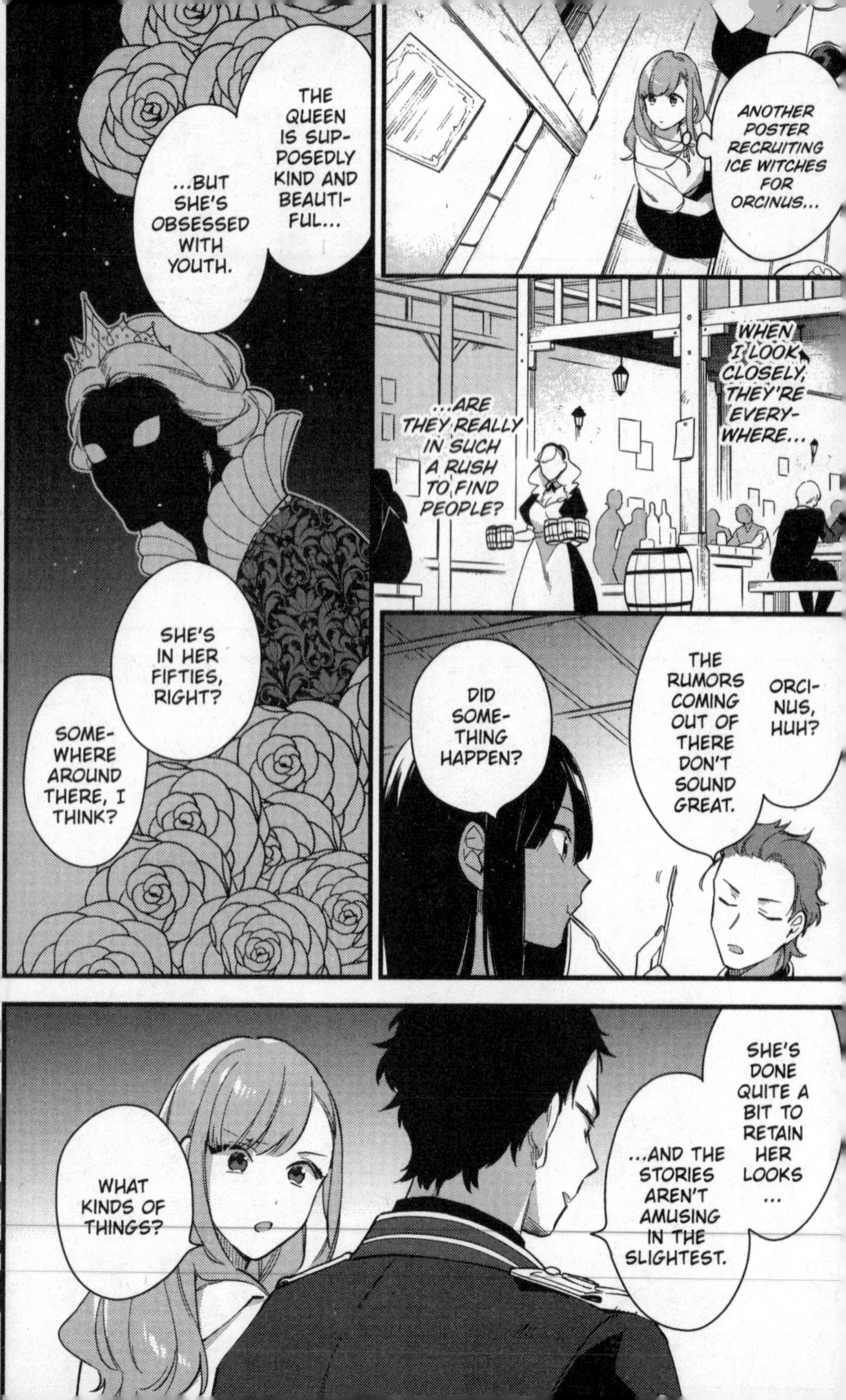
ANOTHER POSTER RECRUITING ICE WITCHES FOR ORCINUS...
WHEN I LOOK CLOSELY, THEY'RE EVERYWHERE...
...ARE THEY REALLY IN SUCH A RUSH TO FIND PEOPLE?
ORCINUS, HUH?
THE RUMORS COMING OUT OF THERE DON'T SOUND GREAT.
DID SOMETHING HAPPEN?
THE QUEEN IS SUPPOSEDLY KIND AND BEAUTIFUL...
...BUT SHE'S OBSESSED WITH YOUTH.
SHE'S IN HER FIFTIES, RIGHT?
SOMEWHERE AROUND THERE, I THINK?
SHE'S DONE QUITE A BIT TO RETAIN HER LOOKS...
...AND THE STORIES AREN'T AMUSING IN THE SLIGHTEST.
WHAT KINDS OF THINGS?

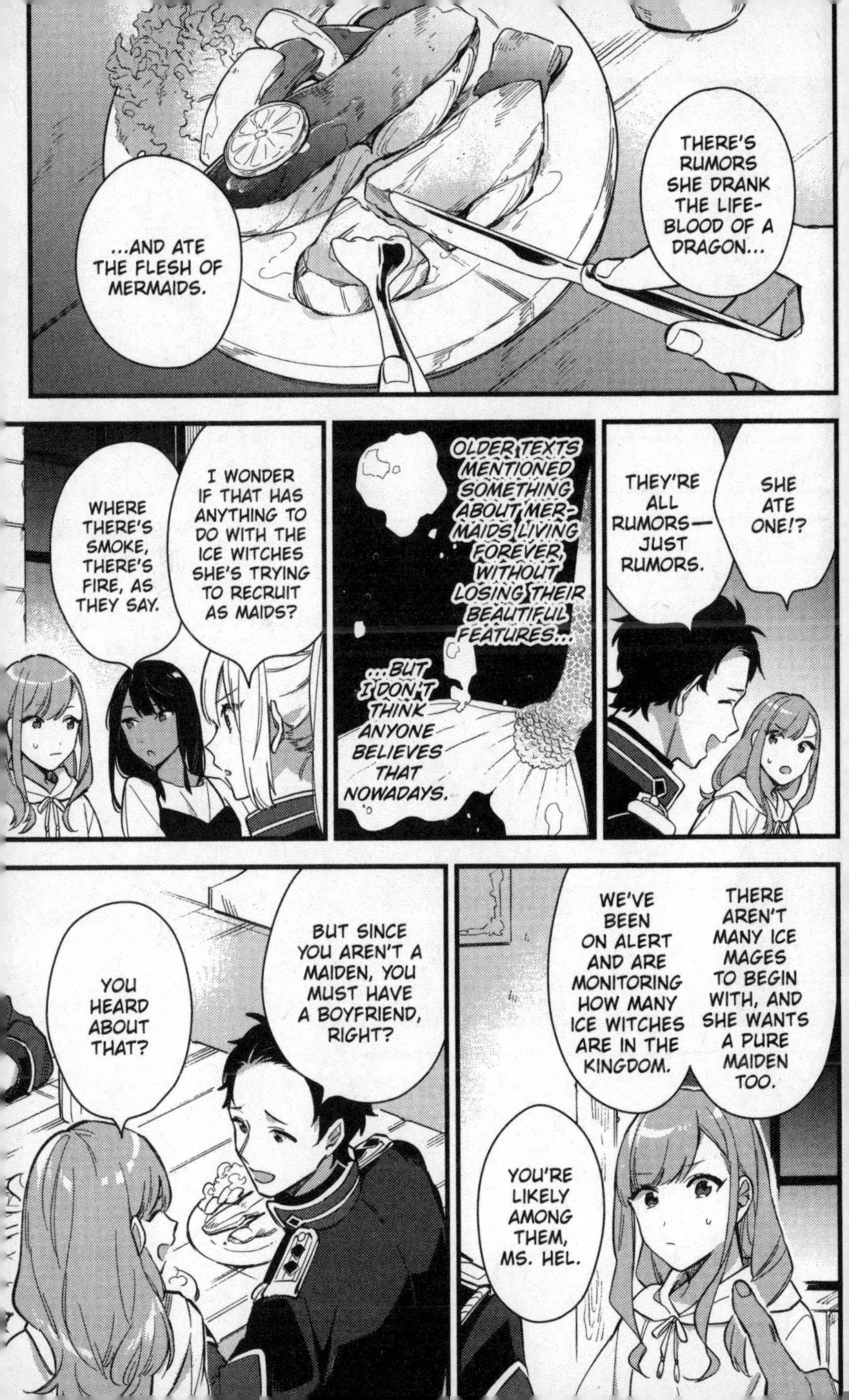
THERE'S RUMORS SHE DRANK THE LIFE-BLOOD OF A DRAGON...
...AND ATE THE FLESH OF MERMAIDS.
SHE ATE ONE!?
THEY'RE ALL RUMORS— JUST RUMORS.
OLDER TEXTS MENTIONED SOMETHING ABOUT MER-MAIDS LIVING FOREVER, WITHOUT LOSING THEIR BEAUTIFUL FEATURES...
...BUT I DON'T THINK ANYONE BELIEVES THAT NOWADAYS.
I WONDER IF THAT HAS ANYTHING TO DO WITH THE ICE WITCHES SHE'S TRYING TO RECRUIT AS MAIDS?
WHERE THERE'S SMOKE, THERE'S FIRE, AS THEY SAY.
THERE AREN'T MANY ICE MAGES TO BEGIN WITH, AND SHE WANTS A PURE MAIDEN TOO.
WE'VE BEEN ON ALERT AND ARE MONITORING HOW MANY ICE WITCHES ARE IN THE KINGDOM.
YOU'RE LIKELY AMONG THEM, MS. HEL.
BUT SINCE YOU AREN'T A MAIDEN, YOU MUST HAVE A BOYFRIEND, RIGHT?
YOU HEARD ABOUT THAT?

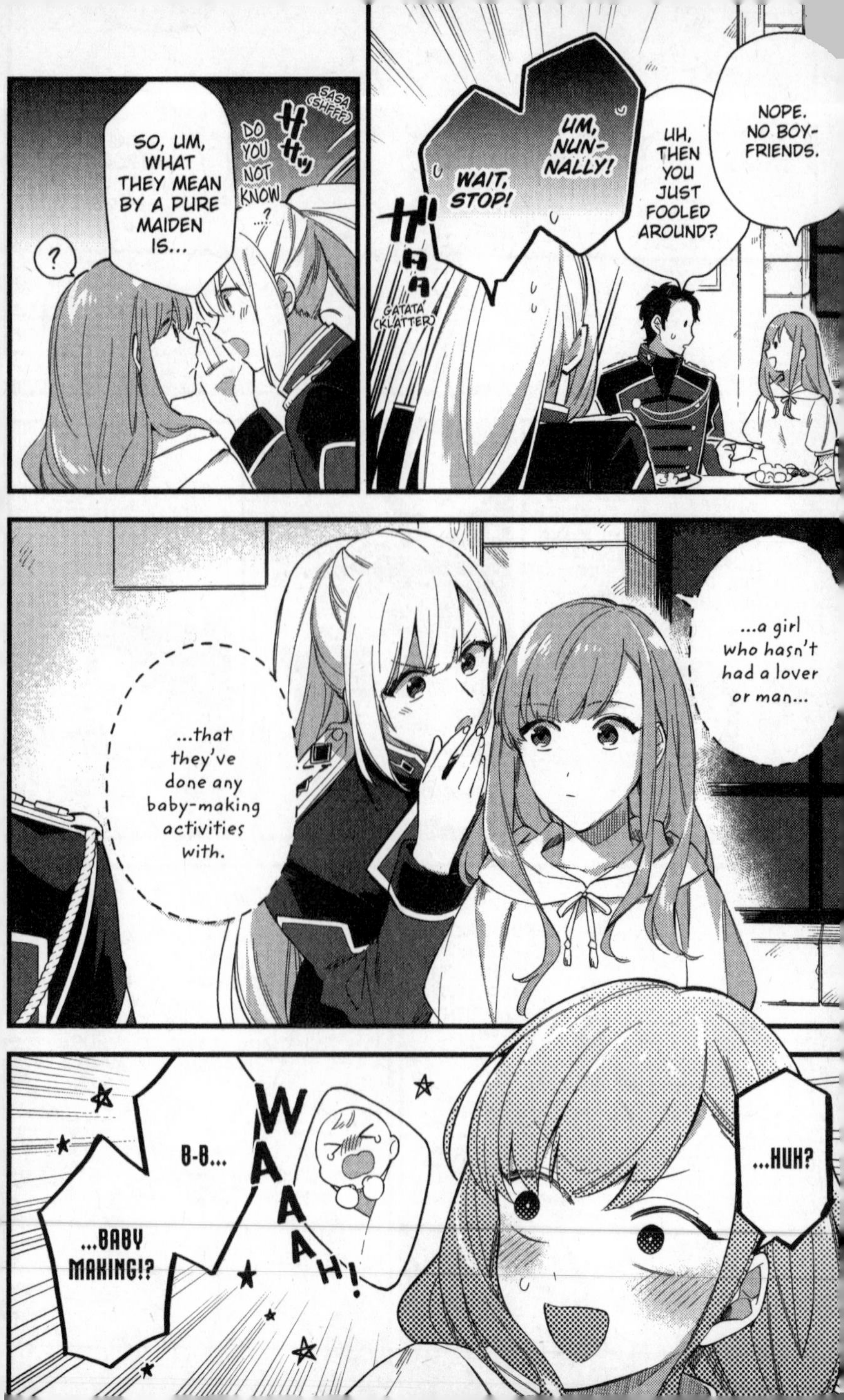
NOPE. NO BOY-FRIENDS.
UH, THEN YOU JUST FOOLED AROUND?
UM, NUN-NALLY!
WAIT, STOP!
GATATA (KLATTER)
DO YOU NOT KNOW ...?
SASA (SHFFF)
SO, UM, WHAT THEY MEAN BY A PURE MAIDEN IS...
?
...a girl who hasn't had a lover or man...
...that they've done any baby-making activities with.
...HUH?
WAAAAH!
B-B...
...BABY MAKING!?

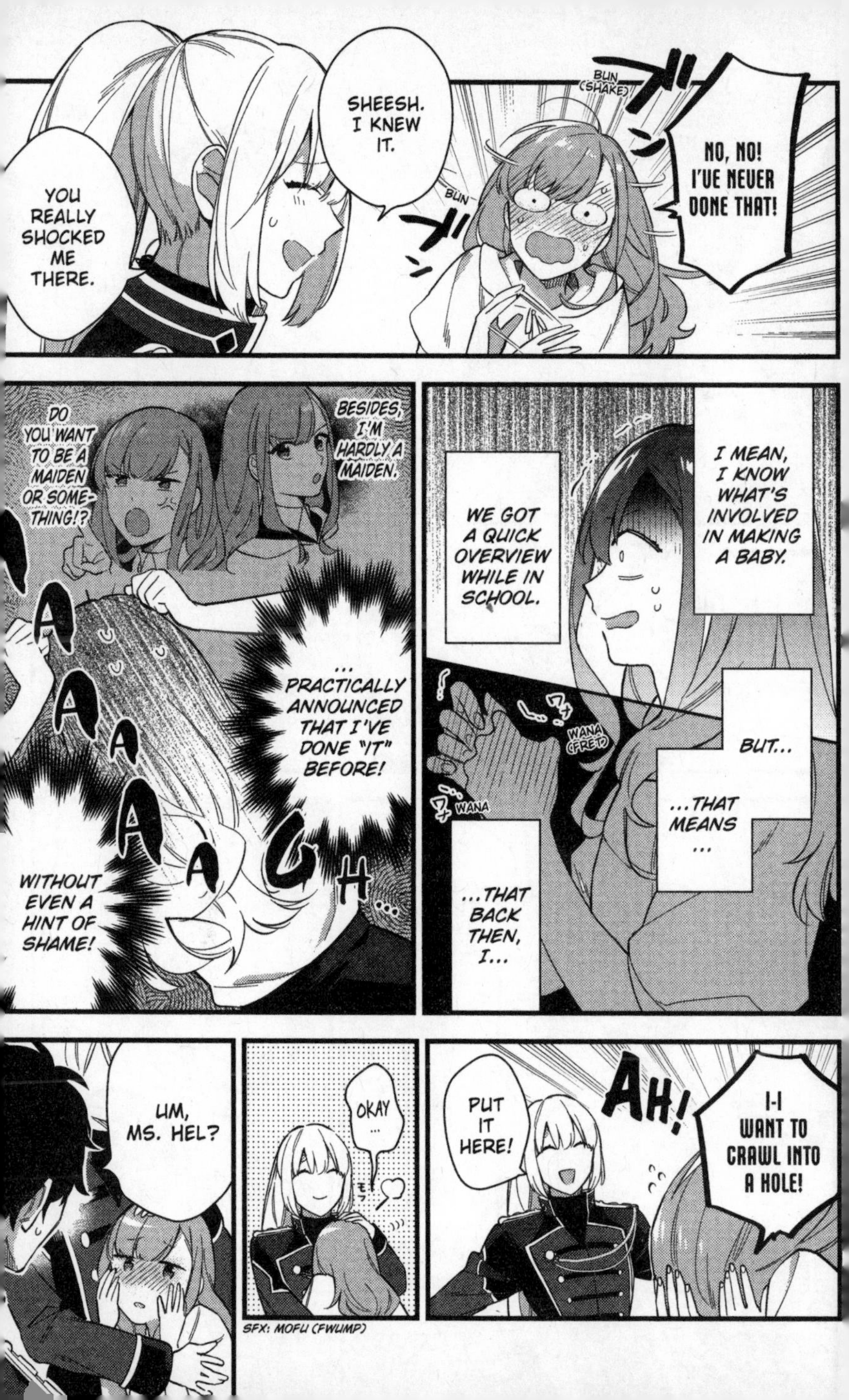
BUN (SHAKE)
NO, NO! I'VE NEVER DONE THAT!
BUN
SHEESH. I KNEW IT.
YOU REALLY SHOCKED ME THERE.
I MEAN, I KNOW WHAT'S INVOLVED IN MAKING A BABY.
WE GOT A QUICK OVERVIEW WHILE IN SCHOOL.
BUT...
...THAT MEANS ...
WANA (FRET)
WANA
...THAT BACK THEN, I...
BESIDES, I'M HARDLY A MAIDEN.
DO YOU WANT TO BE A MAIDEN OR SOME-THING!?
... PRACTICALLY ANNOUNCED THAT I'VE DONE "IT" BEFORE!
WITHOUT EVEN A HINT OF SHAME!
AAAAAAGH...
I-I WANT TO CRAWL INTO A HOLE!
AH!
PUT IT HERE!
OKAY ...
UM, MS. HEL?
SFX: MOFU (FWUMP)

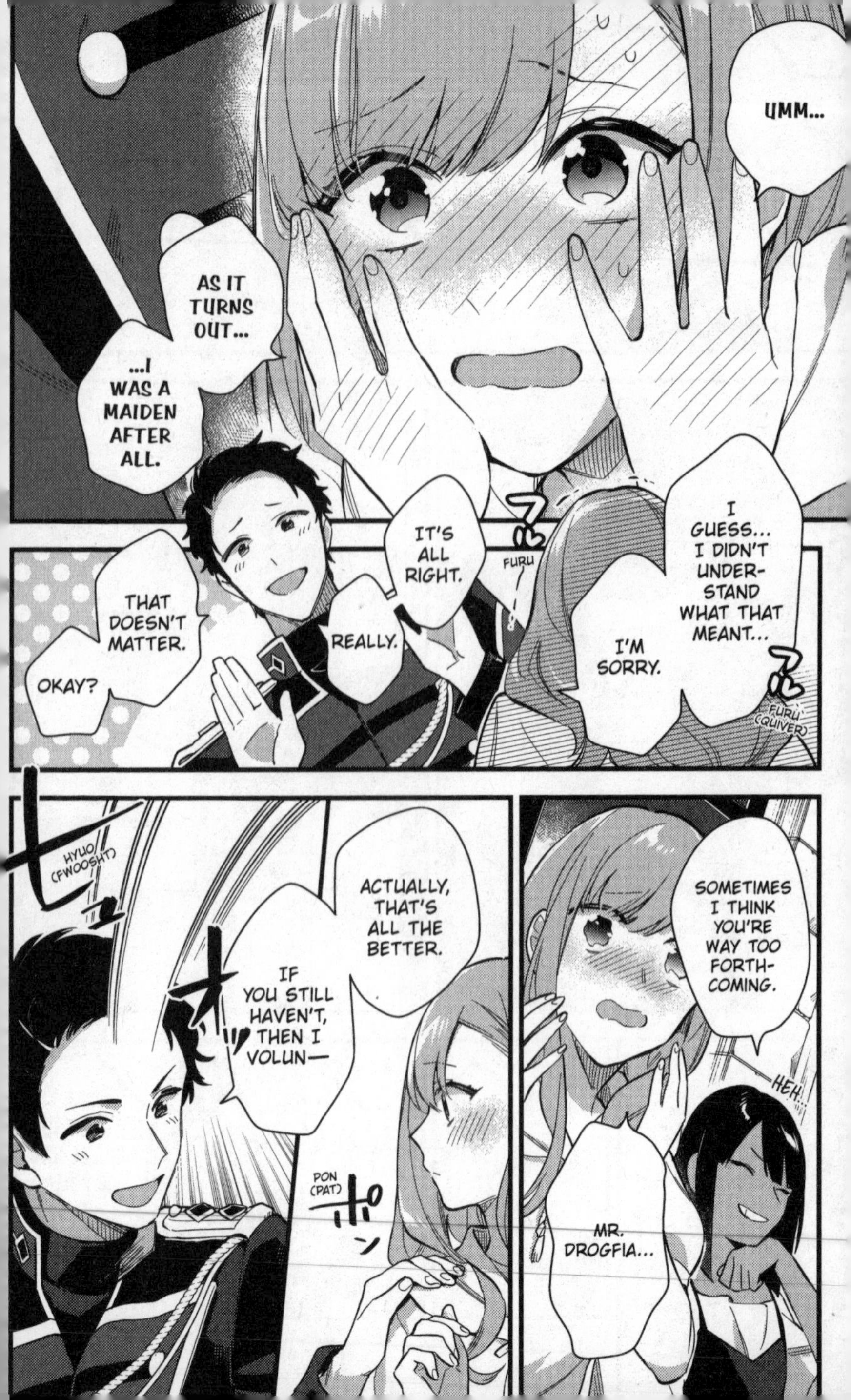
UMM...
AS IT TURNS OUT...
...I WAS A MAIDEN AFTER ALL.
I GUESS... I DIDN'T UNDER-STAND WHAT THAT MEANT...
I'M SORRY.
FURU (QUIVER)
FURU
IT'S ALL RIGHT.
REALLY.
THAT DOESN'T MATTER.
OKAY?
SOMETIMES I THINK YOU'RE WAY TOO FORTH-COMING.
HEH...
MR. DROGFIA...
ACTUALLY, THAT'S ALL THE BETTER.
IF YOU STILL HAVEN'T, THEN I VOLUN—
HYUO (FWOOSHT)
PON (PAT)

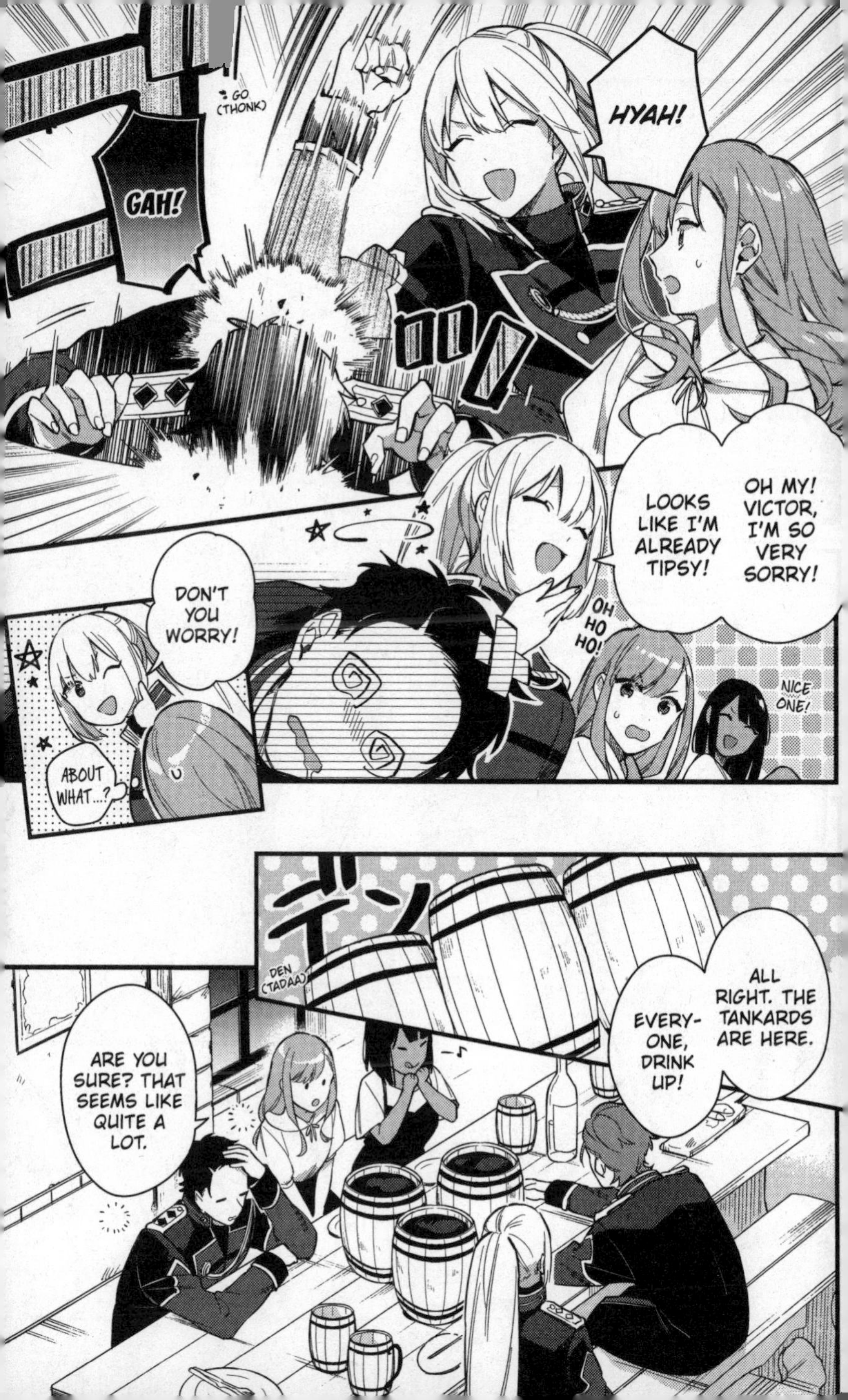
HYAH!
GO (THONK)
GAH!
OH MY! VICTOR, I'M SO VERY SORRY!
LOOKS LIKE I'M ALREADY TIPSY!
OH HO HO!
NICE ONE!
DON'T YOU WORRY!
ABOUT WHAT...?
DEN (TADAA)
ALL RIGHT. THE TANKARDS ARE HERE.
EVERY-ONE, DRINK UP!
ARE YOU SURE? THAT SEEMS LIKE QUITE A LOT.

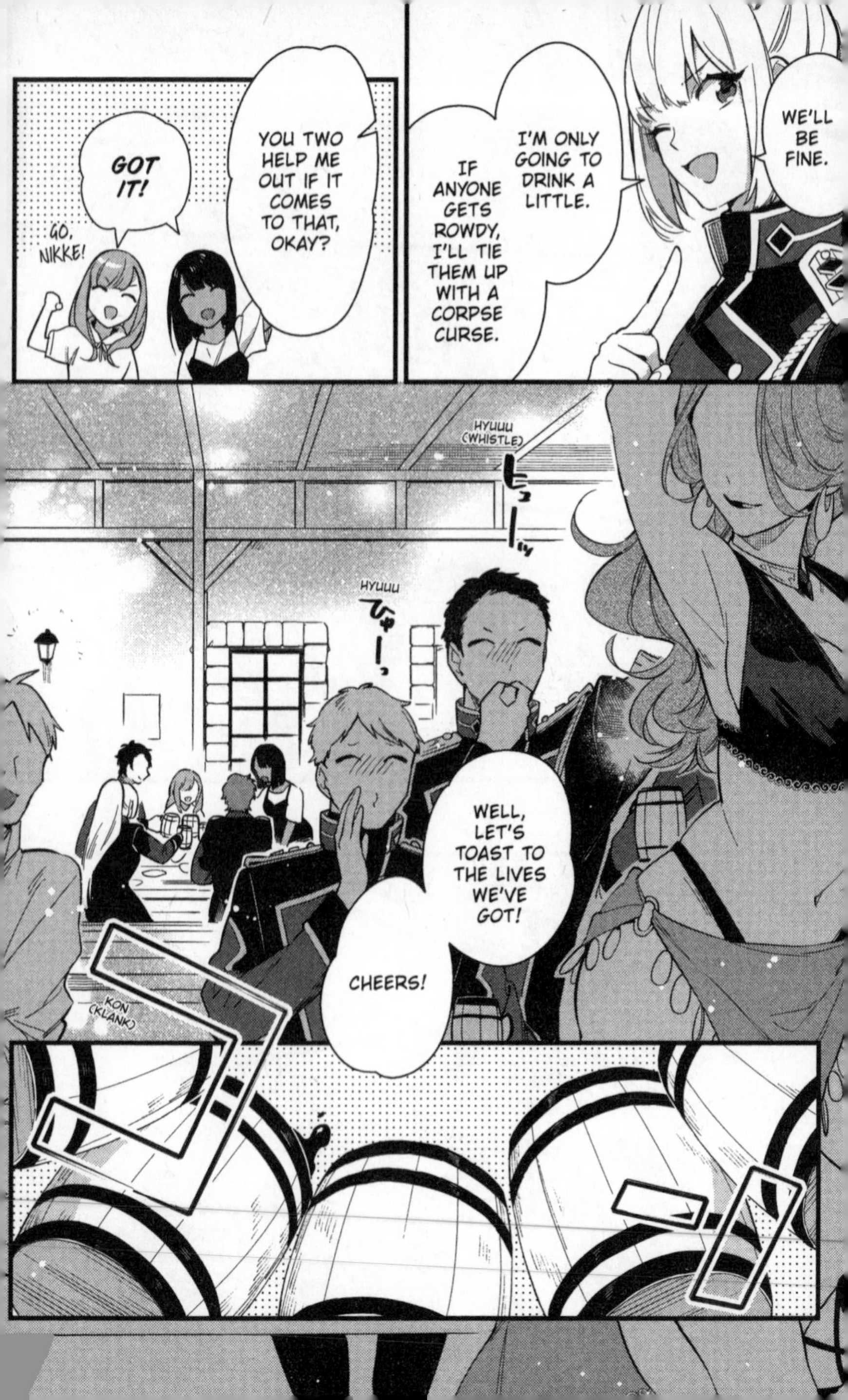
WE'LL BE FINE.
I'M ONLY GOING TO DRINK A LITTLE.
IF ANYONE GETS ROWDY, I'LL TIE THEM UP WITH A CORPSE CURSE.
YOU TWO HELP ME OUT IF IT COMES TO THAT, OKAY?
GOT IT!
GO, NIKKE!
HYUUU (WHISTLE)
HYUUU
WELL, LET'S TOAST TO THE LIVES WE'VE GOT!
CHEERS!
KON (KLANK)

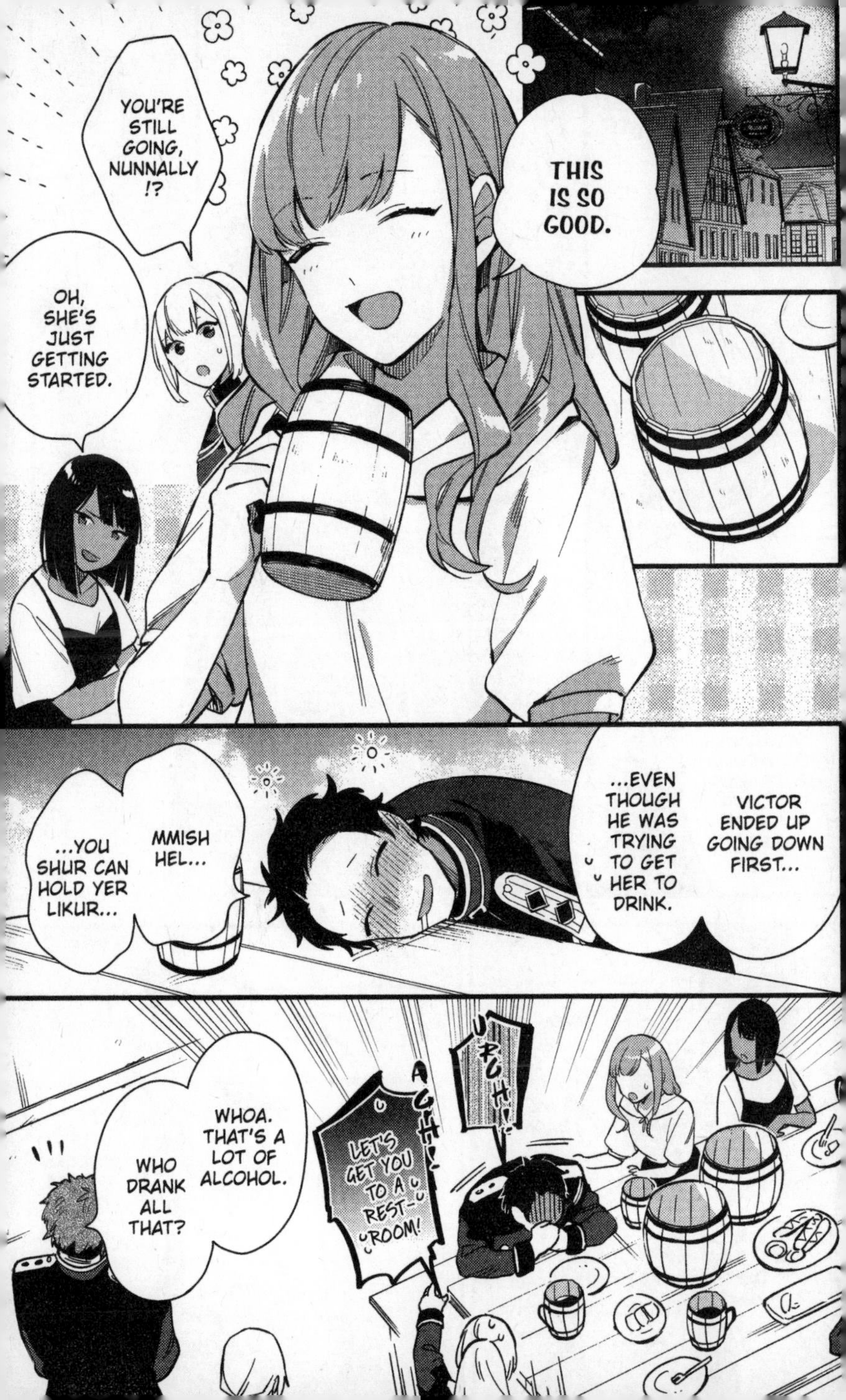
THIS IS SO GOOD.
YOU'RE STILL GOING, NUNNALLY !?
OH, SHE'S JUST GETTING STARTED.
VICTOR ENDED UP GOING DOWN FIRST...
...EVEN THOUGH HE WAS TRYING TO GET HER TO DRINK.
MMISH HEL...
...YOU SHUR CAN HOLD YER LIKUR...
URCH!
AUGH!
LET'S GET YOU TO A REST-ROOM!
WHOA. THAT'S A LOT OF ALCOHOL.
WHO DRANK ALL THAT?

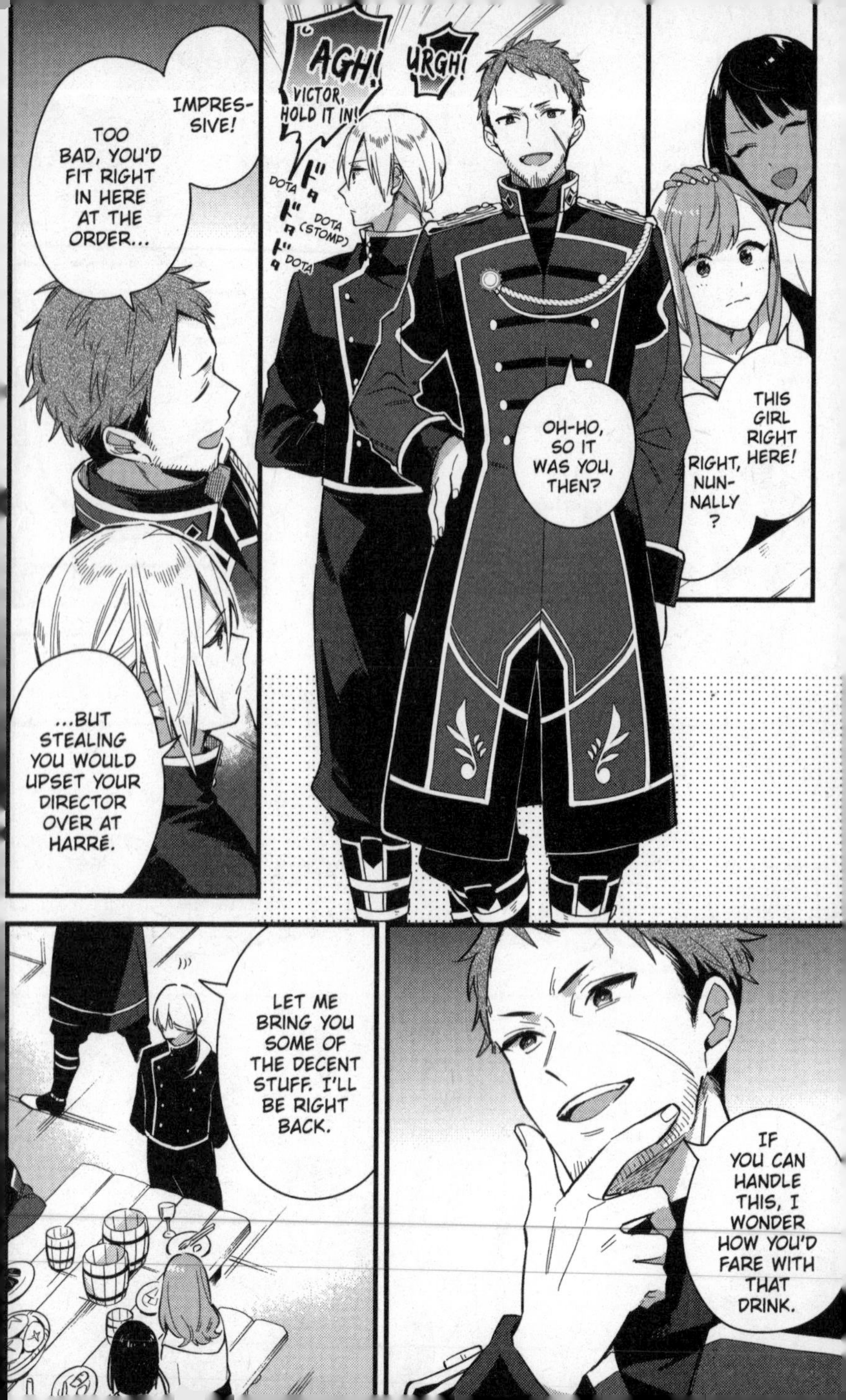
THIS GIRL RIGHT HERE!
RIGHT, NUNNALLY?
OH-HO, SO IT WAS YOU, THEN?
AGH!
URGH!
VICTOR, HOLD IT IN!
ドタ DOTA ドタ DOTA (STOMP) ドタ DOTA
IMPRESSIVE!
TOO BAD, YOU'D FIT RIGHT IN HERE AT THE ORDER...
...BUT STEALING YOU WOULD UPSET YOUR DIRECTOR OVER AT HARRÉ.
IF YOU CAN HANDLE THIS, I WONDER HOW YOU'D FARE WITH THAT DRINK.
LET ME BRING YOU SOME OF THE DECENT STUFF. I'LL BE RIGHT BACK.

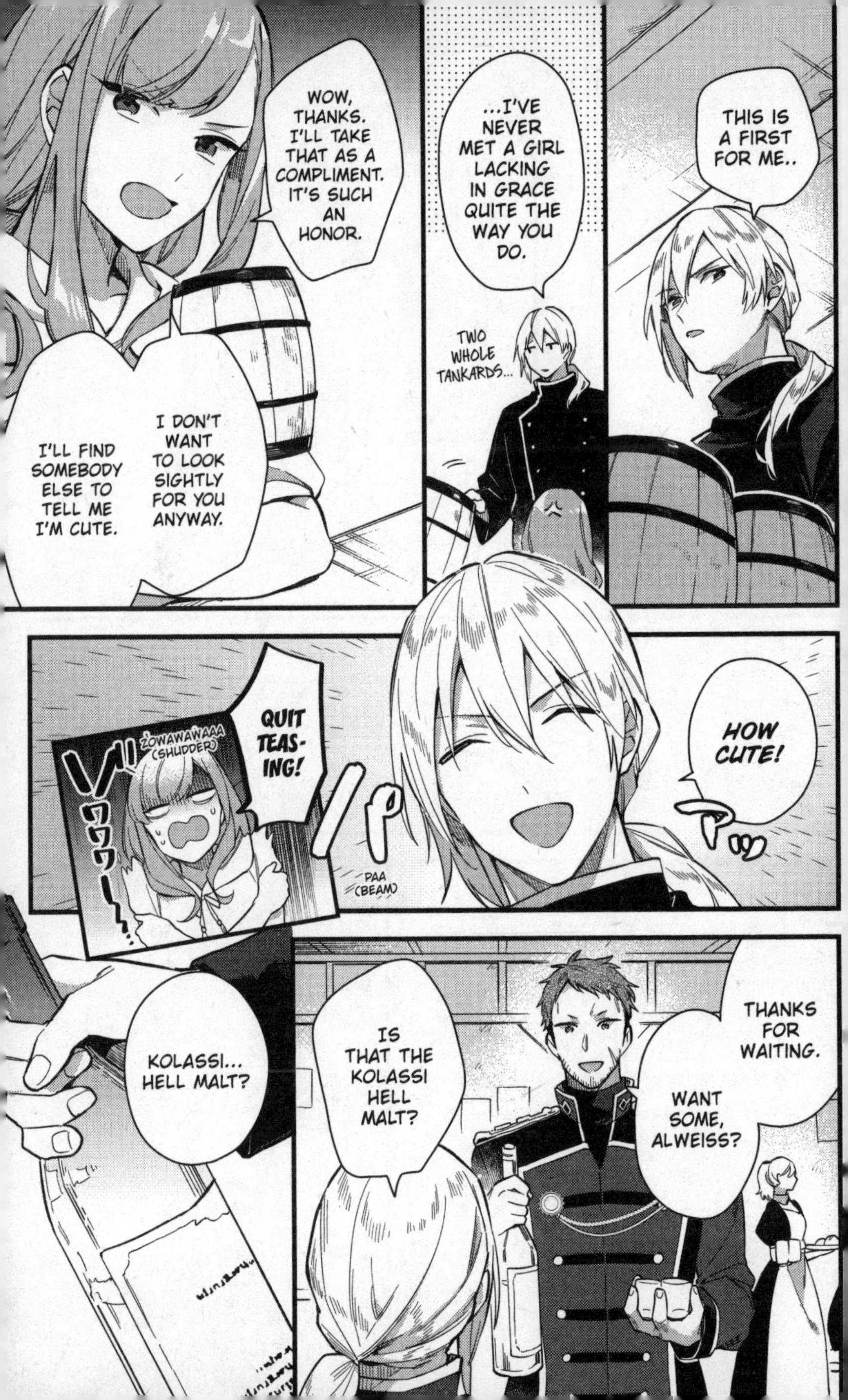
THIS IS A FIRST FOR ME..
...I'VE NEVER MET A GIRL LACKING IN GRACE QUITE THE WAY YOU DO.
TWO WHOLE TANKARDS...
WOW, THANKS. I'LL TAKE THAT AS A COMPLIMENT. IT'S SUCH AN HONOR.
I DON'T WANT TO LOOK SIGHTLY FOR YOU ANYWAY.
I'LL FIND SOMEBODY ELSE TO TELL ME I'M CUTE.
HOW CUTE!
PAA (BEAM)
QUIT TEAS-ING!
ZOWAWAWAAA (SHUDDER)
THANKS FOR WAITING.
WANT SOME, ALWEISS?
IS THAT THE KOLASSI HELL MALT?
KOLASSI... HELL MALT?

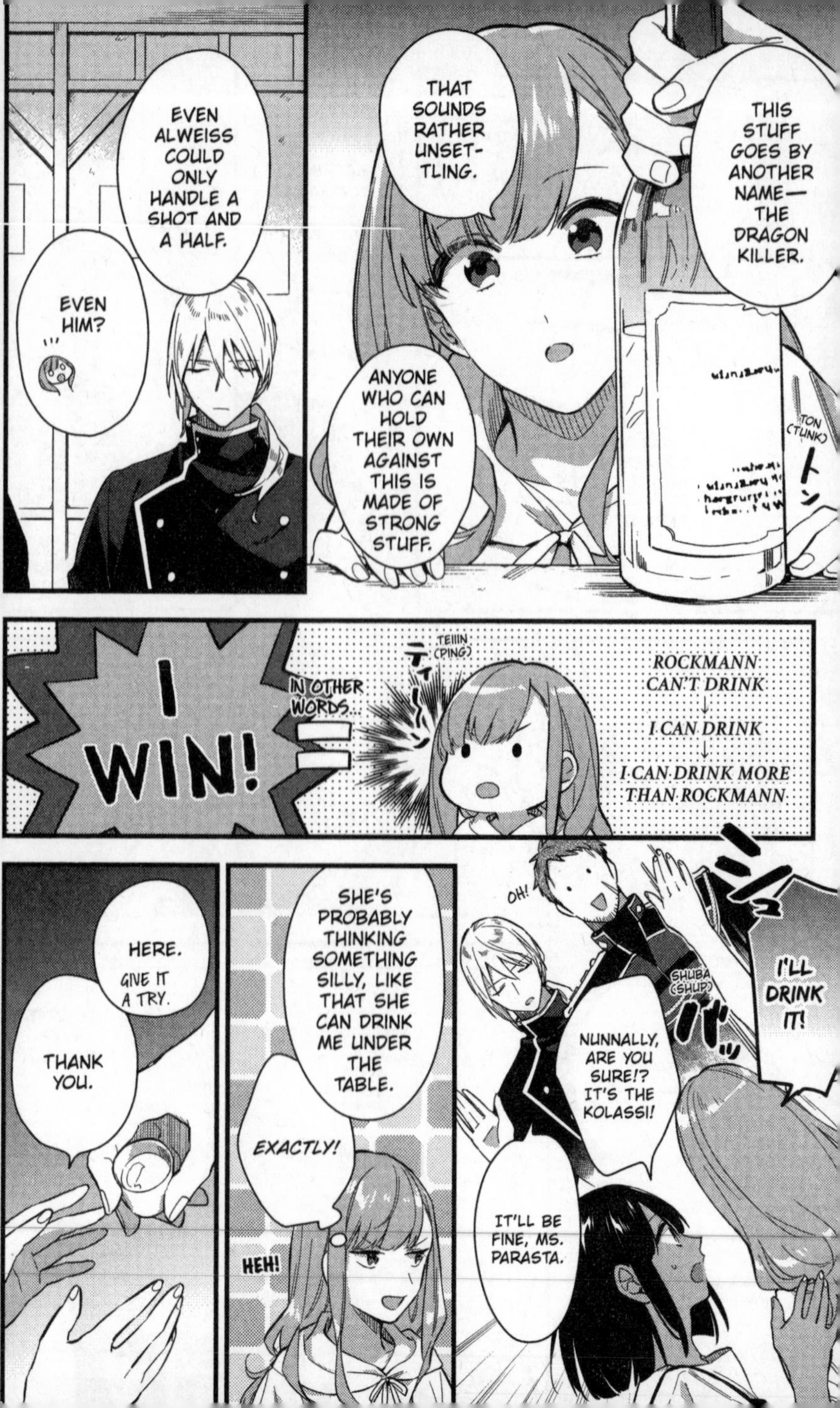
THIS STUFF GOES BY ANOTHER NAME—THE DRAGON KILLER.
TON (TUNK)
THAT SOUNDS RATHER UNSET-TLING.
ANYONE WHO CAN HOLD THEIR OWN AGAINST THIS IS MADE OF STRONG STUFF.
EVEN ALWEISS COULD ONLY HANDLE A SHOT AND A HALF.
EVEN HIM?
ROCKMANN CAN'T DRINK ↓ I CAN DRINK ↓ I CAN DRINK MORE THAN ROCKMANN
TEIIIN (PING)
IN OTHER WORDS...
I WIN!
I'LL DRINK IT!
SHUBA (SHUP)
OH!
NUNNALLY, ARE YOU SURE!? IT'S THE KOLASSI!
IT'LL BE FINE, MS. PARASTA.
SHE'S PROBABLY THINKING SOMETHING SILLY, LIKE THAT SHE CAN DRINK ME UNDER THE TABLE.
EXACTLY!
HEH!
HERE. GIVE IT A TRY.
THANK YOU.

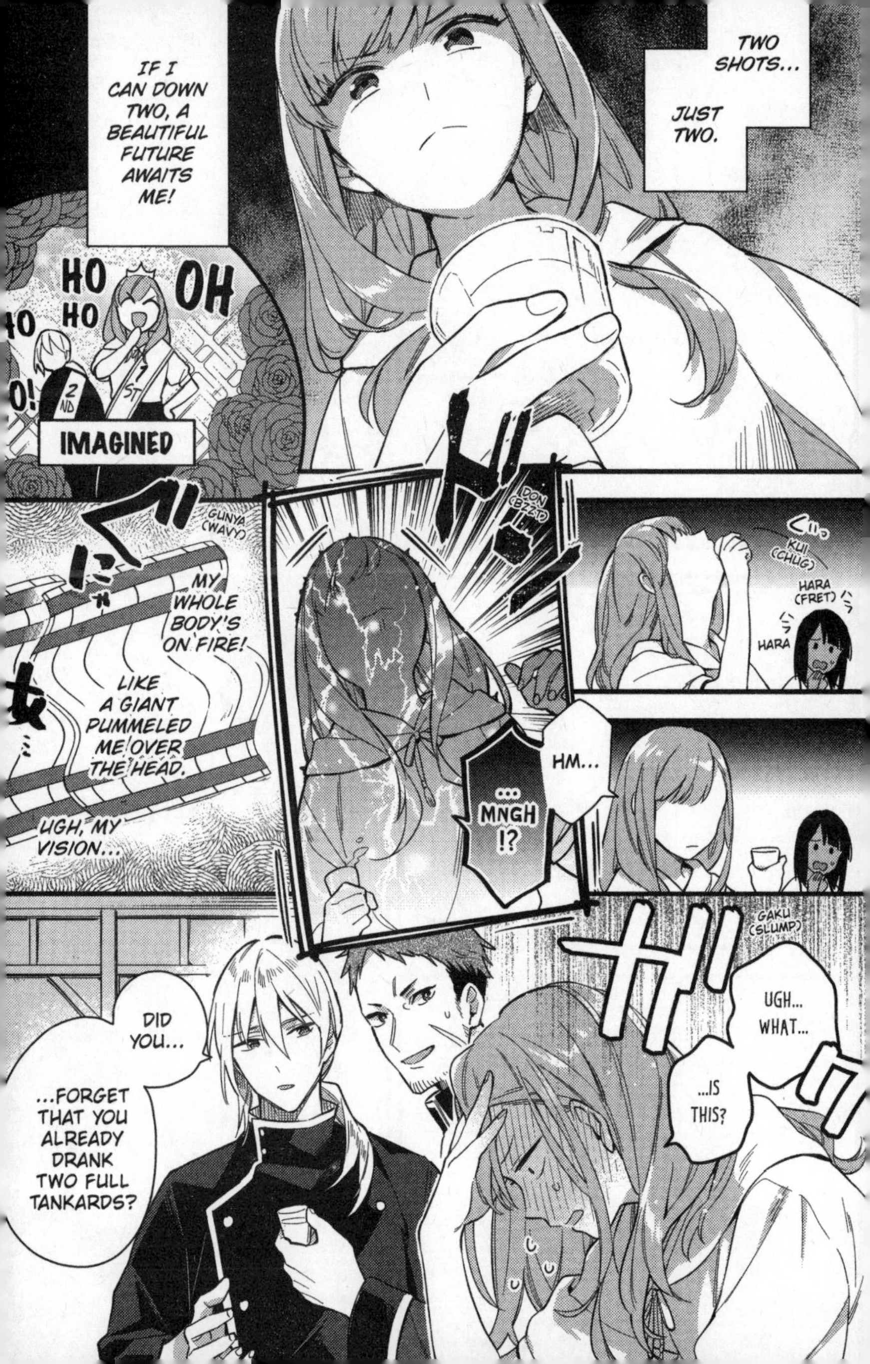
TWO SHOTS...
JUST TWO.
IF I CAN DOWN TWO, A BEAUTIFUL FUTURE AWAITS ME!
HO HO
HO HO OH
2ND
1ST
IMAGINED
KUI (CHUG)
HARA (FRET)
HARA
HM...
...MNGH!?
DON (BZZT)
GUNYA (WAVY)
MY WHOLE BODY'S ON FIRE!
LIKE A GIANT PUMMELED ME OVER THE HEAD.
UGH, MY VISION...
GAKU (SLUMP)
UGH... WHAT...
...IS THIS?
DID YOU...
...FORGET THAT YOU ALREADY DRANK TWO FULL TANKARDS?

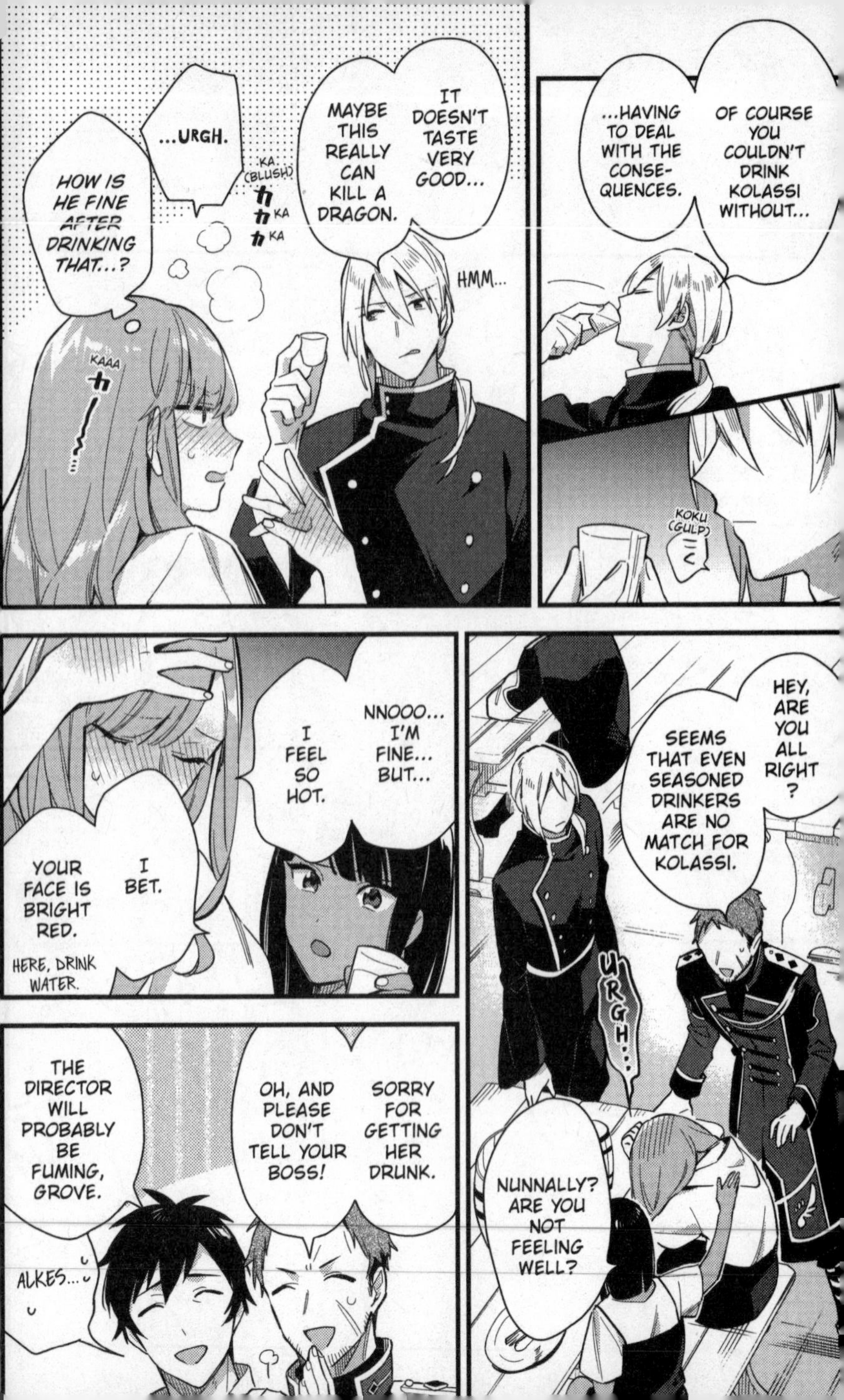
OF COURSE YOU COULDN'T DRINK KOLASSI WITHOUT...
...HAVING TO DEAL WITH THE CONSE-QUENCES.
KOKU (GULP)
IT DOESN'T TASTE VERY GOOD...
MAYBE THIS REALLY CAN KILL A DRAGON.
HMM...
...URGH.
KA (BLUSH) KA KA
HOW IS HE FINE AFTER DRINKING THAT...?
KAAA
HEY, ARE YOU ALL RIGHT?
SEEMS THAT EVEN SEASONED DRINKERS ARE NO MATCH FOR KOLASSI.
URGH...
NUNNALLY? ARE YOU NOT FEELING WELL?
NNOOO... I'M FINE... BUT...
I FEEL SO HOT.
I BET.
YOUR FACE IS BRIGHT RED.
HERE, DRINK WATER.
SORRY FOR GETTING HER DRUNK.
OH, AND PLEASE DON'T TELL YOUR BOSS!
THE DIRECTOR WILL PROBABLY BE FUMING, GROVE.
ALKES...

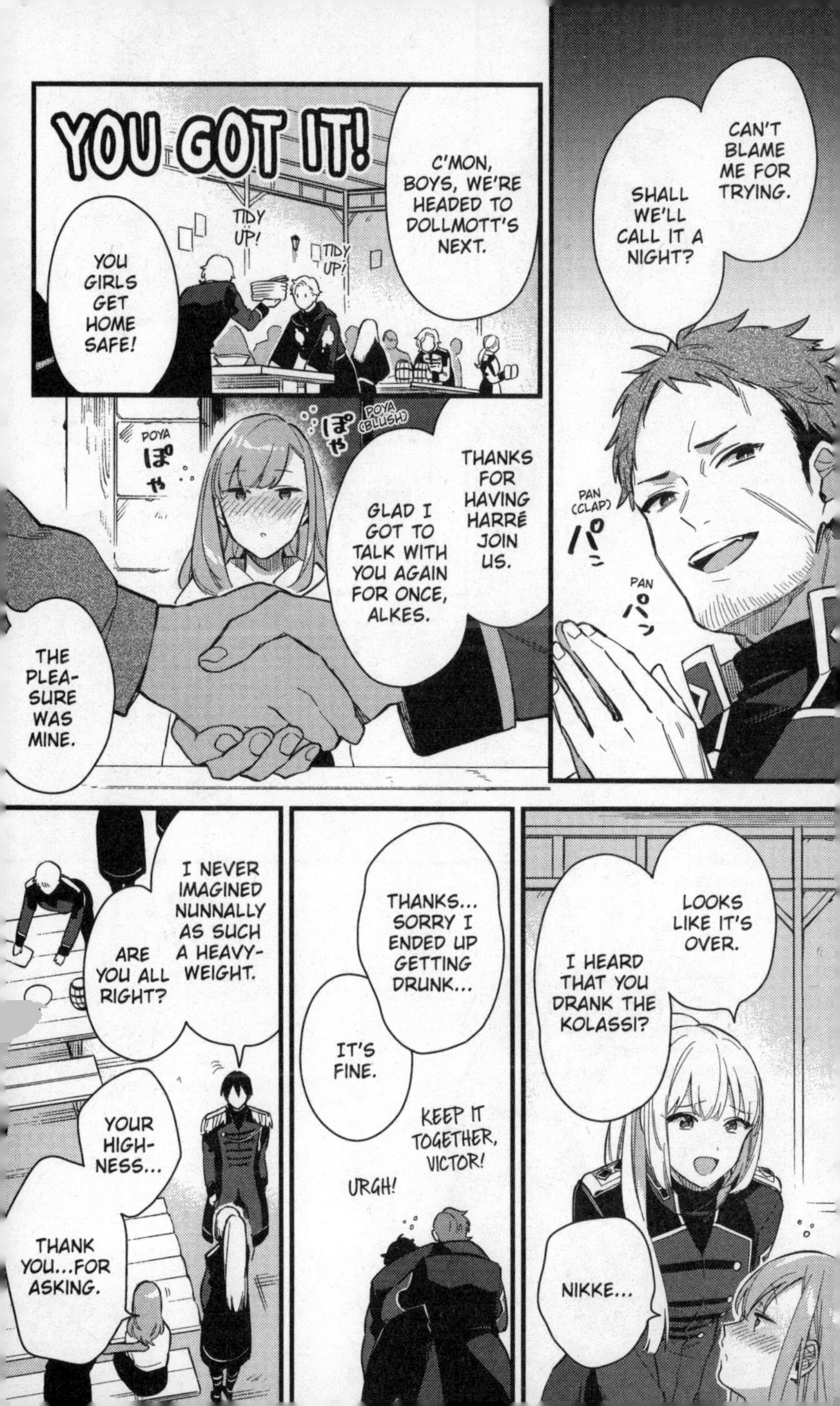
CAN'T BLAME ME FOR TRYING.
SHALL WE'LL CALL IT A NIGHT?
PAN (CLAP) パ
PAN パン
C'MON, BOYS, WE'RE HEADED TO DOLLMOTT'S NEXT.
YOU GOT IT!
TIDY UP!
TIDY UP!
YOU GIRLS GET HOME SAFE!
THANKS FOR HAVING HARRÉ JOIN US.
GLAD I GOT TO TALK WITH YOU AGAIN FOR ONCE, ALKES.
POYA (BLUSH) ぽや
POYA ぽや
THE PLEA-SURE WAS MINE.
LOOKS LIKE IT'S OVER.
I HEARD THAT YOU DRANK THE KOLASSI?
NIKKE...
THANKS... SORRY I ENDED UP GETTING DRUNK...
IT'S FINE.
KEEP IT TOGETHER, VICTOR!
URGH!
I NEVER IMAGINED NUNNALLY AS SUCH A HEAVY-WEIGHT.
ARE YOU ALL RIGHT?
YOUR HIGH-NESS...
THANK YOU...FOR ASKING.

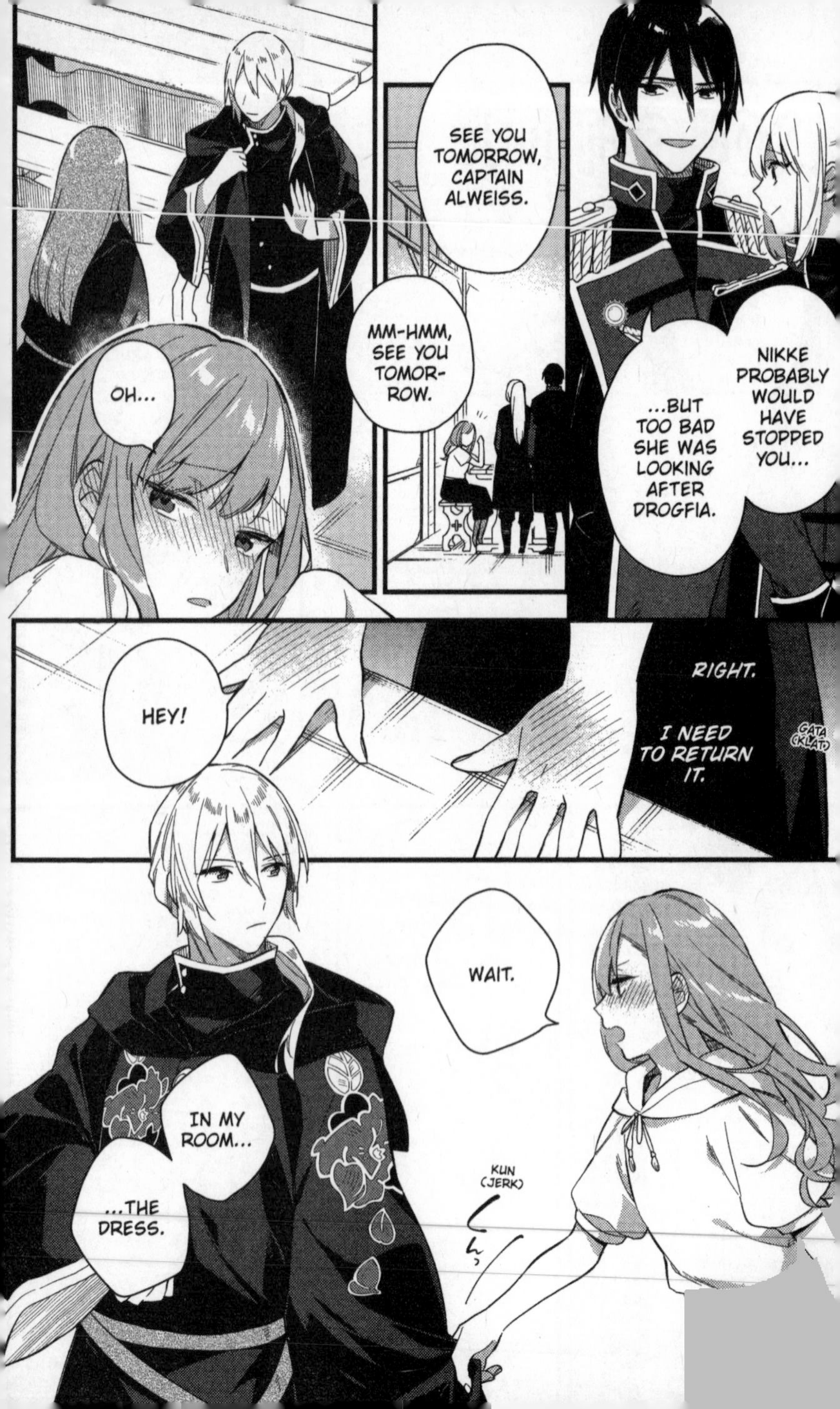
NIKKE PROBABLY WOULD HAVE STOPPED YOU...
...BUT TOO BAD SHE WAS LOOKING AFTER DROGFIA.
SEE YOU TOMORROW, CAPTAIN ALWEISS.
MM-HMM, SEE YOU TOMOR-ROW.
OH...
GATA (KLAT)
RIGHT.
I NEED TO RETURN IT.
HEY!
WAIT.
KUN (JERK)
IN MY ROOM...
...THE DRESS.

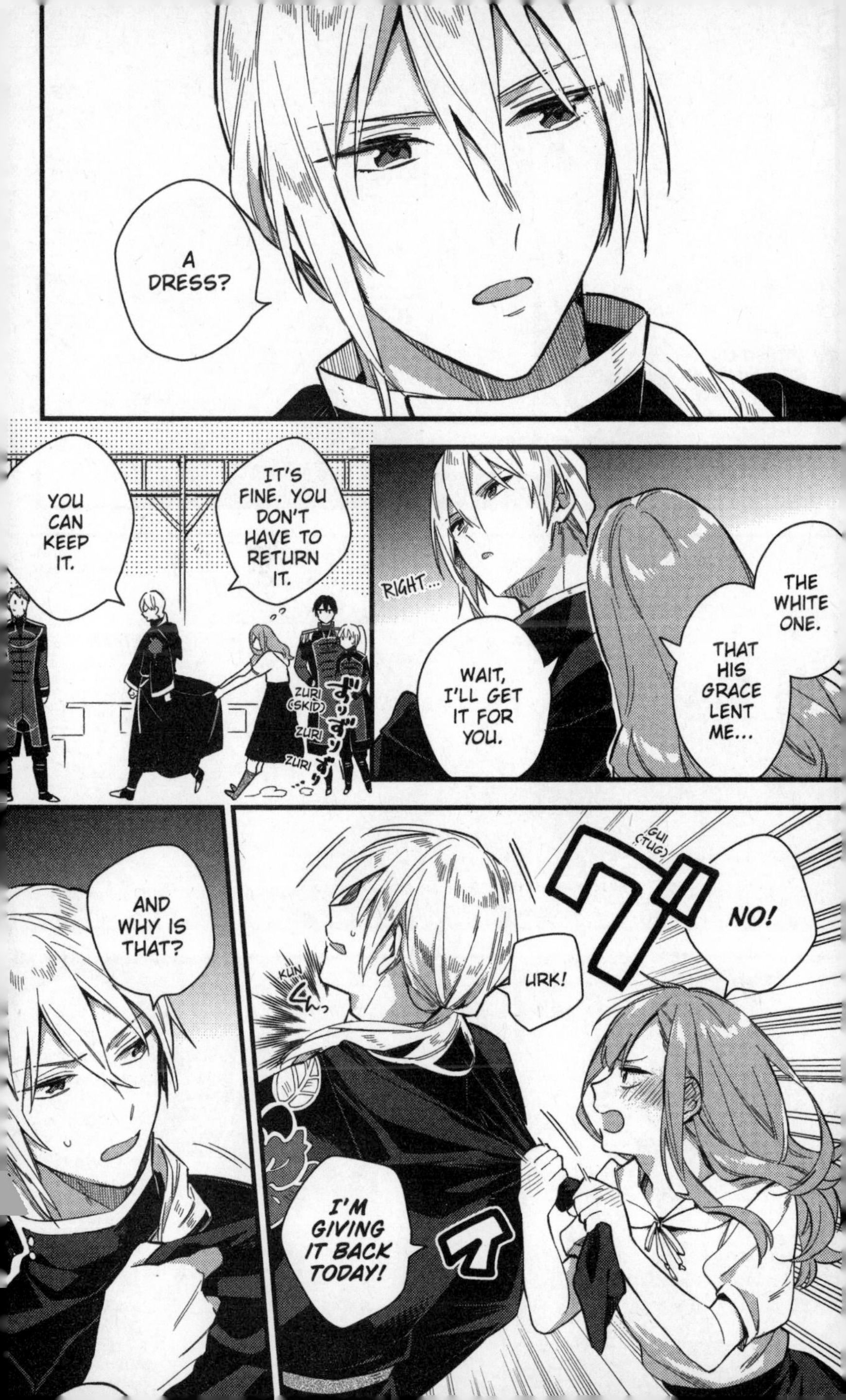
A DRESS?
THE WHITE ONE.
THAT HIS GRACE LENT ME...
RIGHT...
WAIT, I'LL GET IT FOR YOU.
IT'S FINE. YOU DON'T HAVE TO RETURN IT.
ZURI (SKID) ZURI ZURI
YOU CAN KEEP IT.
GUI (TUG)
NO!
URK!
KUN
I'M GIVING IT BACK TODAY!
AND WHY IS THAT?

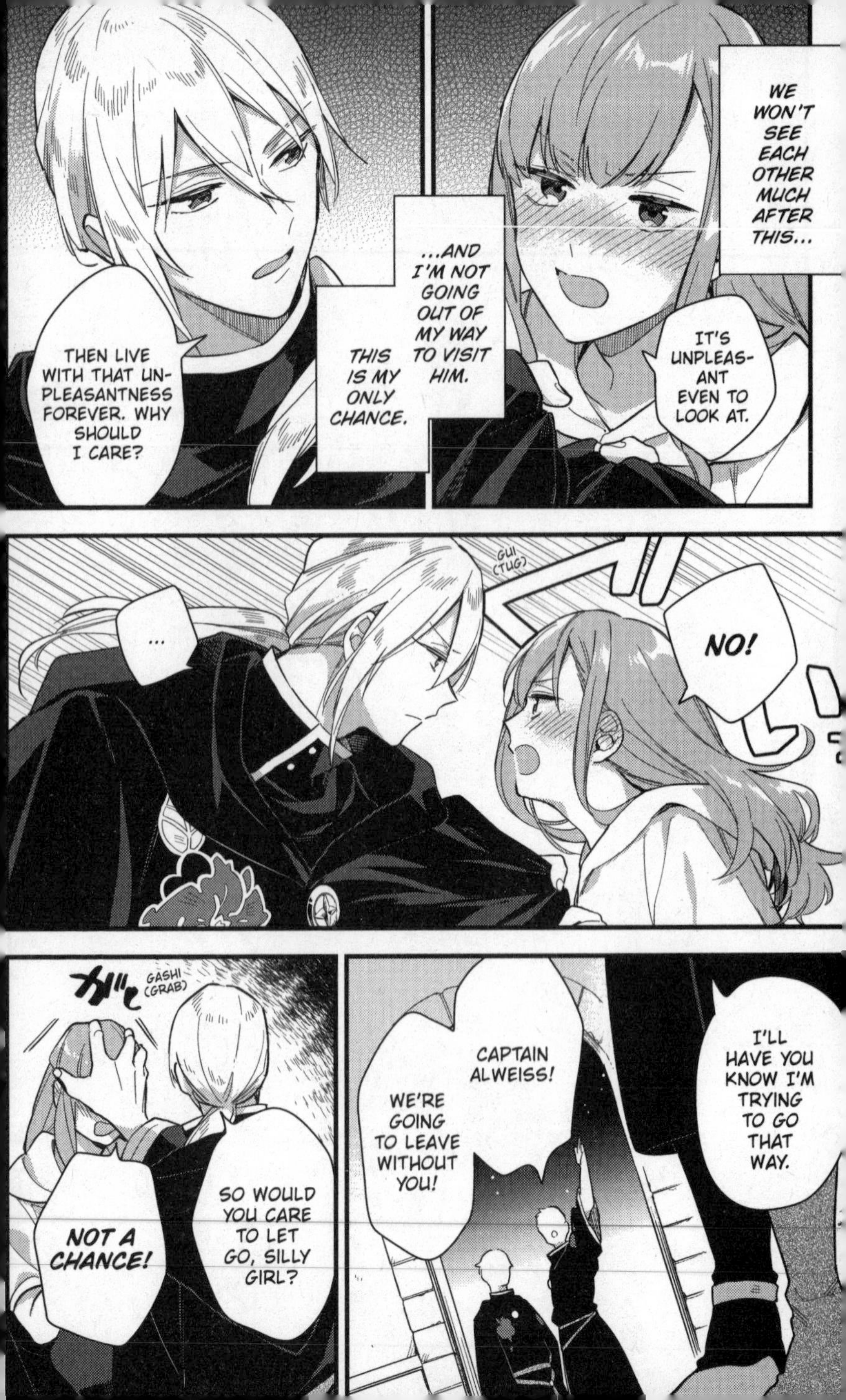
WE WON'T SEE EACH OTHER MUCH AFTER THIS...
IT'S UNPLEASANT EVEN TO LOOK AT.
...AND I'M NOT GOING OUT OF MY WAY TO VISIT HIM.
THIS IS MY ONLY CHANCE.
THEN LIVE WITH THAT UNPLEASANTNESS FOREVER. WHY SHOULD I CARE?
GUI (TUG)
NO!
...
I'LL HAVE YOU KNOW I'M TRYING TO GO THAT WAY.
CAPTAIN ALWEISS!
WE'RE GOING TO LEAVE WITHOUT YOU!
GASHI (GRAB)
SO WOULD YOU CARE TO LET GO, SILLY GIRL?
NOT A CHANCE!

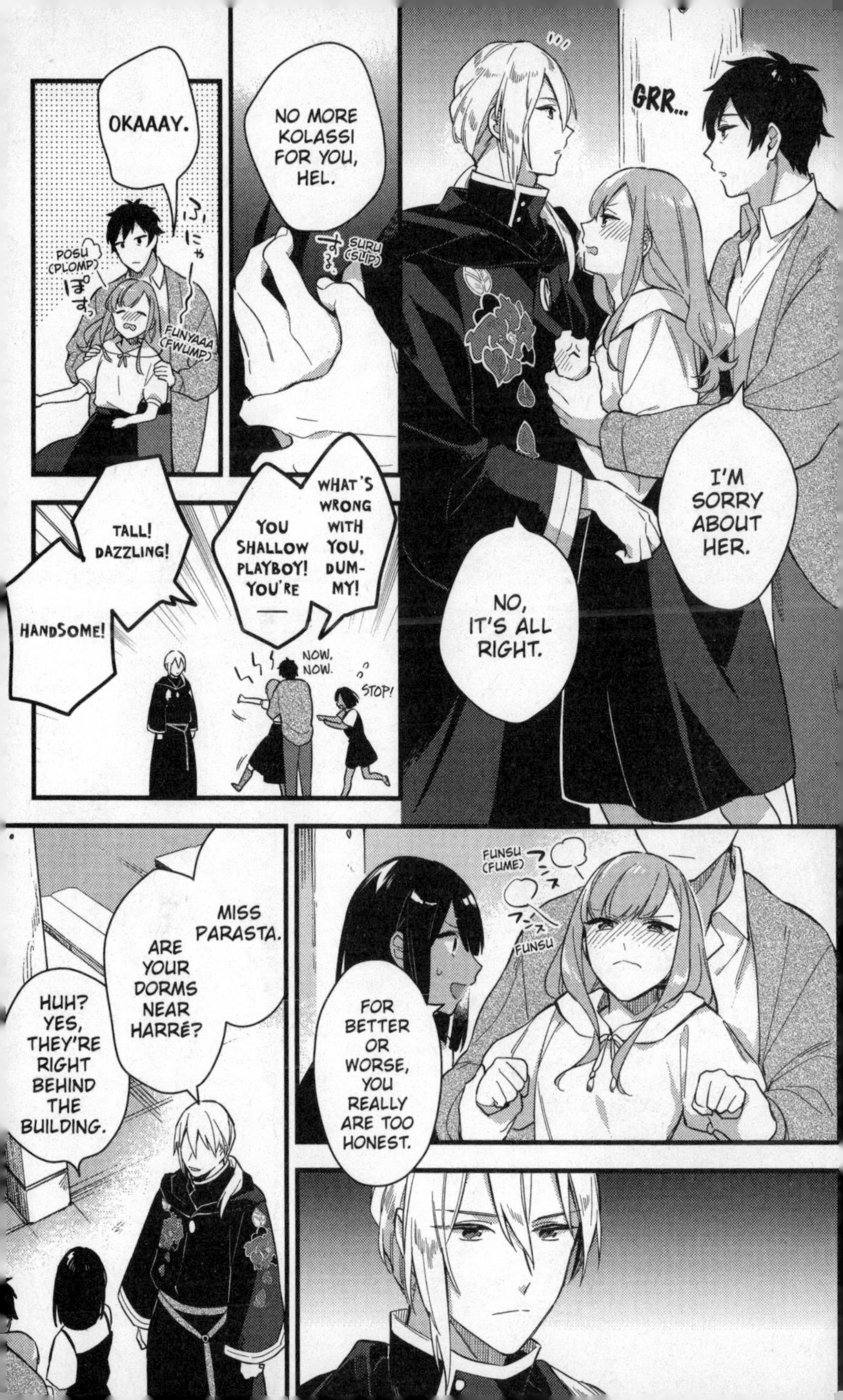
GRR...
I'M SORRY ABOUT HER.
NO, IT'S ALL RIGHT.
NO MORE KOLASSI FOR YOU, HEL.
SURU (SLIP)
OKAAAY.
POSU (PLOMP)
FUNYAAA (FWUMP)
WHAT'S WRONG WITH YOU, DUMMY! YOU'RE
YOU SHALLOW PLAYBOY!
TALL! DAZZLING!
HANDSOME!
NOW, NOW.
STOP!
FUNSU (FUME)
FUNSU
FOR BETTER OR WORSE, YOU REALLY ARE TOO HONEST.
MISS PARASTA.
ARE YOUR DORMS NEAR HARRÉ?
HUH? YES, THEY'RE RIGHT BEHIND THE BUILDING.

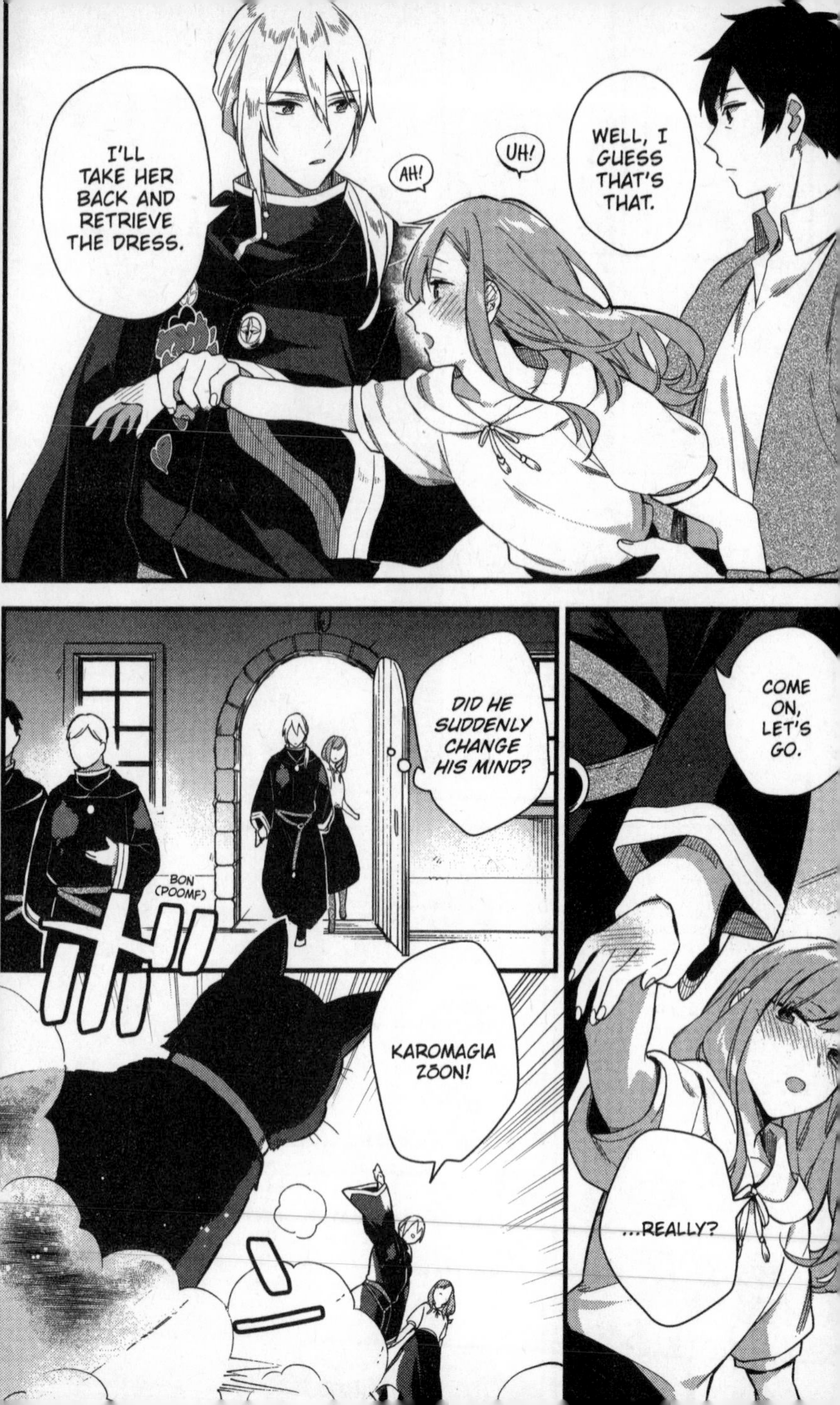
WELL, I GUESS THAT'S THAT.
UH!
AH!
I'LL TAKE HER BACK AND RETRIEVE THE DRESS.
COME ON, LET'S GO.
...REALLY?
DID HE SUDDENLY CHANGE HIS MIND?
KAROMAGIA ZOON!
BON (POOMF)

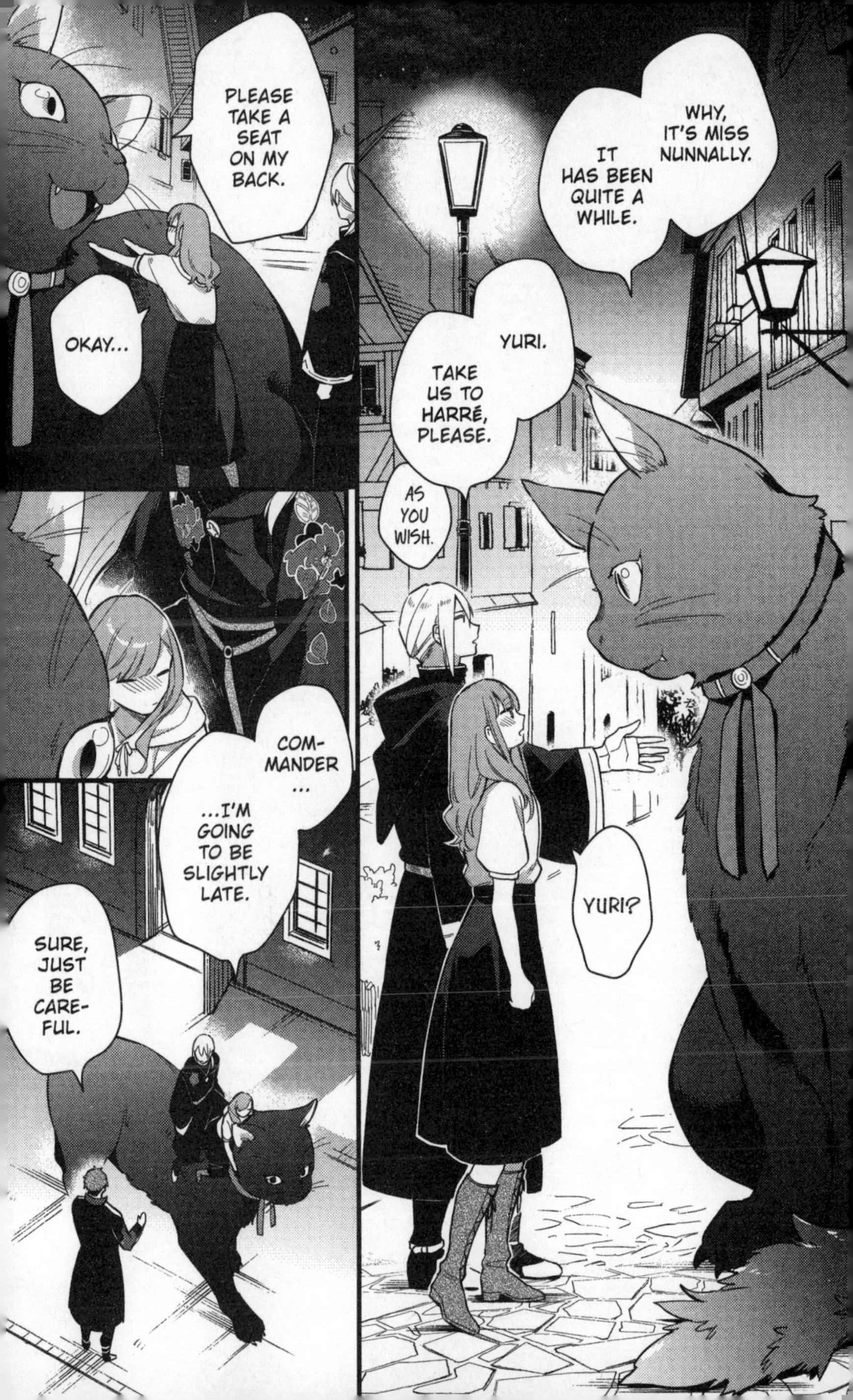
WHY, IT'S MISS NUNNALLY.
IT HAS BEEN QUITE A WHILE.
YURI.
TAKE US TO HARRÉ, PLEASE.
AS YOU WISH.
YURI?
PLEASE TAKE A SEAT ON MY BACK.
OKAY...
COM-MANDER ...
...I'M GOING TO BE SLIGHTLY LATE.
SURE, JUST BE CARE-FUL.

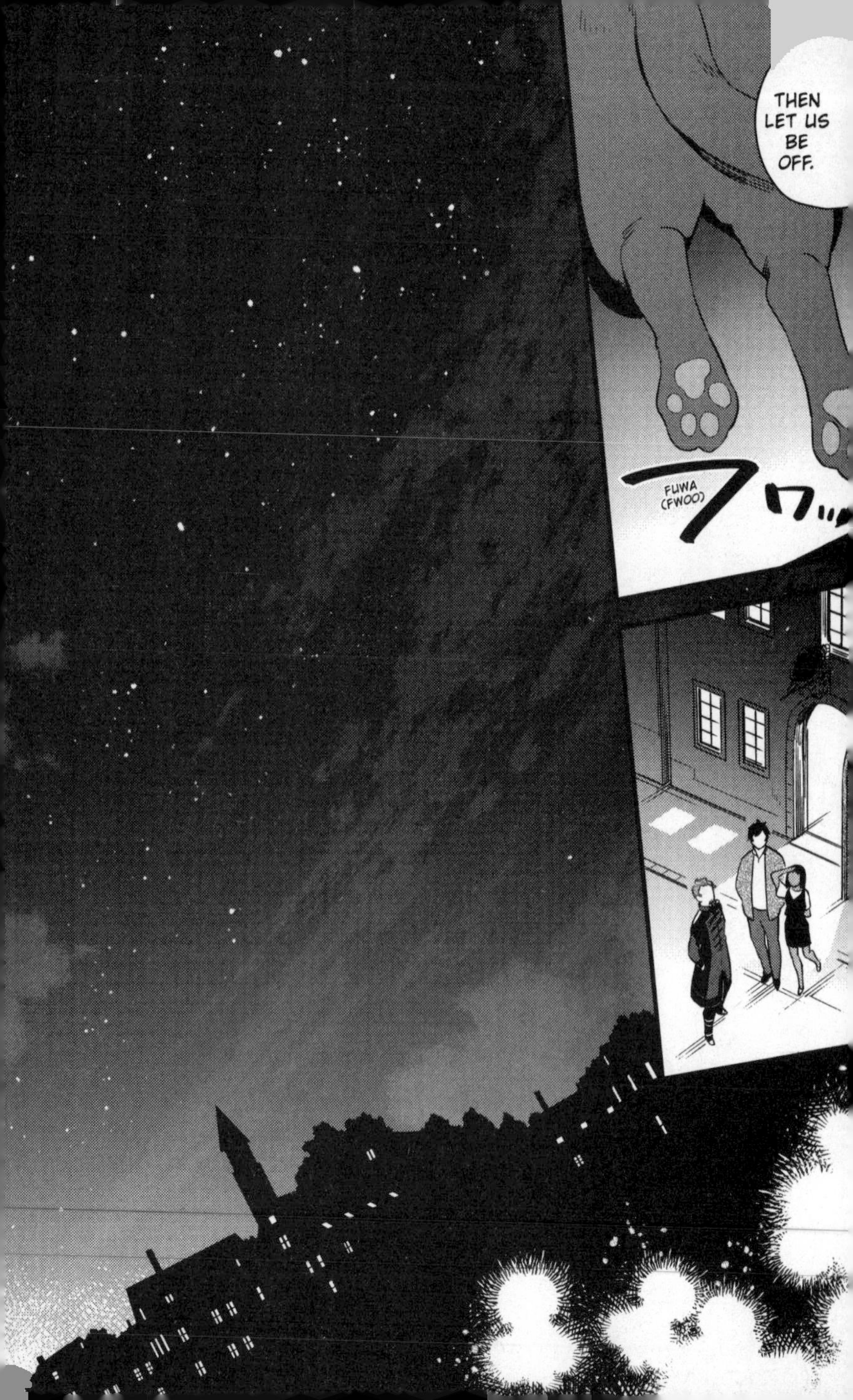
THEN LET US BE OFF.
FUWA (FWOO)

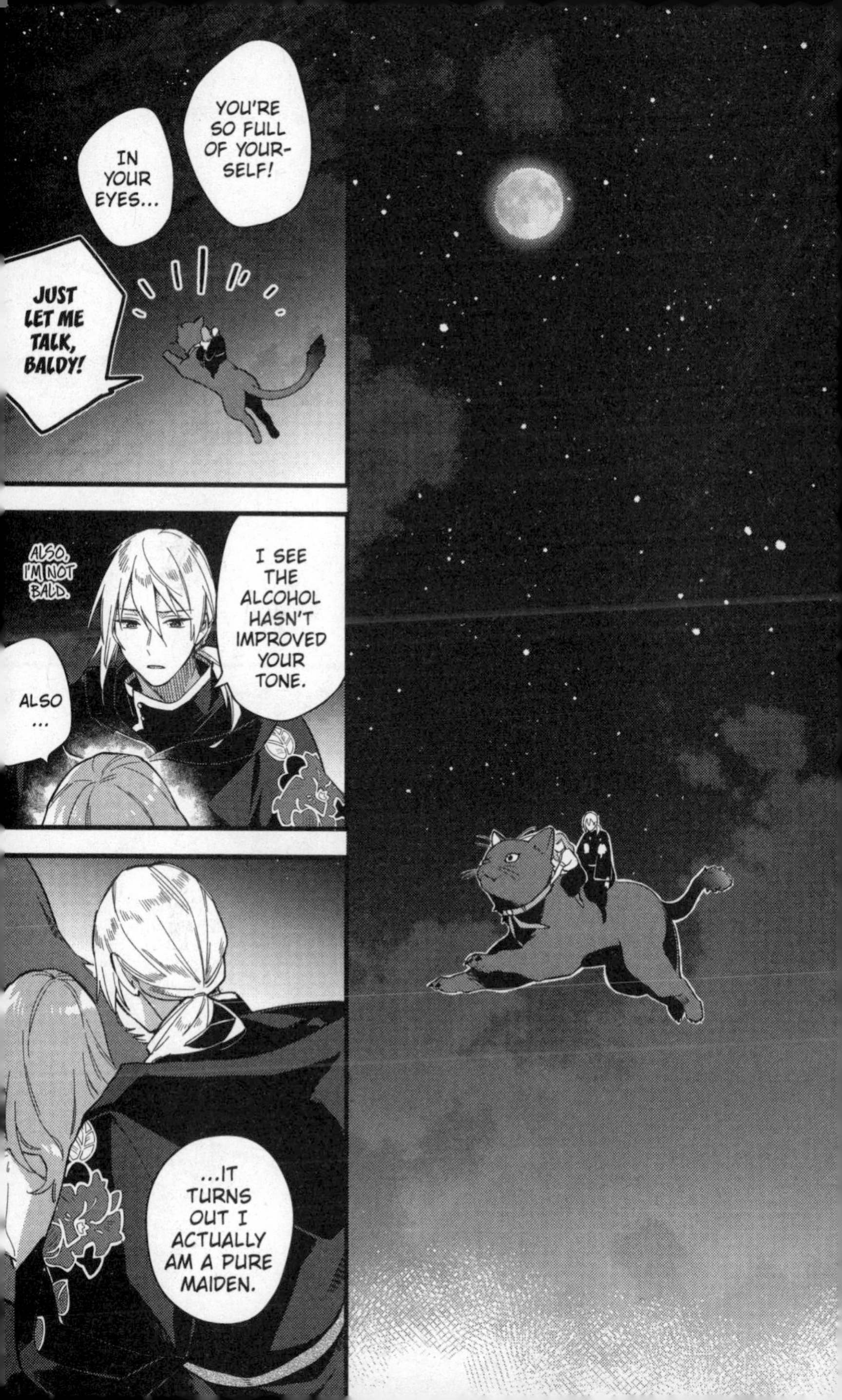
YOU'RE SO FULL OF YOUR-SELF!
IN YOUR EYES...
JUST LET ME TALK, BALDY!
I SEE THE ALCOHOL HASN'T IMPROVED YOUR TONE.
ALSO, I'M NOT BALD.
ALSO ...
...IT TURNS OUT I ACTUALLY AM A PURE MAIDEN.

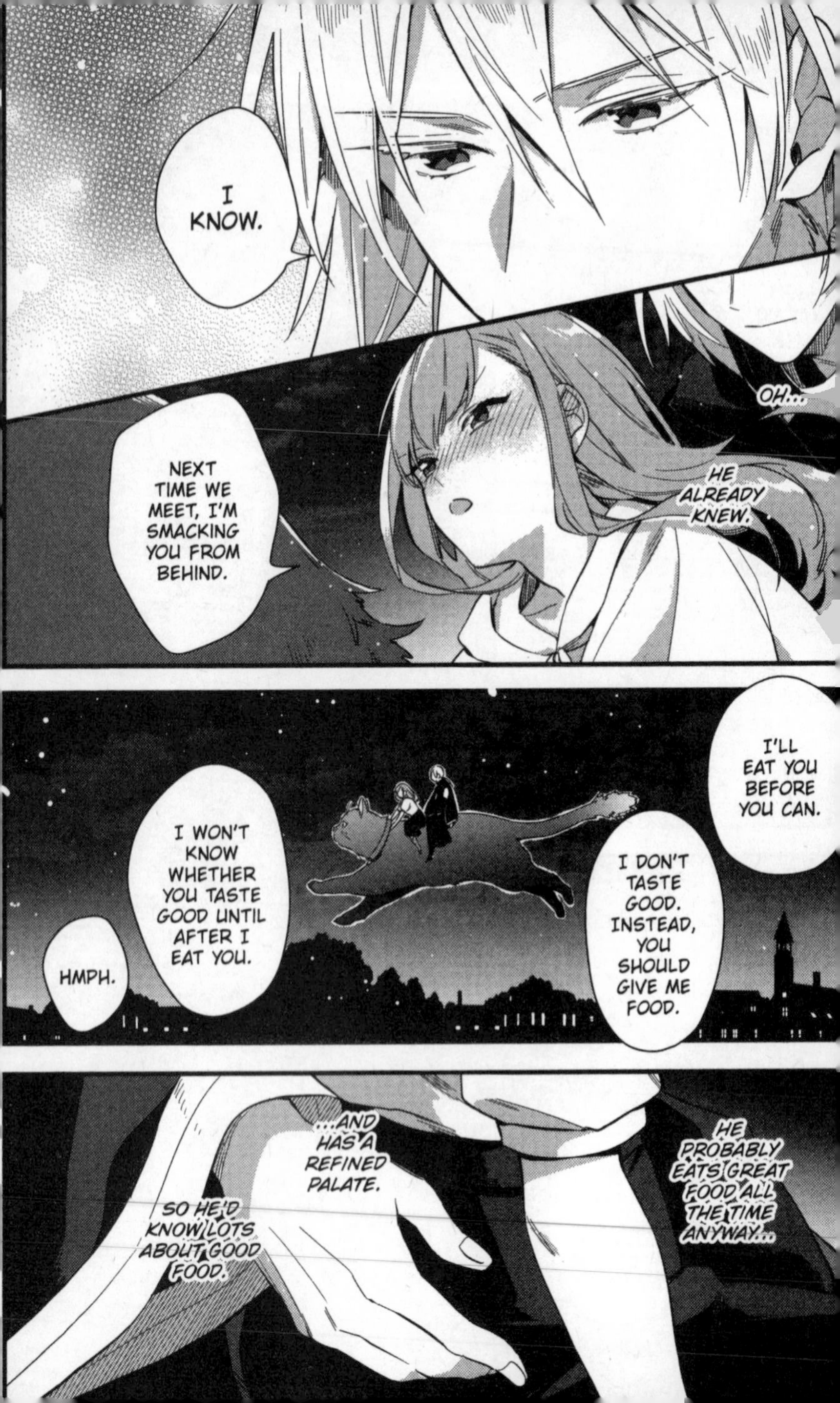
I KNOW.
OH...
HE ALREADY KNEW.
NEXT TIME WE MEET, I'M SMACKING YOU FROM BEHIND.
I'LL EAT YOU BEFORE YOU CAN.
I DON'T TASTE GOOD. INSTEAD, YOU SHOULD GIVE ME FOOD.
I WON'T KNOW WHETHER YOU TASTE GOOD UNTIL AFTER I EAT YOU.
HMPH.
HE PROBABLY EATS GREAT FOOD ALL THE TIME ANYWAY...
...AND HAS A REFINED PALATE.
SO HE'D KNOW LOTS ABOUT GOOD FOOD.

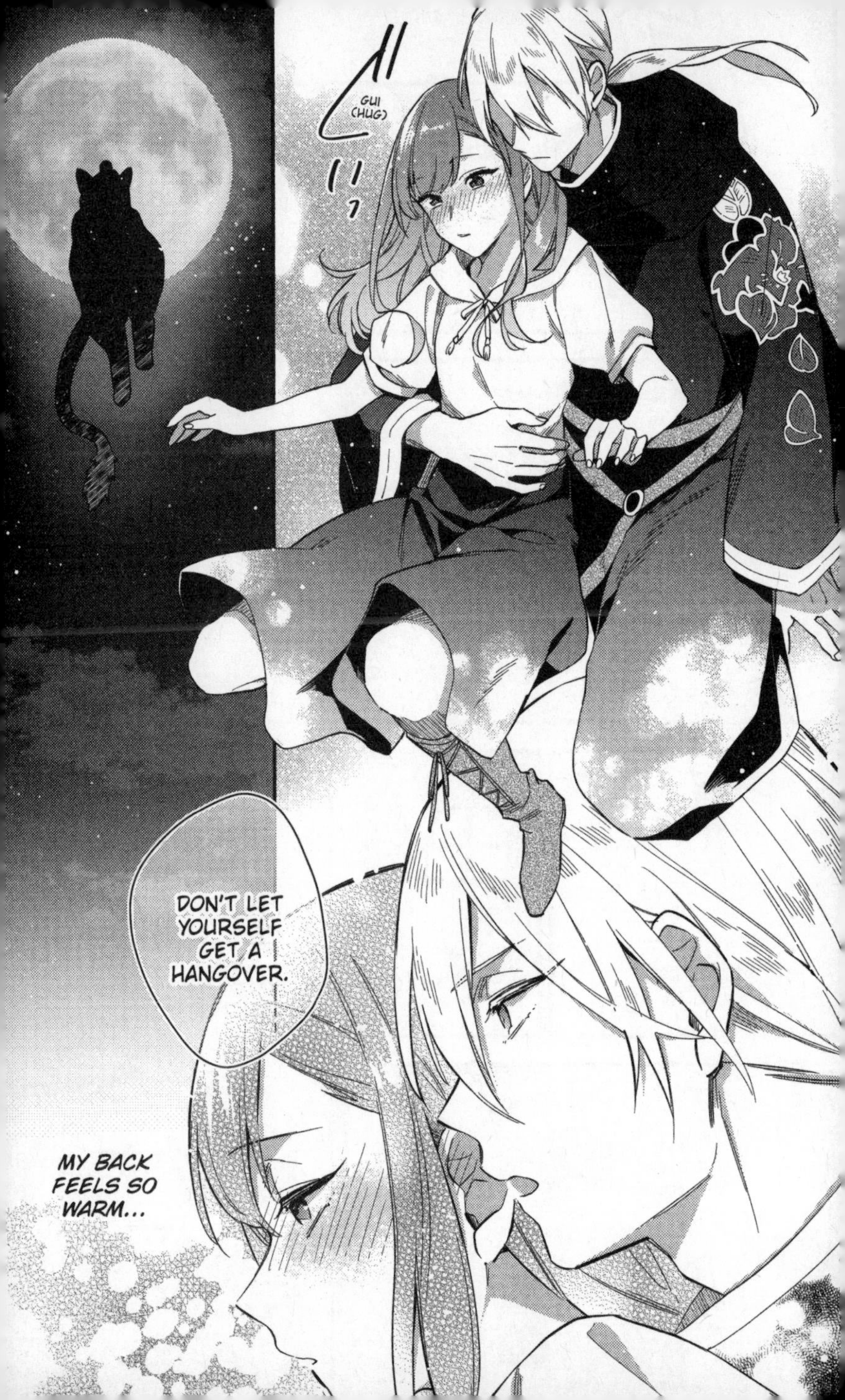
GUI (HUG)
DON'T LET YOURSELF GET A HANGOVER.
MY BACK FEELS SO WARM...

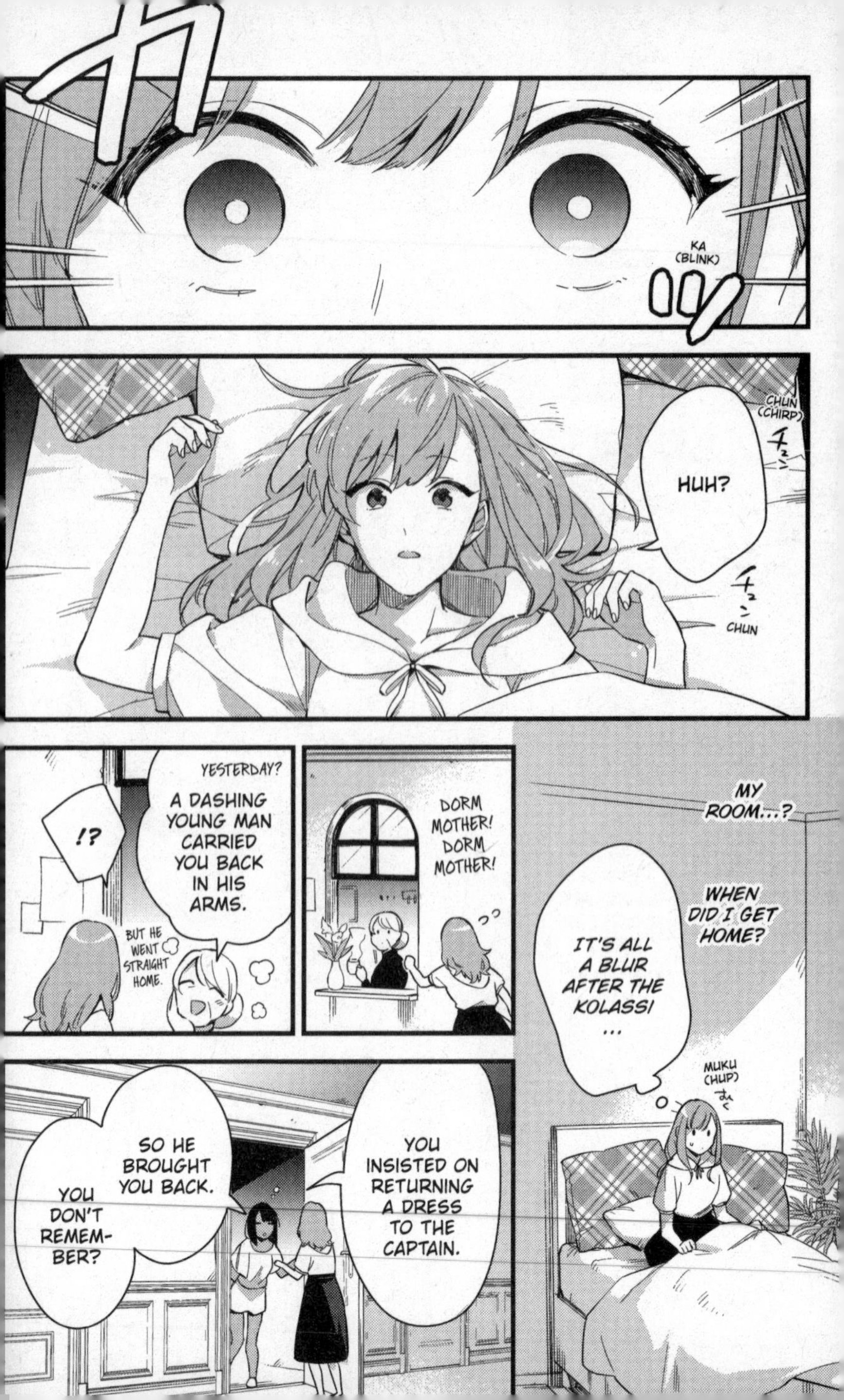
KA (BLINK)
CHUN (CHIRP)
HUH?
CHUN
MY ROOM...?
WHEN DID I GET HOME?
IT'S ALL A BLUR AFTER THE KOLASSI ...
MUKU (CHUP)
DORM MOTHER! DORM MOTHER!
YESTERDAY?
A DASHING YOUNG MAN CARRIED YOU BACK IN HIS ARMS.
!?
BUT HE WENT STRAIGHT HOME.
YOU INSISTED ON RETURNING A DRESS TO THE CAPTAIN.
SO HE BROUGHT YOU BACK.
YOU DON'T REMEMBER?

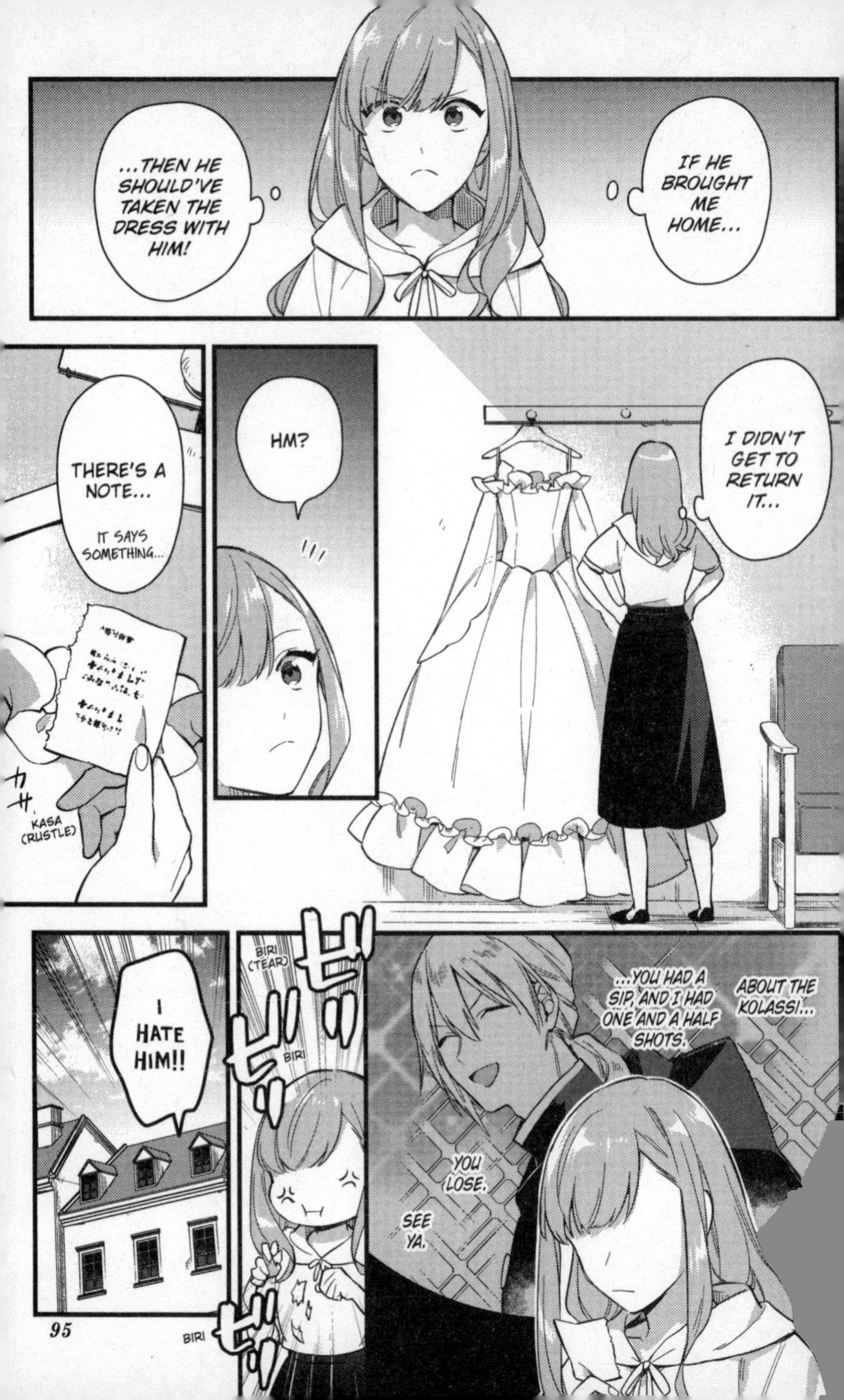
IF HE BROUGHT ME HOME...
...THEN HE SHOULD'VE TAKEN THE DRESS WITH HIM!
I DIDN'T GET TO RETURN IT...
HM?
THERE'S A NOTE...
IT SAYS SOMETHING...
KASA (RUSTLE)
ABOUT THE KOLASSI...
...YOU HAD A SIP, AND I HAD ONE AND A HALF SHOTS.
YOU LOSE.
SEE YA.
BIRI (TEAR)
BIRI
BIRI
I HATE HIM!!

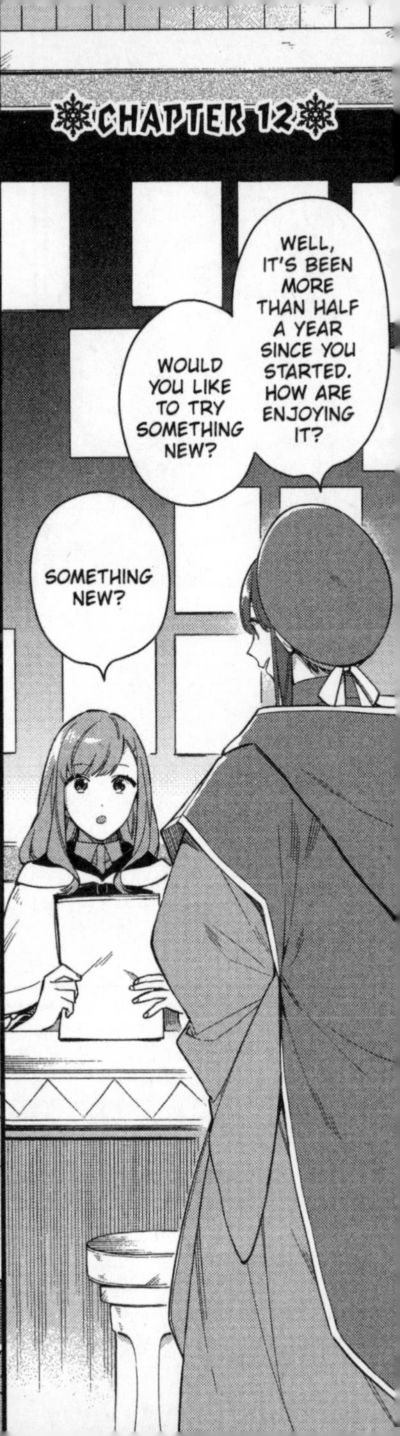
CHAPTER 12
WELL, IT'S BEEN MORE THAN HALF A YEAR SINCE YOU STARTED. HOW ARE ENJOYING IT?
WOULD YOU LIKE TO TRY SOMETHING NEW?
SOMETHING NEW?

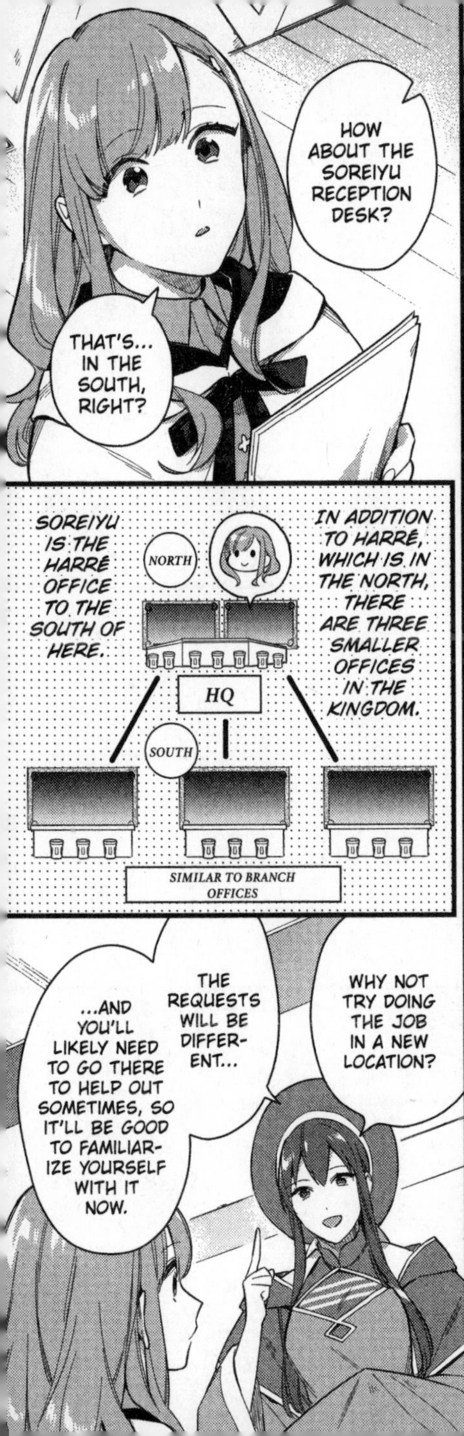
HOW ABOUT THE SOREIYU RECEPTION DESK?
THAT'S... IN THE SOUTH, RIGHT?
IN ADDITION TO HARRÉ, WHICH IS IN THE NORTH, THERE ARE THREE SMALLER OFFICES IN THE KINGDOM.
SOREIYU IS THE HARRÉ OFFICE TO THE SOUTH OF HERE.
NORTH
HQ
SOUTH
SIMILAR TO BRANCH OFFICES
WHY NOT TRY DOING THE JOB IN A NEW LOCATION?
THE REQUESTS WILL BE DIFFER-ENT...
...AND YOU'LL LIKELY NEED TO GO THERE TO HELP OUT SOMETIMES, SO IT'LL BE GOOD TO FAMILIAR-IZE YOURSELF WITH IT NOW.

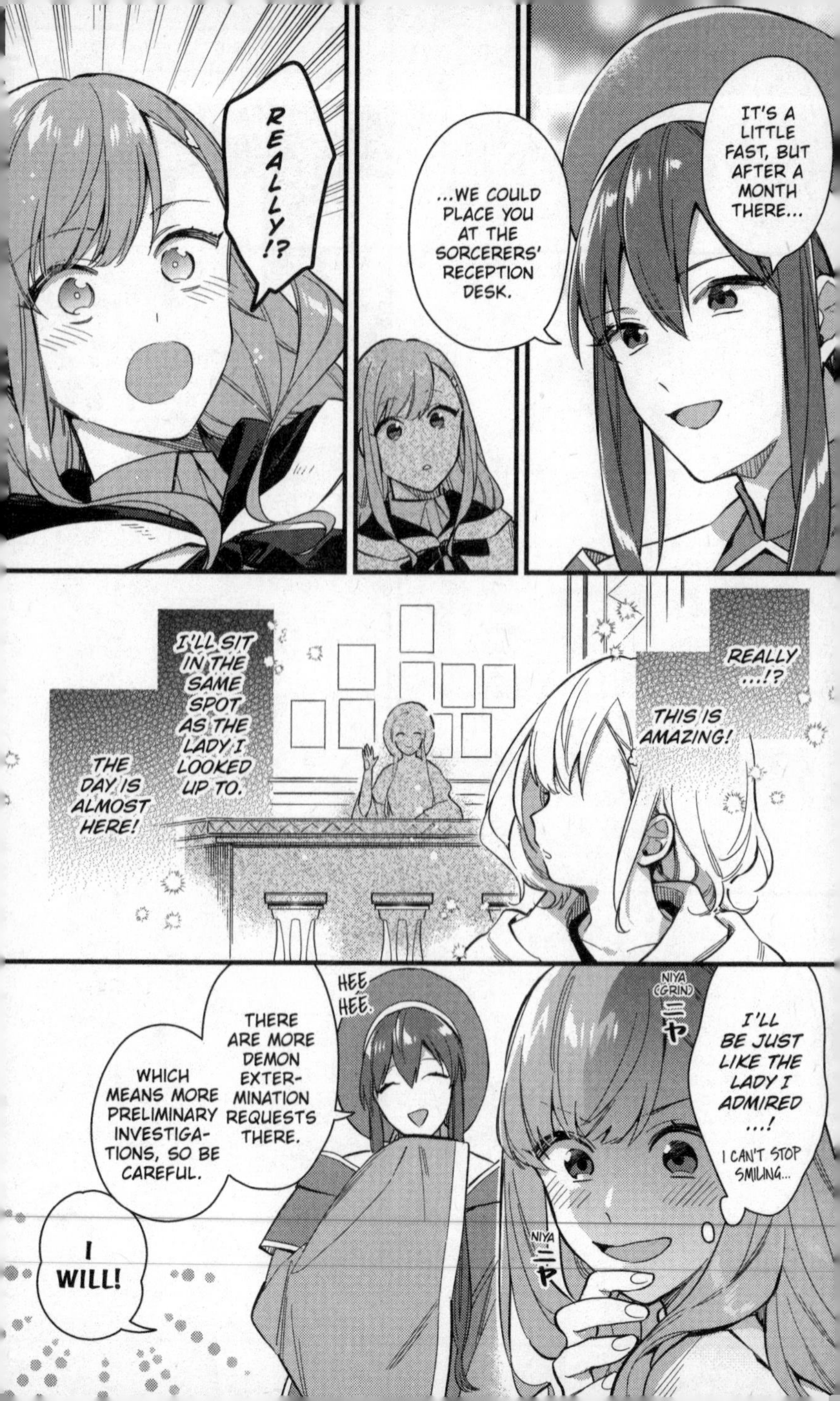
IT'S A LITTLE FAST, BUT AFTER A MONTH THERE...
...WE COULD PLACE YOU AT THE SORCERERS' RECEPTION DESK.
REALLY!?
REALLY ...!?
THIS IS AMAZING!
I'LL SIT IN THE SAME SPOT AS THE LADY I LOOKED UP TO.
THE DAY IS ALMOST HERE!
NIYA (GRIN)
ニヤ
I'LL BE JUST LIKE THE LADY I ADMIRED ...!
I CAN'T STOP SMILING...
NIYA
ニヤ
HEE HEE.
THERE ARE MORE DEMON EXTER-MINATION REQUESTS THERE.
WHICH MEANS MORE PRELIMINARY INVESTIGA-TIONS, SO BE CAREFUL.
I WILL!

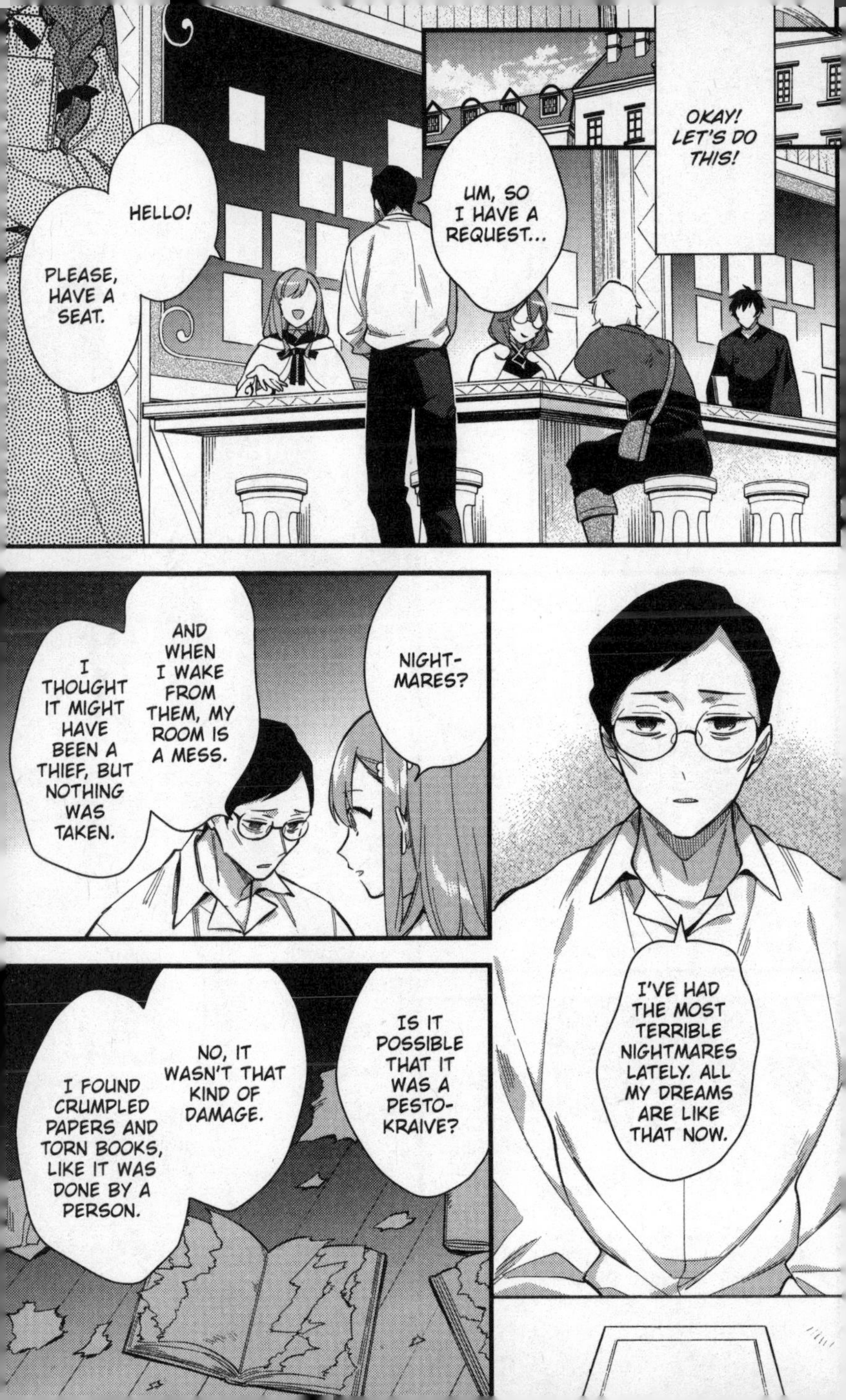
OKAY! LET'S DO THIS!
UM, SO I HAVE A REQUEST...
HELLO!
PLEASE, HAVE A SEAT.
I'VE HAD THE MOST TERRIBLE NIGHTMARES LATELY. ALL MY DREAMS ARE LIKE THAT NOW.
NIGHT-MARES?
AND WHEN I WAKE FROM THEM, MY ROOM IS A MESS.
I THOUGHT IT MIGHT HAVE BEEN A THIEF, BUT NOTHING WAS TAKEN.
IS IT POSSIBLE THAT IT WAS A PESTO-KRAIVE?
NO, IT WASN'T THAT KIND OF DAMAGE.
I FOUND CRUMPLED PAPERS AND TORN BOOKS, LIKE IT WAS DONE BY A PERSON.

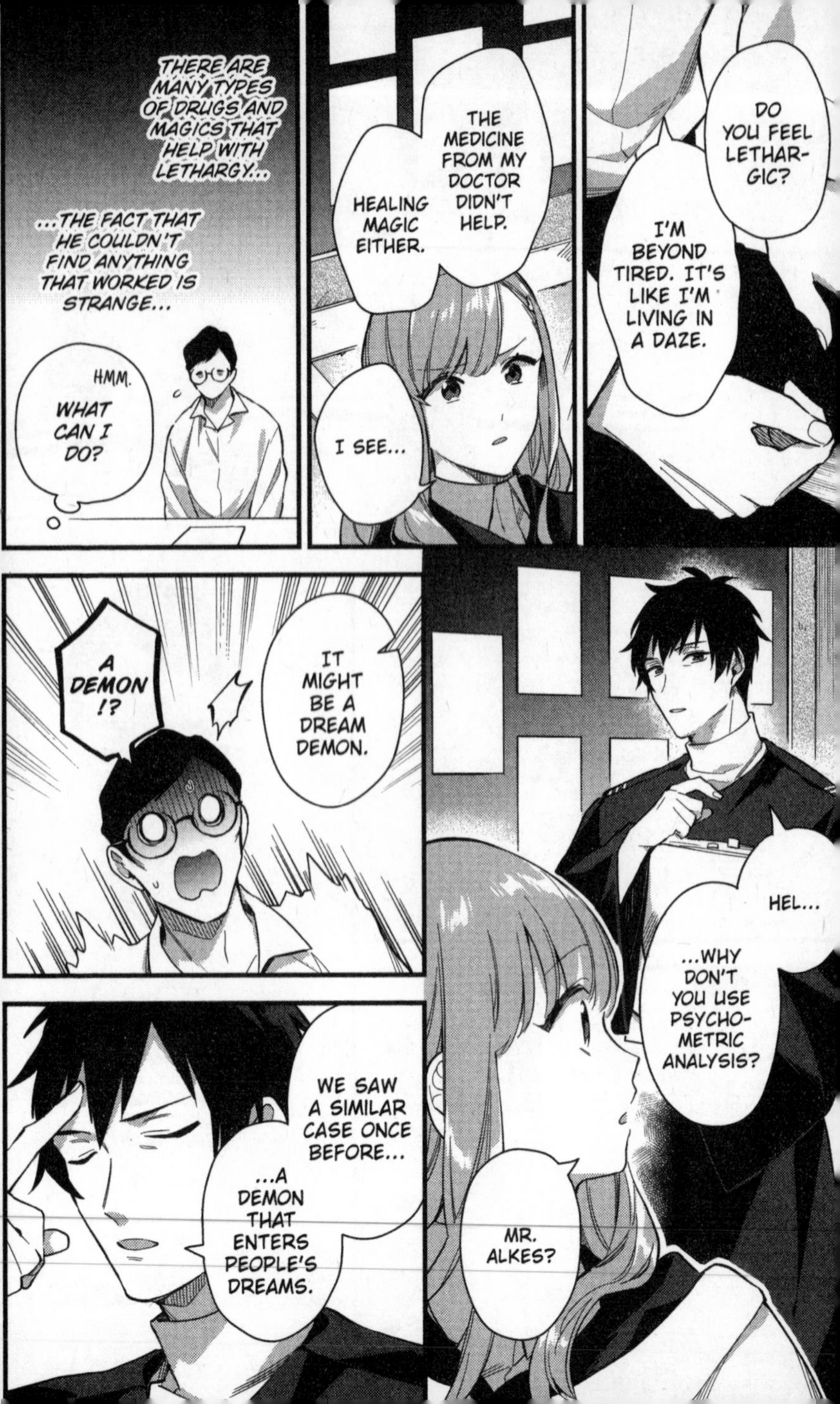
DO YOU FEEL LETHARGIC?
I'M BEYOND TIRED. IT'S LIKE I'M LIVING IN A DAZE.
THE MEDICINE FROM MY DOCTOR DIDN'T HELP.
HEALING MAGIC EITHER.
I SEE...
THERE ARE MANY TYPES OF DRUGS AND MAGICS THAT HELP WITH LETHARGY...
...THE FACT THAT HE COULDN'T FIND ANYTHING THAT WORKED IS STRANGE...
HMM.
WHAT CAN I DO?
HEL...
...WHY DON'T YOU USE PSYCHOMETRIC ANALYSIS?
MR. ALKES?
IT MIGHT BE A DREAM DEMON.
A DEMON!?
WE SAW A SIMILAR CASE ONCE BEFORE...
...A DEMON THAT ENTERS PEOPLE'S DREAMS.

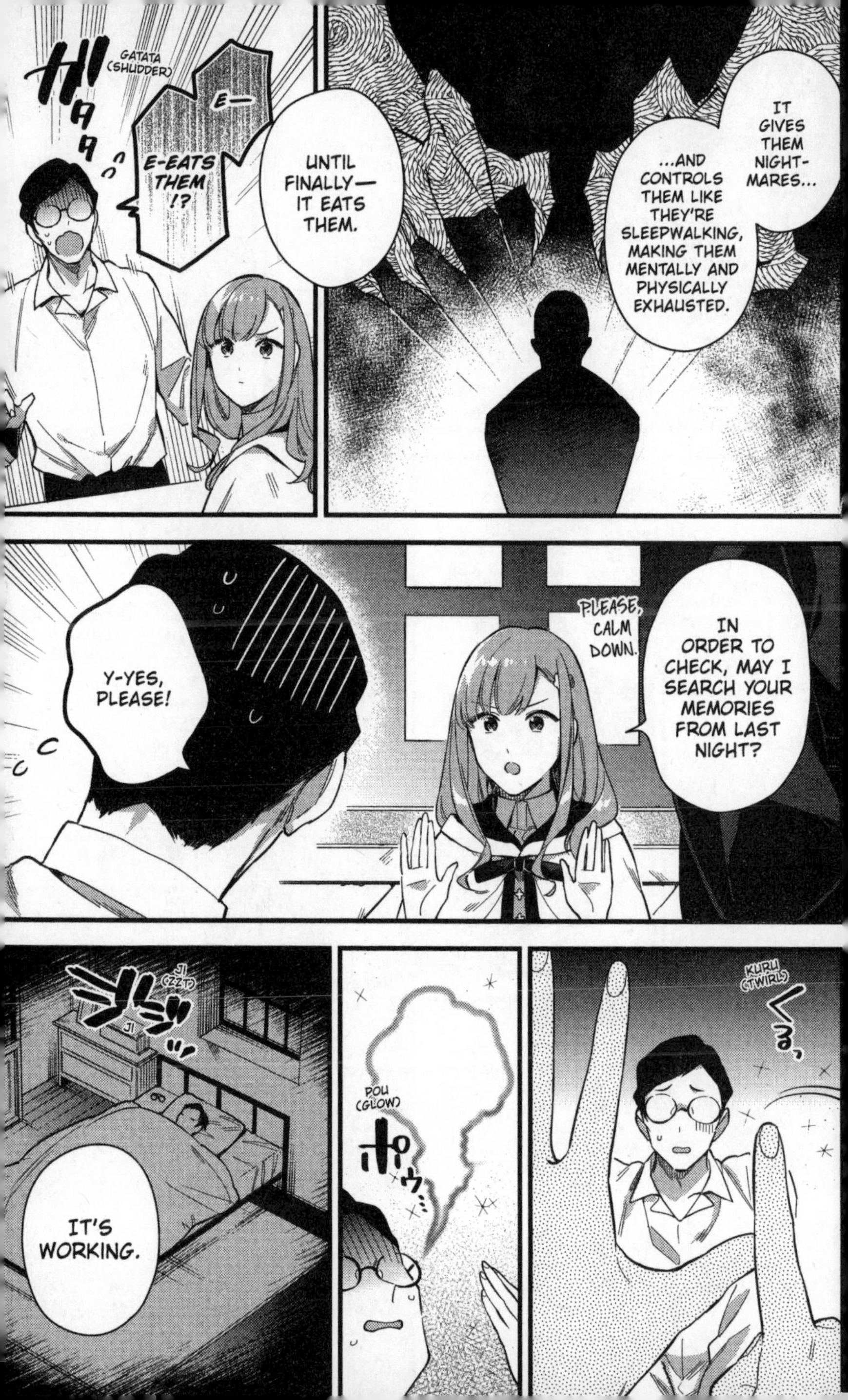
IT GIVES THEM NIGHT-MARES...
...AND CONTROLS THEM LIKE THEY'RE SLEEPWALKING, MAKING THEM MENTALLY AND PHYSICALLY EXHAUSTED.
UNTIL FINALLY— IT EATS THEM.
E—
E-EATS THEM !?
GATATA (SHUDDER)
IN ORDER TO CHECK, MAY I SEARCH YOUR MEMORIES FROM LAST NIGHT?
PLEASE, CALM DOWN.
Y-YES, PLEASE!
KURU (TWIRL)
POU (GLOW)
JI (ZZZT)
JI
IT'S WORKING.

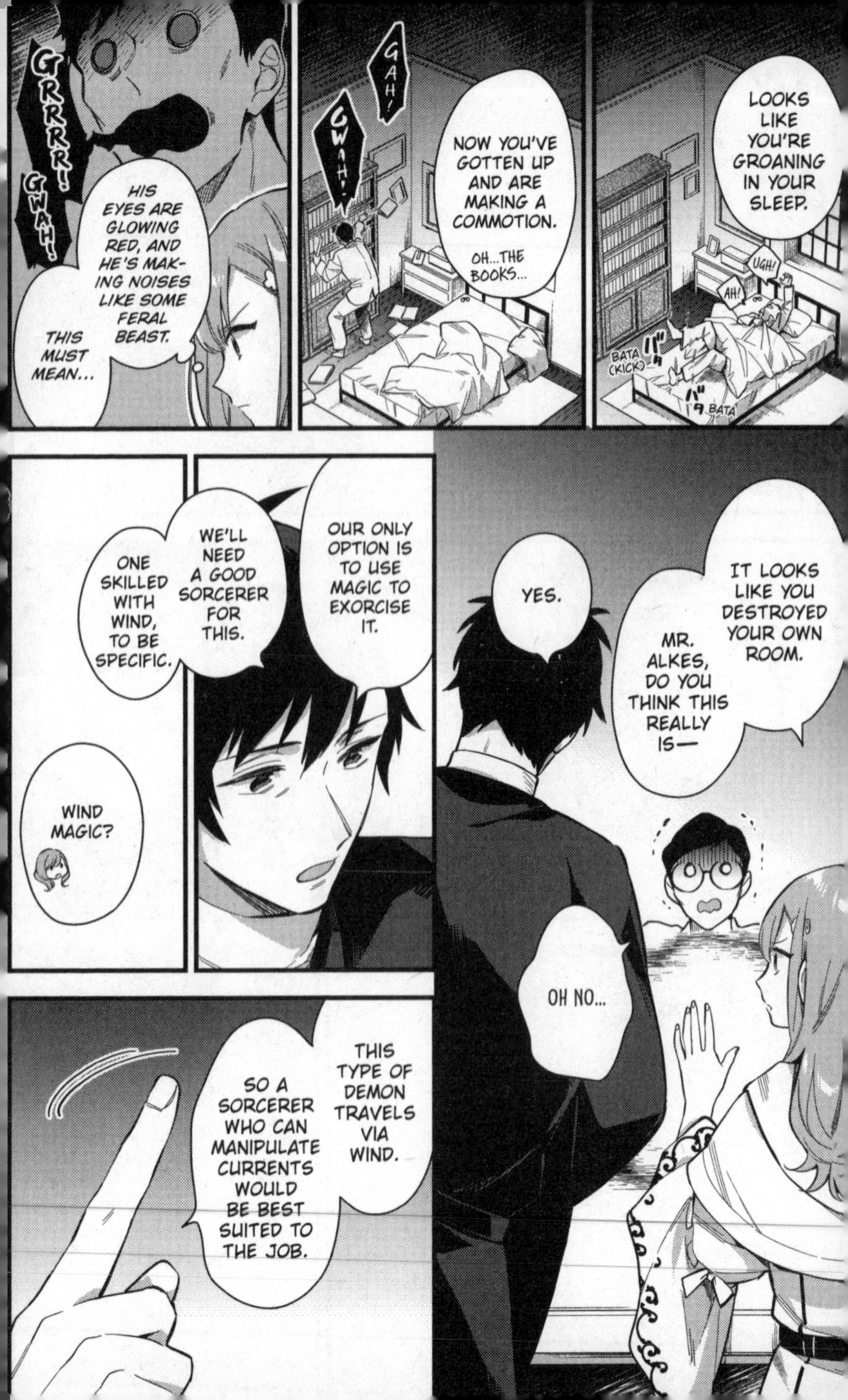
LOOKS LIKE YOU'RE GROANING IN YOUR SLEEP.
UGH!
AH!
BATA (KICK)
BATA
NOW YOU'VE GOTTEN UP AND ARE MAKING A COMMOTION.
OH...THE BOOKS...
GAH!
GWAH!
GRRRR!
GWAH!
HIS EYES ARE GLOWING RED, AND HE'S MAKING NOISES LIKE SOME FERAL BEAST.
THIS MUST MEAN...
IT LOOKS LIKE YOU DESTROYED YOUR OWN ROOM.
MR. ALKES, DO YOU THINK THIS REALLY IS—
YES.
OH NO...
OUR ONLY OPTION IS TO USE MAGIC TO EXORCISE IT.
WE'LL NEED A GOOD SORCERER FOR THIS.
ONE SKILLED WITH WIND, TO BE SPECIFIC.
WIND MAGIC?
THIS TYPE OF DEMON TRAVELS VIA WIND.
SO A SORCERER WHO CAN MANIPULATE CURRENTS WOULD BE BEST SUITED TO THE JOB.

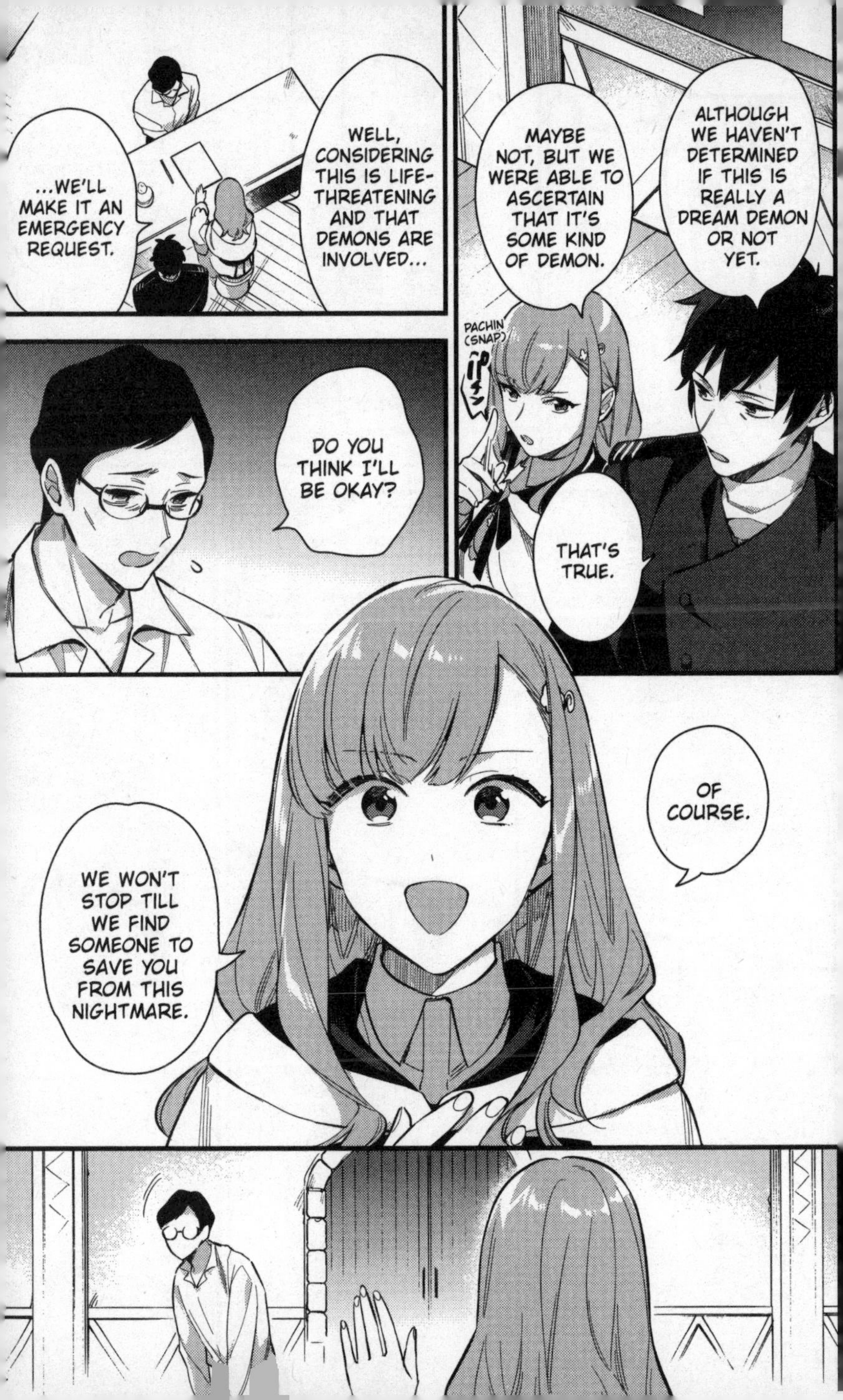
ALTHOUGH WE HAVEN'T DETERMINED IF THIS IS REALLY A DREAM DEMON OR NOT YET.
MAYBE NOT, BUT WE WERE ABLE TO ASCERTAIN THAT IT'S SOME KIND OF DEMON.
PACHIN (SNAP)
THAT'S TRUE.
WELL, CONSIDERING THIS IS LIFE-THREATENING AND THAT DEMONS ARE INVOLVED...
...WE'LL MAKE IT AN EMERGENCY REQUEST.
DO YOU THINK I'LL BE OKAY?
OF COURSE.
WE WON'T STOP TILL WE FIND SOMEONE TO SAVE YOU FROM THIS NIGHTMARE.

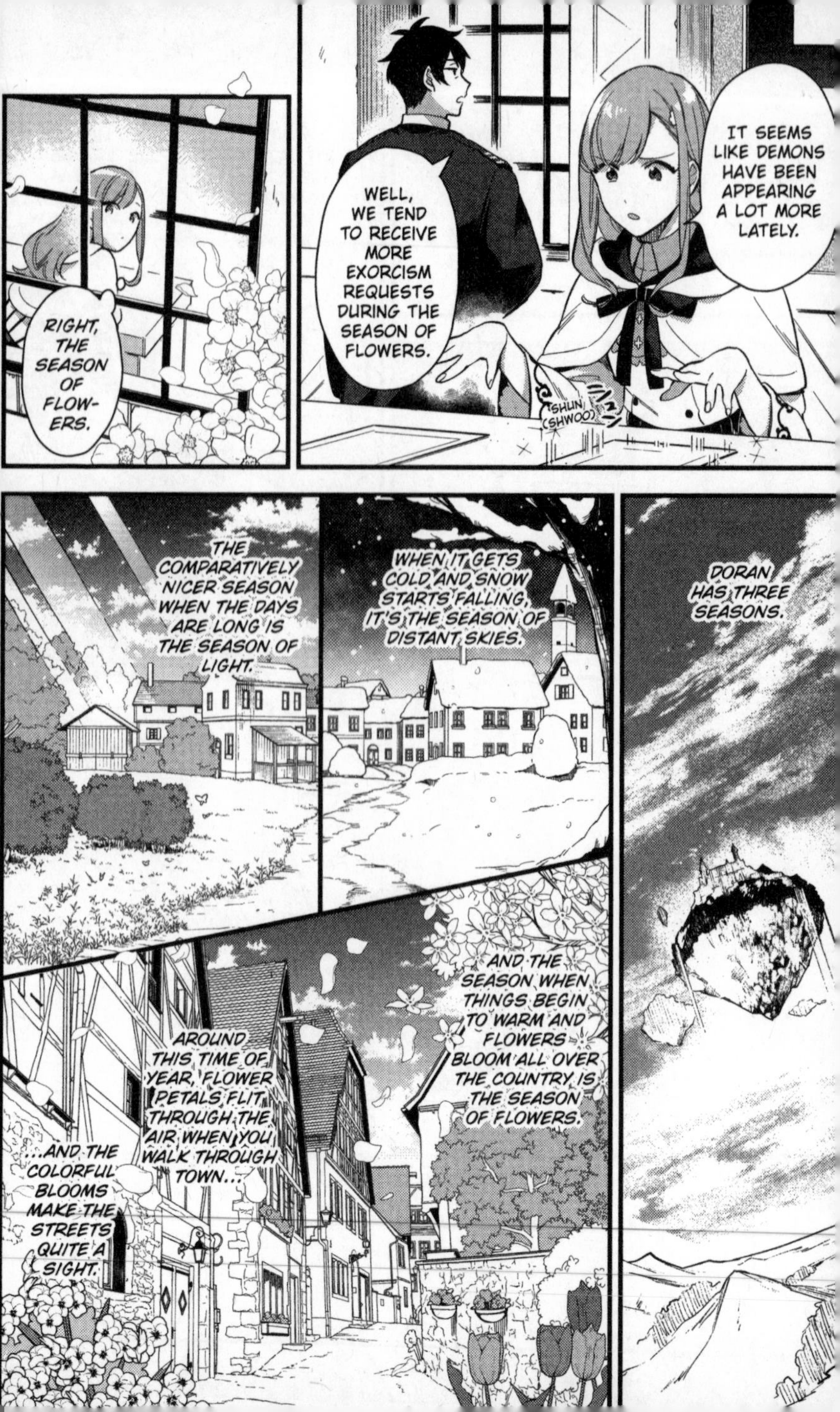
IT SEEMS LIKE DEMONS HAVE BEEN APPEARING A LOT MORE LATELY.
SHUN (SHWOO)
WELL, WE TEND TO RECEIVE MORE EXORCISM REQUESTS DURING THE SEASON OF FLOWERS.
RIGHT, THE SEASON OF FLOW-ERS.
DORAN HAS THREE SEASONS.
WHEN IT GETS COLD AND SNOW STARTS FALLING, IT'S THE SEASON OF DISTANT SKIES.
THE COMPARATIVELY NICER SEASON WHEN THE DAYS ARE LONG IS THE SEASON OF LIGHT.
AND THE SEASON WHEN THINGS BEGIN TO WARM AND FLOWERS BLOOM ALL OVER THE COUNTRY IS THE SEASON OF FLOWERS.
AROUND THIS TIME OF YEAR, FLOWER PETALS FLIT THROUGH THE AIR WHEN YOU WALK THROUGH TOWN...
...AND THE COLORFUL BLOOMS MAKE THE STREETS QUITE A SIGHT.

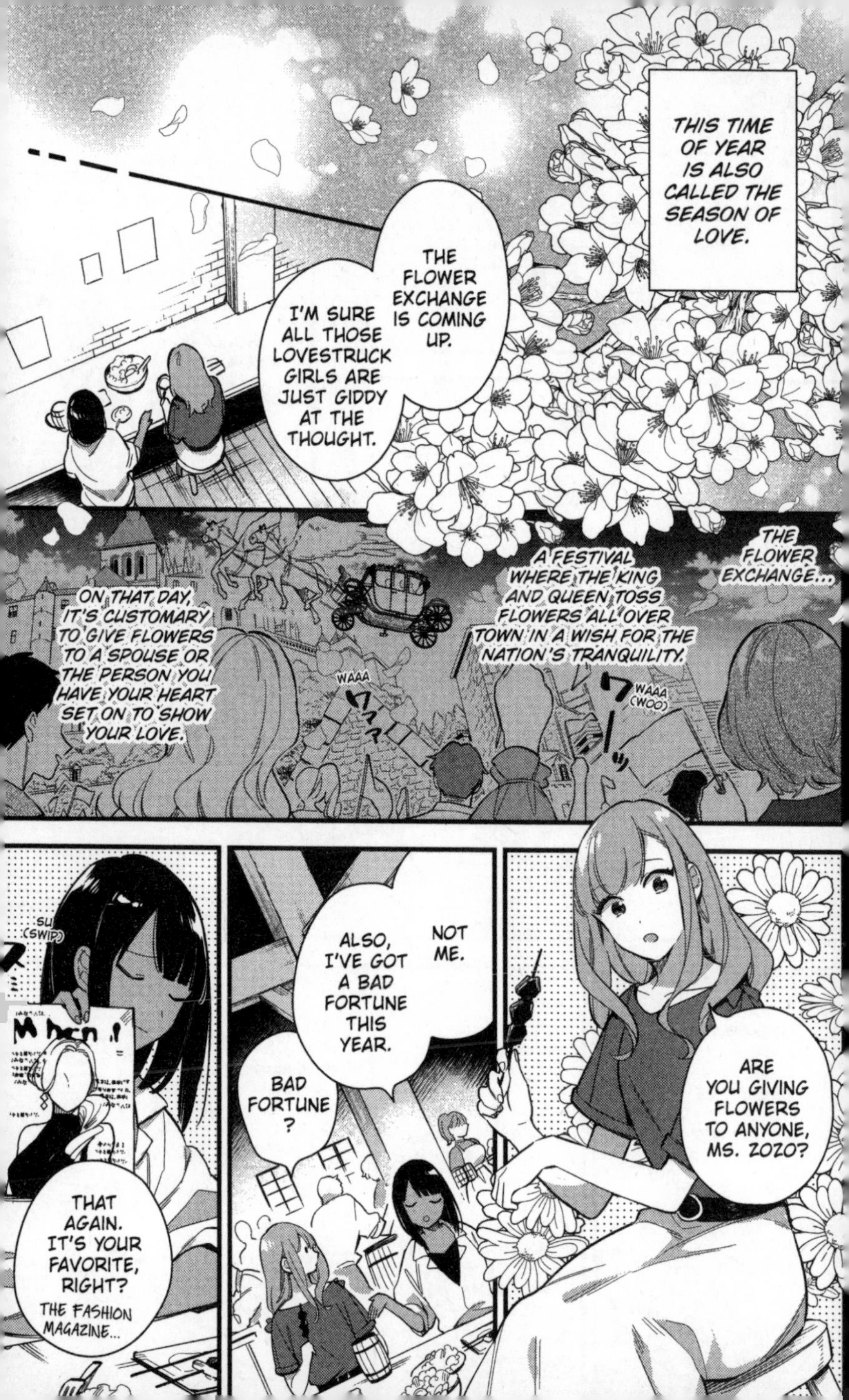
THIS TIME OF YEAR IS ALSO CALLED THE SEASON OF LOVE.
THE FLOWER EXCHANGE IS COMING UP.
I'M SURE ALL THOSE LOVESTRUCK GIRLS ARE JUST GIDDY AT THE THOUGHT.
THE FLOWER EXCHANGE...
A FESTIVAL WHERE THE KING AND QUEEN TOSS FLOWERS ALL OVER TOWN IN A WISH FOR THE NATION'S TRANQUILITY.
WAAA (WOO)
WAAA
ON THAT DAY, IT'S CUSTOMARY TO GIVE FLOWERS TO A SPOUSE OR THE PERSON YOU HAVE YOUR HEART SET ON TO SHOW YOUR LOVE.
ARE YOU GIVING FLOWERS TO ANYONE, MS. ZOZO?
NOT ME.
ALSO, I'VE GOT A BAD FORTUNE THIS YEAR.
BAD FORTUNE ?
SU (SWIP)
THAT AGAIN. IT'S YOUR FAVORITE, RIGHT?
THE FASHION MAGAZINE...

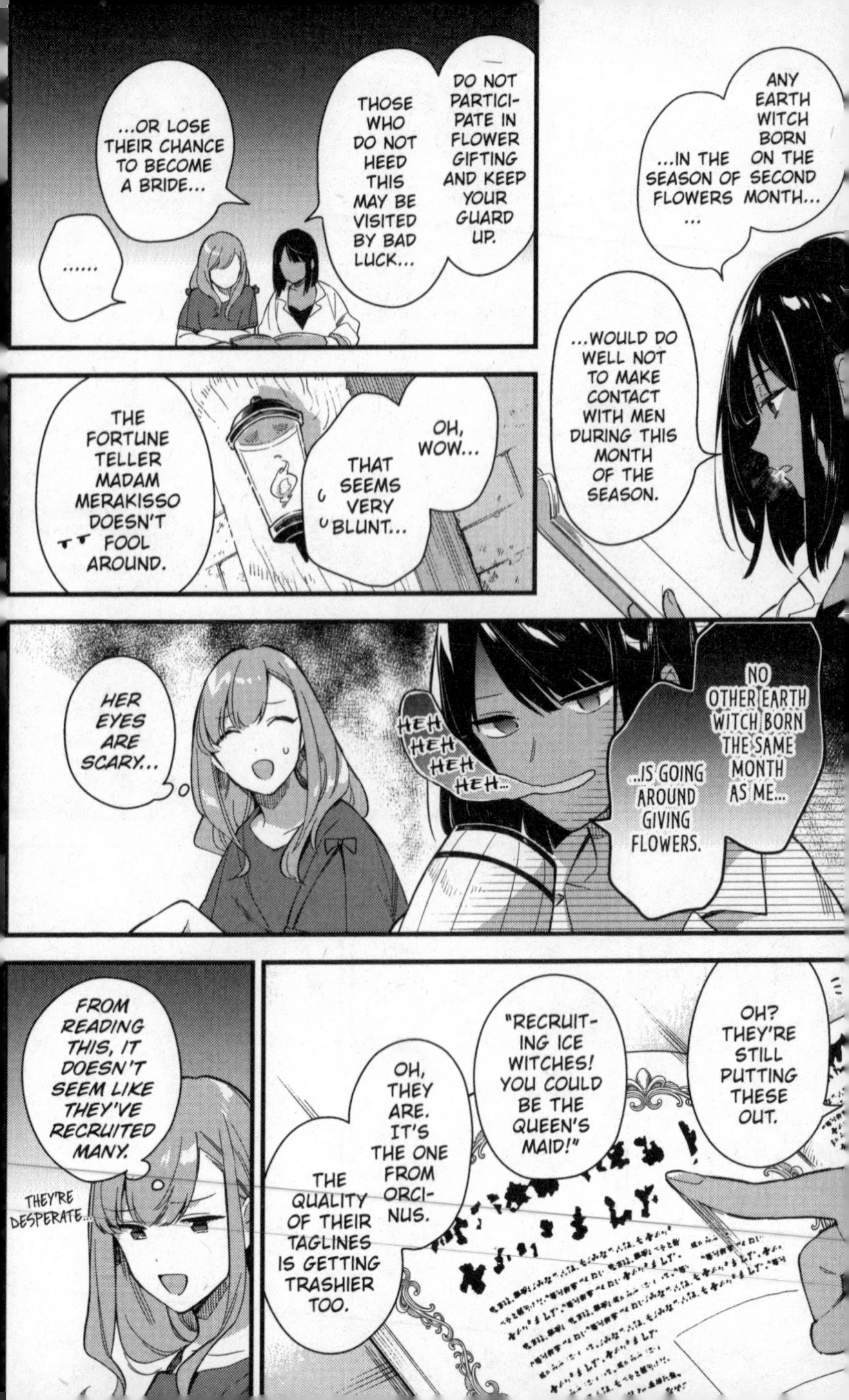
ANY EARTH WITCH BORN ON THE SECOND MONTH...
...IN THE SEASON OF FLOWERS ...
...WOULD DO WELL NOT TO MAKE CONTACT WITH MEN DURING THIS MONTH OF THE SEASON.
DO NOT PARTICIPATE IN FLOWER GIFTING AND KEEP YOUR GUARD UP.
THOSE WHO DO NOT HEED THIS MAY BE VISITED BY BAD LUCK...
...OR LOSE THEIR CHANCE TO BECOME A BRIDE...
......
OH, WOW...
THAT SEEMS VERY BLUNT...
THE FORTUNE TELLER MADAM MERAKISSO DOESN'T FOOL AROUND.
NO OTHER EARTH WITCH BORN THE SAME MONTH AS ME...
...IS GOING AROUND GIVING FLOWERS.
HEH HEH HEH HEH...
HER EYES ARE SCARY...
OH? THEY'RE STILL PUTTING THESE OUT.
"RECRUITING ICE WITCHES! YOU COULD BE THE QUEEN'S MAID!"
OH, THEY ARE. IT'S THE ONE FROM ORCINUS.
THE QUALITY OF THEIR TAGLINES IS GETTING TRASHIER TOO.
FROM READING THIS, IT DOESN'T SEEM LIKE THEY'VE RECRUITED MANY.
THEY'RE DESPERATE...

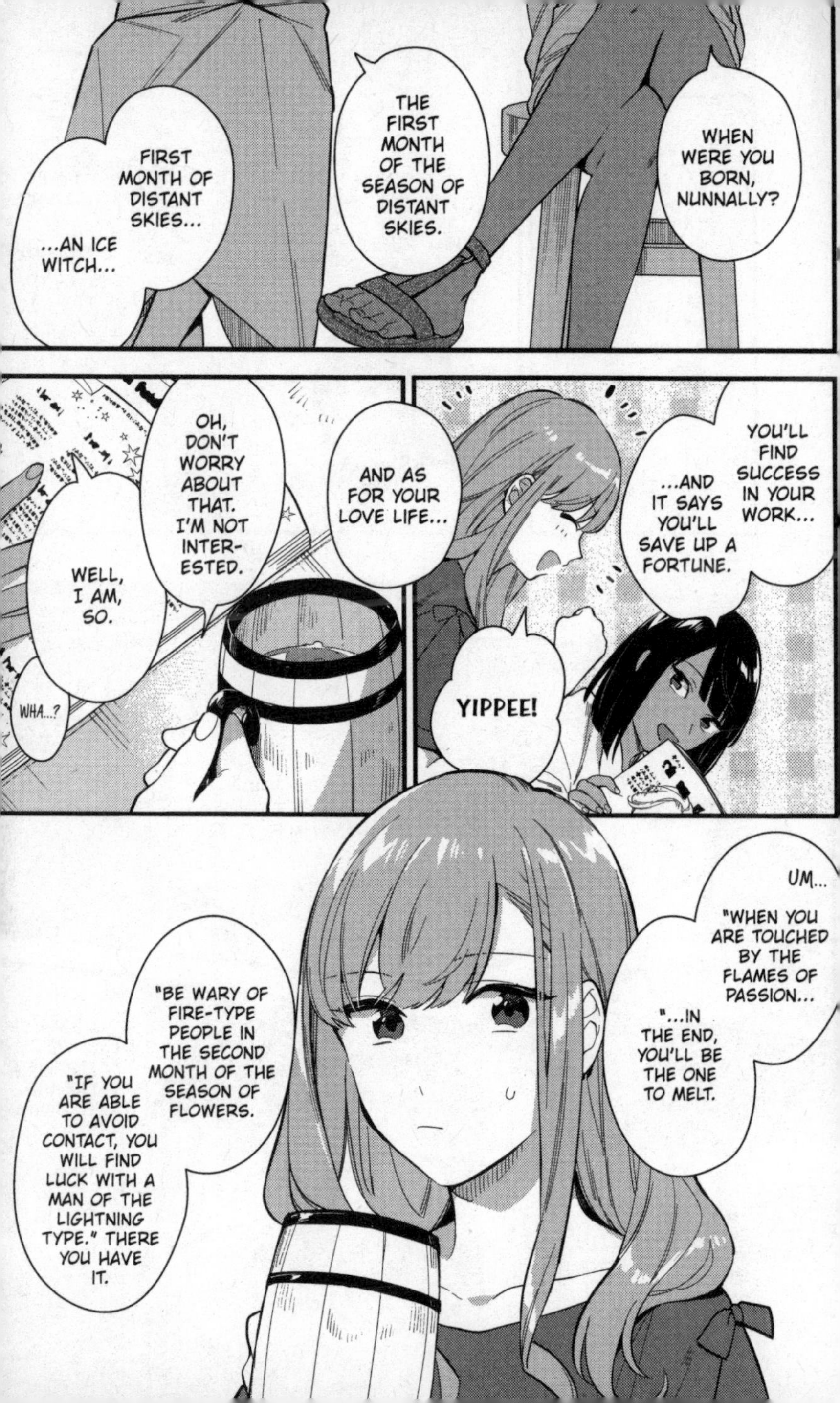
WHEN WERE YOU BORN, NUNNALLY?
THE FIRST MONTH OF THE SEASON OF DISTANT SKIES.
FIRST MONTH OF DISTANT SKIES...
...AN ICE WITCH...
YOU'LL FIND SUCCESS IN YOUR WORK...
...AND IT SAYS YOU'LL SAVE UP A FORTUNE.
YIPPEE!
AND AS FOR YOUR LOVE LIFE...
OH, DON'T WORRY ABOUT THAT. I'M NOT INTER-ESTED.
WELL, I AM, SO.
WHA...?
UM...
"WHEN YOU ARE TOUCHED BY THE FLAMES OF PASSION...
"...IN THE END, YOU'LL BE THE ONE TO MELT.
"BE WARY OF FIRE-TYPE PEOPLE IN THE SECOND MONTH OF THE SEASON OF FLOWERS.
"IF YOU ARE ABLE TO AVOID CONTACT, YOU WILL FIND LUCK WITH A MAN OF THE LIGHTNING TYPE." THERE YOU HAVE IT.

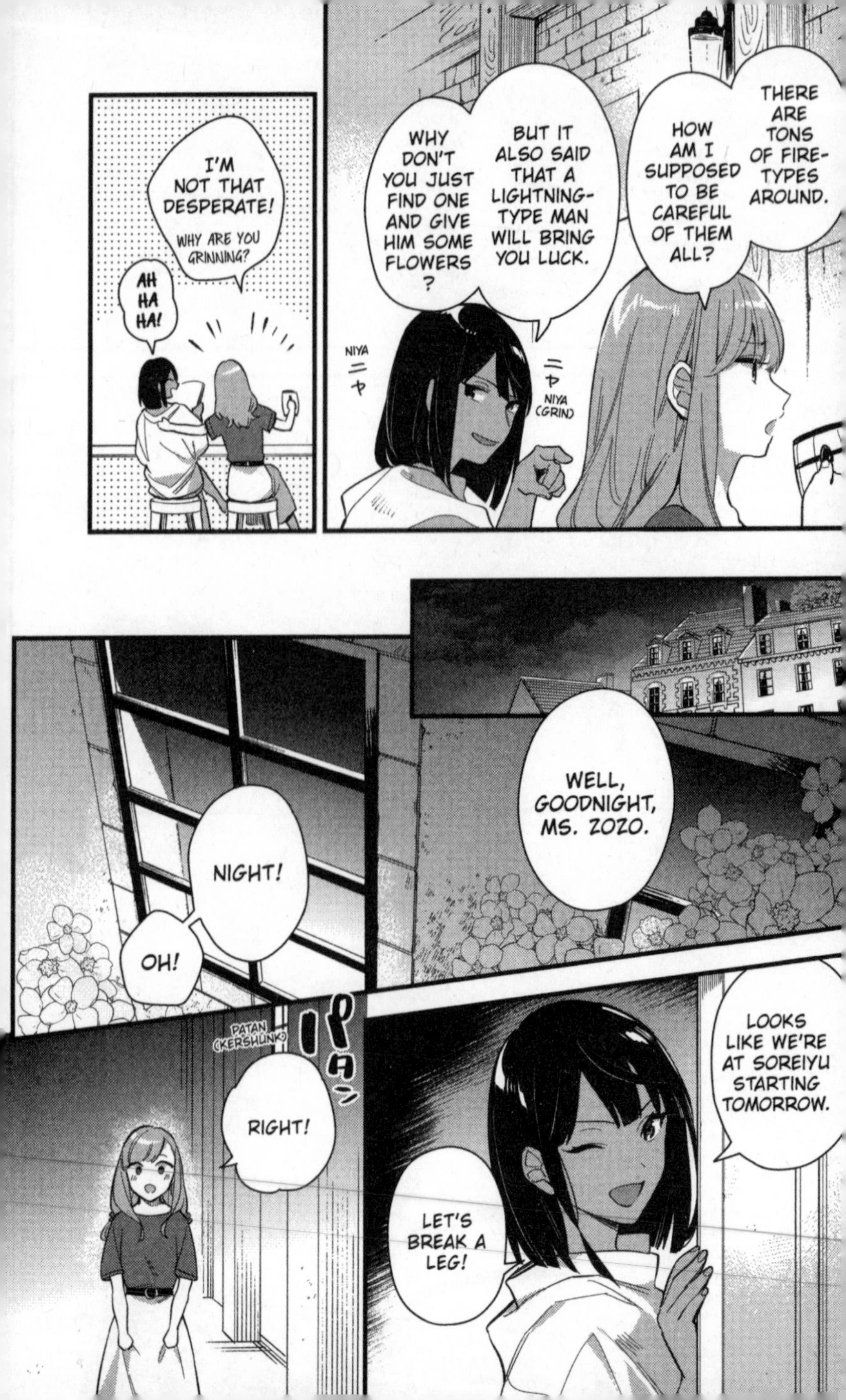
THERE ARE TONS OF FIRE-TYPES AROUND.
HOW AM I SUPPOSED TO BE CAREFUL OF THEM ALL?
BUT IT ALSO SAID THAT A LIGHTNING-TYPE MAN WILL BRING YOU LUCK.
WHY DON'T YOU JUST FIND ONE AND GIVE HIM SOME FLOWERS?
NIYA (GRIN)
NIYA
I'M NOT THAT DESPERATE!
WHY ARE YOU GRINNING?
AH HA HA!
WELL, GOODNIGHT, MS. ZOZO.
NIGHT!
OH!
LOOKS LIKE WE'RE AT SOREIYU STARTING TOMORROW.
LET'S BREAK A LEG!
PATAN (KERSHUNK)
RIGHT!

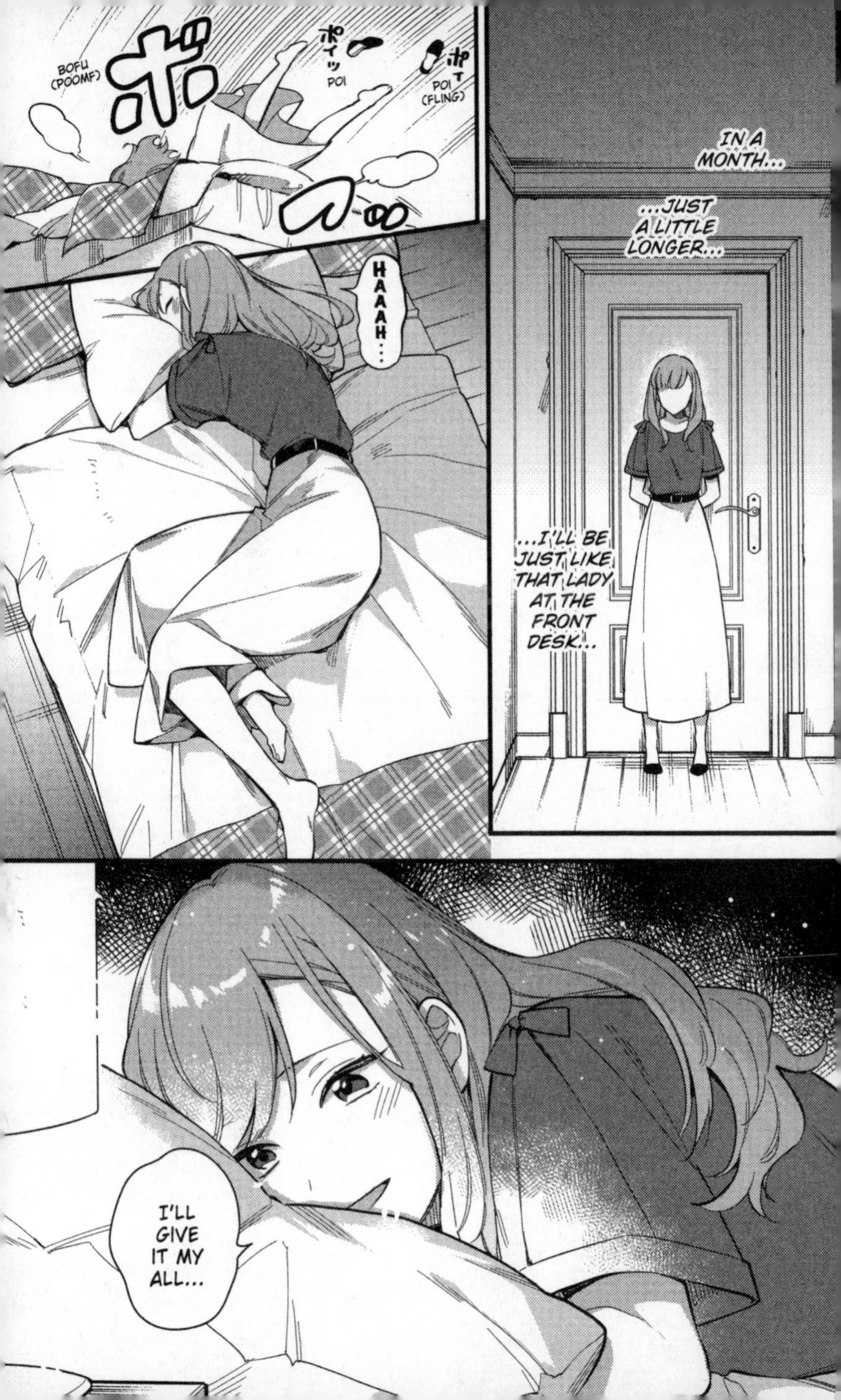
IN A MONTH...
...JUST A LITTLE LONGER...
...I'LL BE JUST LIKE THAT LADY AT THE FRONT DESK...
ポイ
POI (FLING)
ポイッ
POI
ボフ
BOFU (POOMF)
HAAAAH...
I'LL GIVE IT MY ALL...

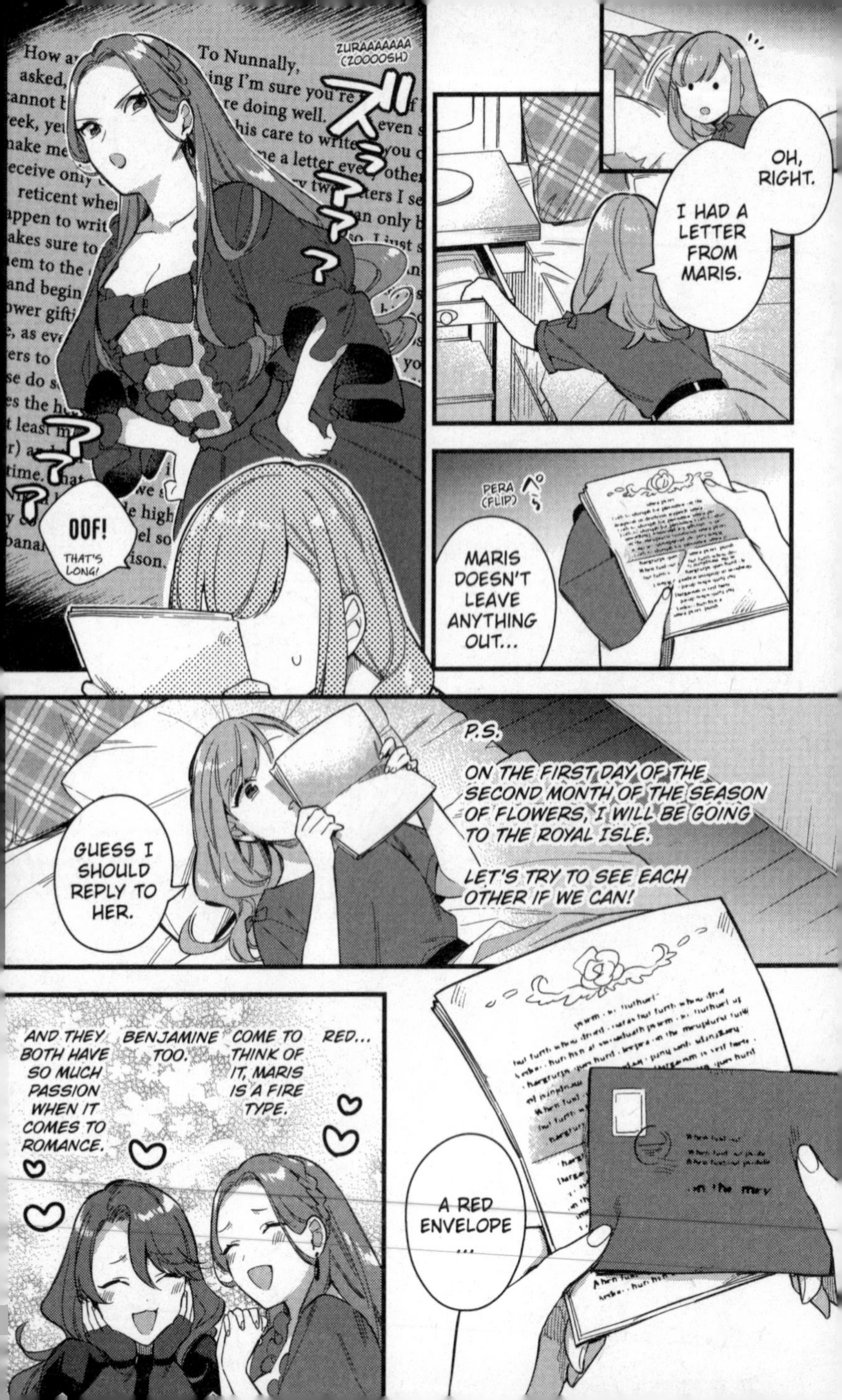

OH, RIGHT.
I HAD A LETTER FROM MARIS.
PERA (FLIP)
MARIS DOESN'T LEAVE ANYTHING OUT...
To Nunnally,
ZURAAAAAAA (ZOOOOSH)
OOF!
THAT'S LONG!
P.S.
ON THE FIRST DAY OF THE SECOND MONTH OF THE SEASON OF FLOWERS, I WILL BE GOING TO THE ROYAL ISLE.
LET'S TRY TO SEE EACH OTHER IF WE CAN!
GUESS I SHOULD REPLY TO HER.
A RED ENVELOPE ...
RED...
COME TO THINK OF IT, MARIS IS A FIRE TYPE.
BENJAMINE TOO.
AND THEY BOTH HAVE SO MUCH PASSION WHEN IT COMES TO ROMANCE.

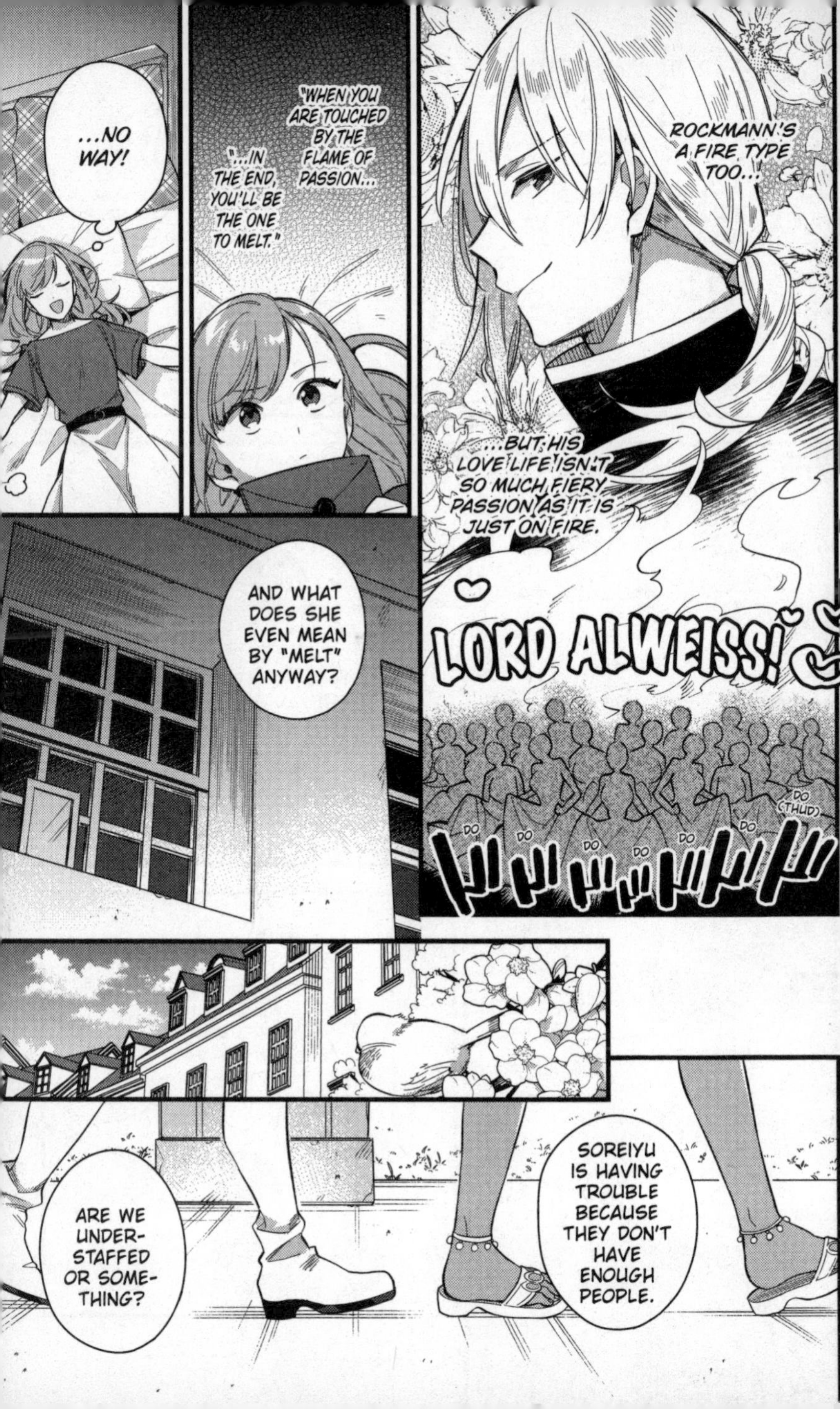
ROCKMANN'S A FIRE TYPE TOO...
...BUT HIS LOVE LIFE ISN'T SO MUCH FIERY PASSION AS IT IS JUST ON FIRE.
LORD ALWEISS!
DO (THUD) DO DO DO DO DO DO
"WHEN YOU ARE TOUCHED BY THE FLAME OF PASSION...
"...IN THE END, YOU'LL BE THE ONE TO MELT."
...NO WAY!
AND WHAT DOES SHE EVEN MEAN BY "MELT" ANYWAY?
SOREIYU IS HAVING TROUBLE BECAUSE THEY DON'T HAVE ENOUGH PEOPLE.
ARE WE UNDER-STAFFED OR SOME-THING?

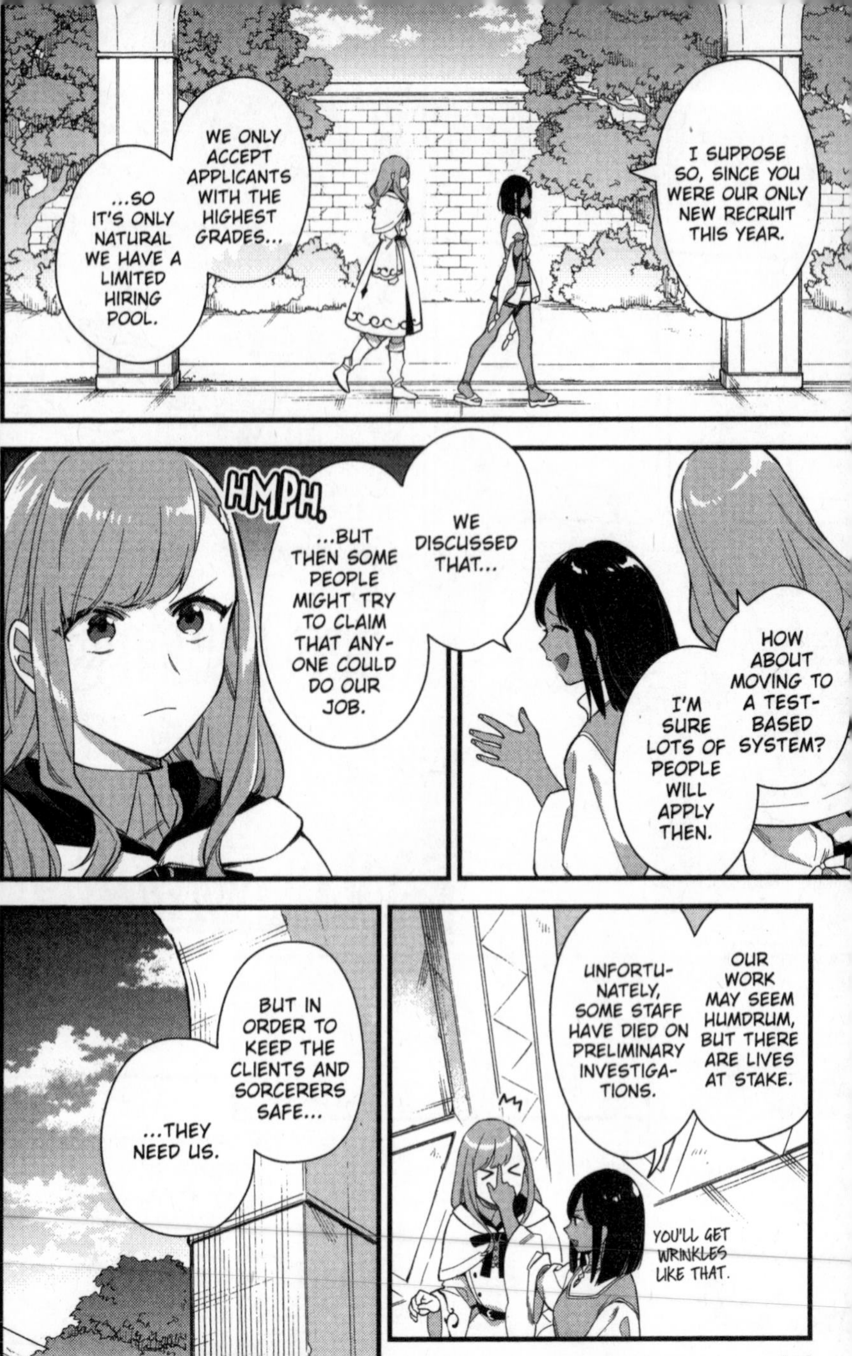
I SUPPOSE SO, SINCE YOU WERE OUR ONLY NEW RECRUIT THIS YEAR.
WE ONLY ACCEPT APPLICANTS WITH THE HIGHEST GRADES...
...SO IT'S ONLY NATURAL WE HAVE A LIMITED HIRING POOL.
HOW ABOUT MOVING TO A TEST-BASED SYSTEM?
I'M SURE LOTS OF PEOPLE WILL APPLY THEN.
WE DISCUSSED THAT...
...BUT THEN SOME PEOPLE MIGHT TRY TO CLAIM THAT ANY-ONE COULD DO OUR JOB.
HMPH.
OUR WORK MAY SEEM HUMDRUM, BUT THERE ARE LIVES AT STAKE.
UNFORTU-NATELY, SOME STAFF HAVE DIED ON PRELIMINARY INVESTIGA-TIONS.
YOU'LL GET WRINKLES LIKE THAT.
BUT IN ORDER TO KEEP THE CLIENTS AND SORCERERS SAFE...
...THEY NEED US.

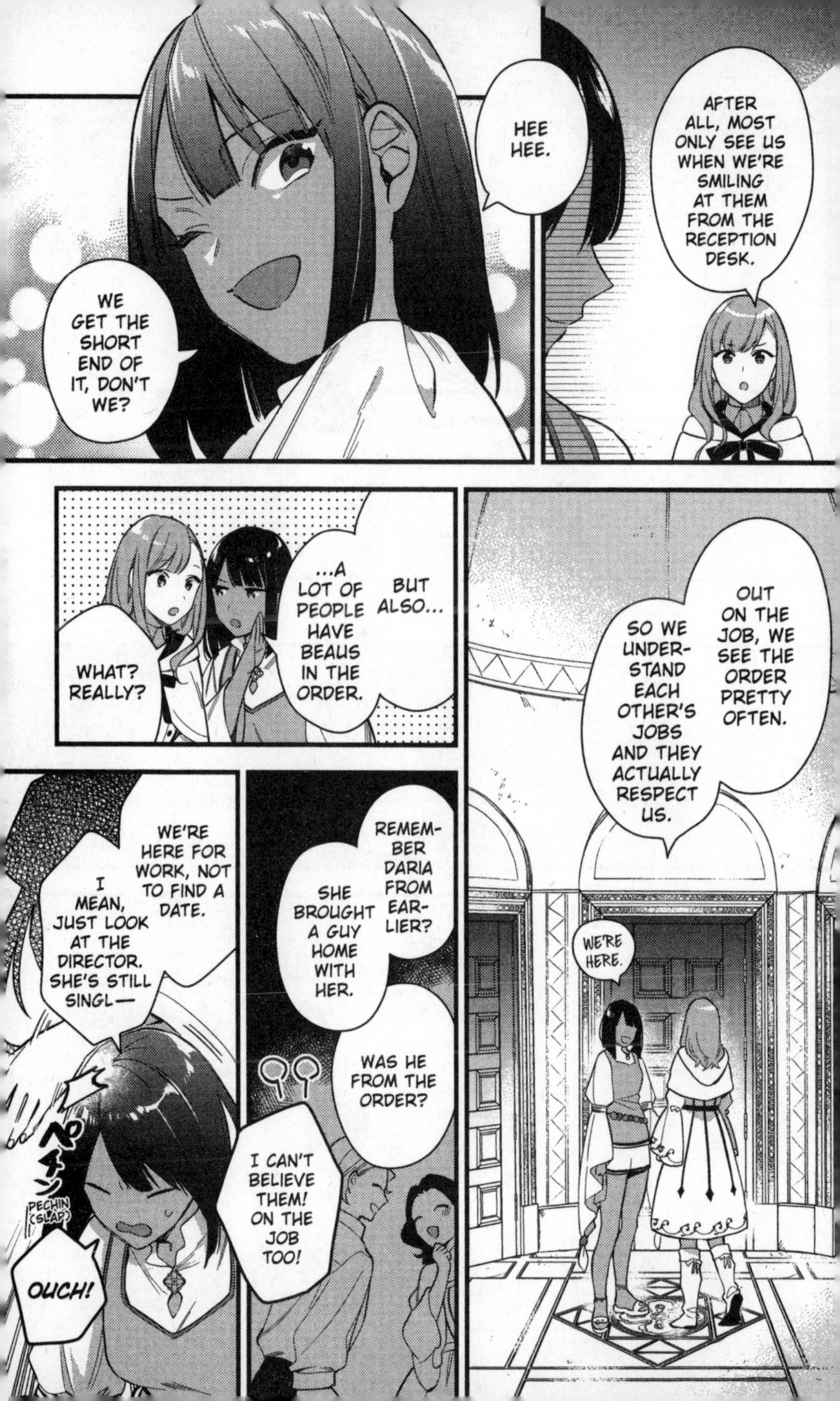
AFTER ALL, MOST ONLY SEE US WHEN WE'RE SMILING AT THEM FROM THE RECEPTION DESK.
HEE HEE.
WE GET THE SHORT END OF IT, DON'T WE?
OUT ON THE JOB, WE SEE THE ORDER PRETTY OFTEN.
SO WE UNDER-STAND EACH OTHER'S JOBS AND THEY ACTUALLY RESPECT US.
WE'RE HERE.
BUT ALSO...
...A LOT OF PEOPLE HAVE BEAUS IN THE ORDER.
WHAT? REALLY?
REMEM-BER DARIA FROM EAR-LIER?
SHE BROUGHT A GUY HOME WITH HER.
WAS HE FROM THE ORDER?
I CAN'T BELIEVE THEM! ON THE JOB TOO!
WE'RE HERE FOR WORK, NOT TO FIND A DATE.
I MEAN, JUST LOOK AT THE DIRECTOR. SHE'S STILL SINGL—
PECHIN (SLAP)
OUCH!

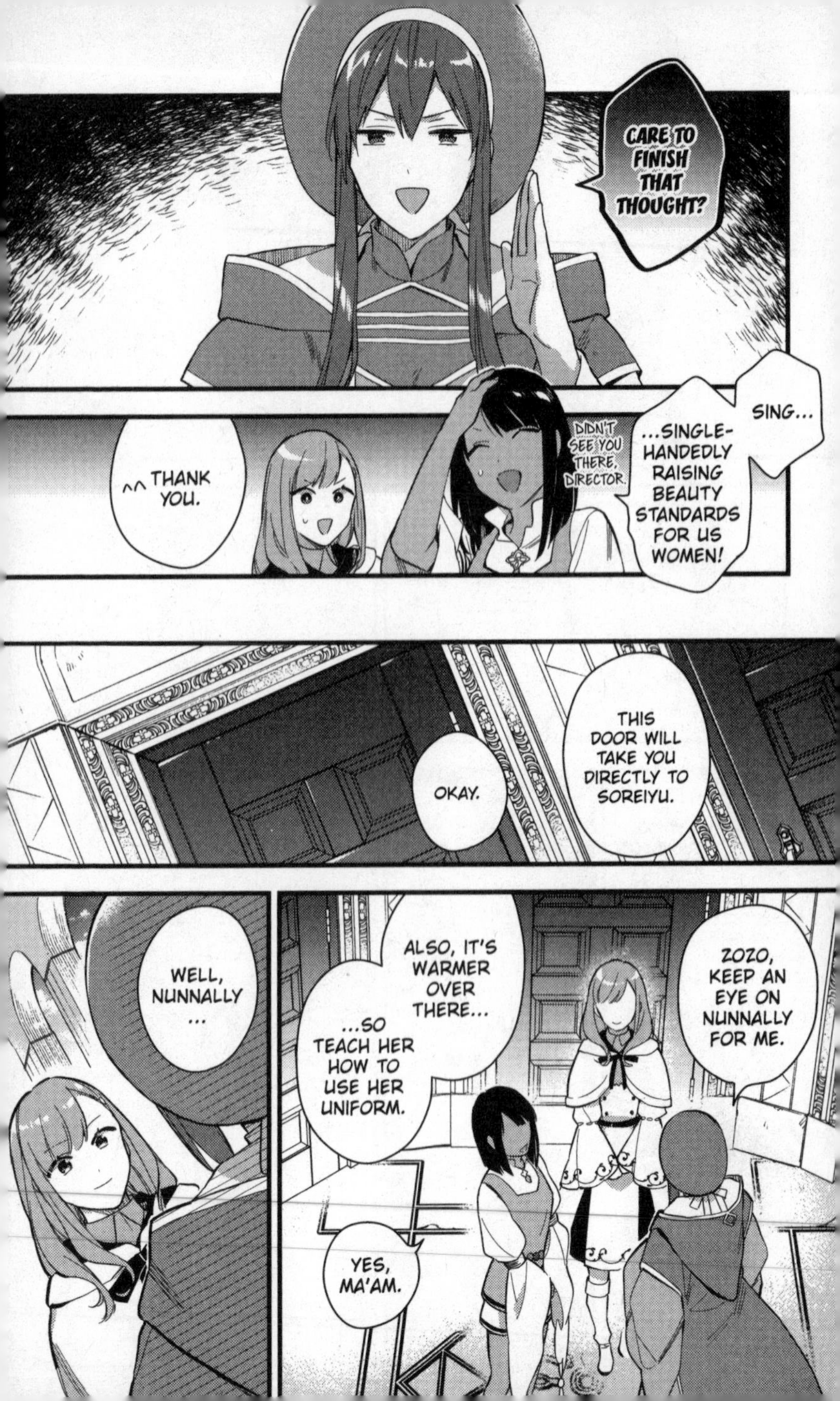
CARE TO FINISH THAT THOUGHT?
SING...
...SINGLE-HANDEDLY RAISING BEAUTY STANDARDS FOR US WOMEN!
DIDN'T SEE YOU THERE, DIRECTOR.
^^ THANK YOU.
THIS DOOR WILL TAKE YOU DIRECTLY TO SOREIYU.
OKAY.
ZOZO, KEEP AN EYE ON NUNNALLY FOR ME.
ALSO, IT'S WARMER OVER THERE...
...SO TEACH HER HOW TO USE HER UNIFORM.
YES, MA'AM.
WELL, NUNNALLY ...

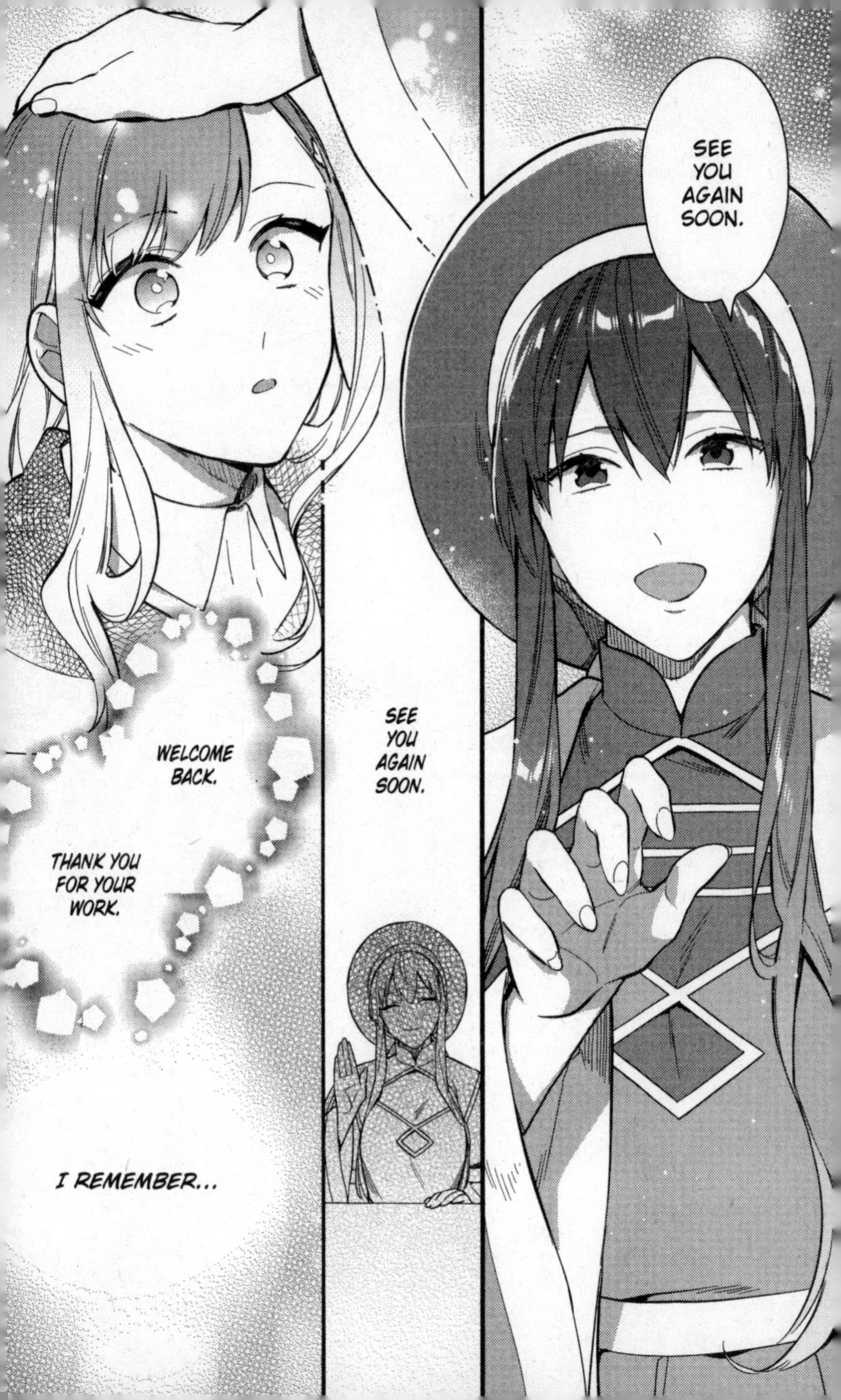
SEE YOU AGAIN SOON.
SEE YOU AGAIN SOON.
WELCOME BACK.
THANK YOU FOR YOUR WORK.
I REMEMBER...

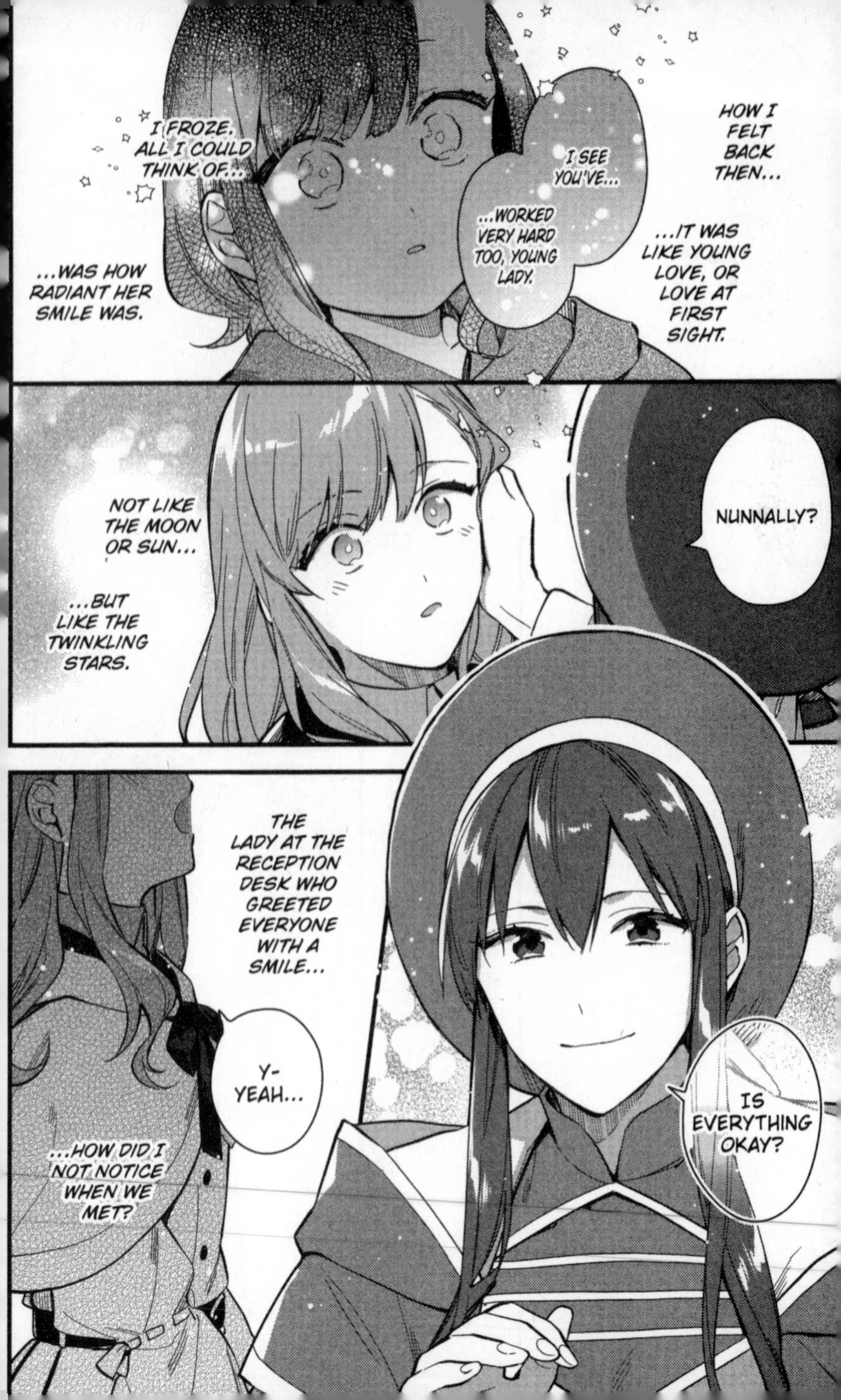
HOW I FELT BACK THEN...
...IT WAS LIKE YOUNG LOVE, OR LOVE AT FIRST SIGHT.
I SEE YOU'VE...
...WORKED VERY HARD TOO, YOUNG LADY.
I FROZE. ALL I COULD THINK OF...
...WAS HOW RADIANT HER SMILE WAS.
NUNNALLY?
NOT LIKE THE MOON OR SUN...
...BUT LIKE THE TWINKLING STARS.
IS EVERYTHING OKAY?
THE LADY AT THE RECEPTION DESK WHO GREETED EVERYONE WITH A SMILE...
Y-YEAH...
...HOW DID I NOT NOTICE WHEN WE MET?

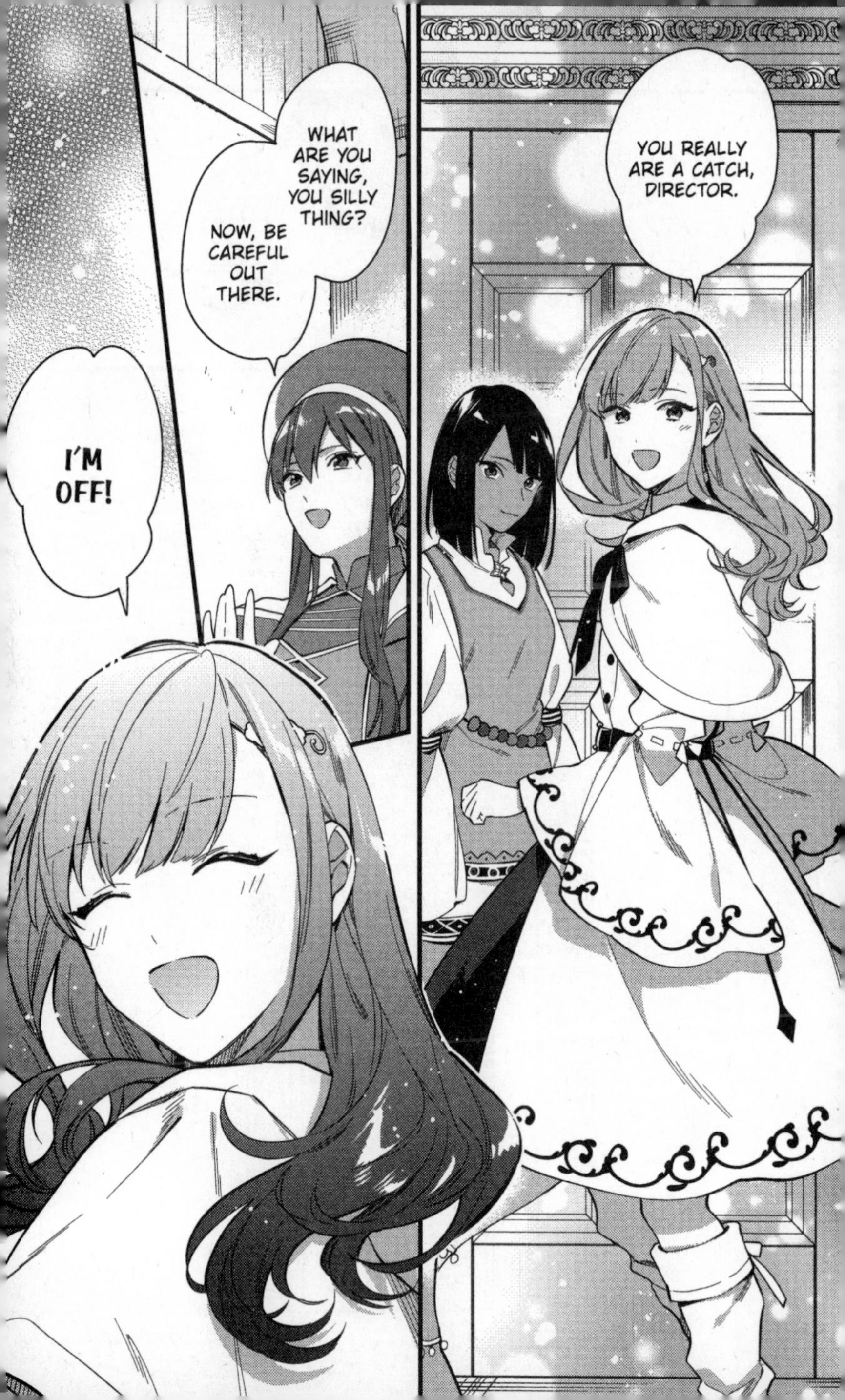
YOU REALLY ARE A CATCH, DIRECTOR.
WHAT ARE YOU SAYING, YOU SILLY THING?
NOW, BE CAREFUL OUT THERE.
I'M OFF!

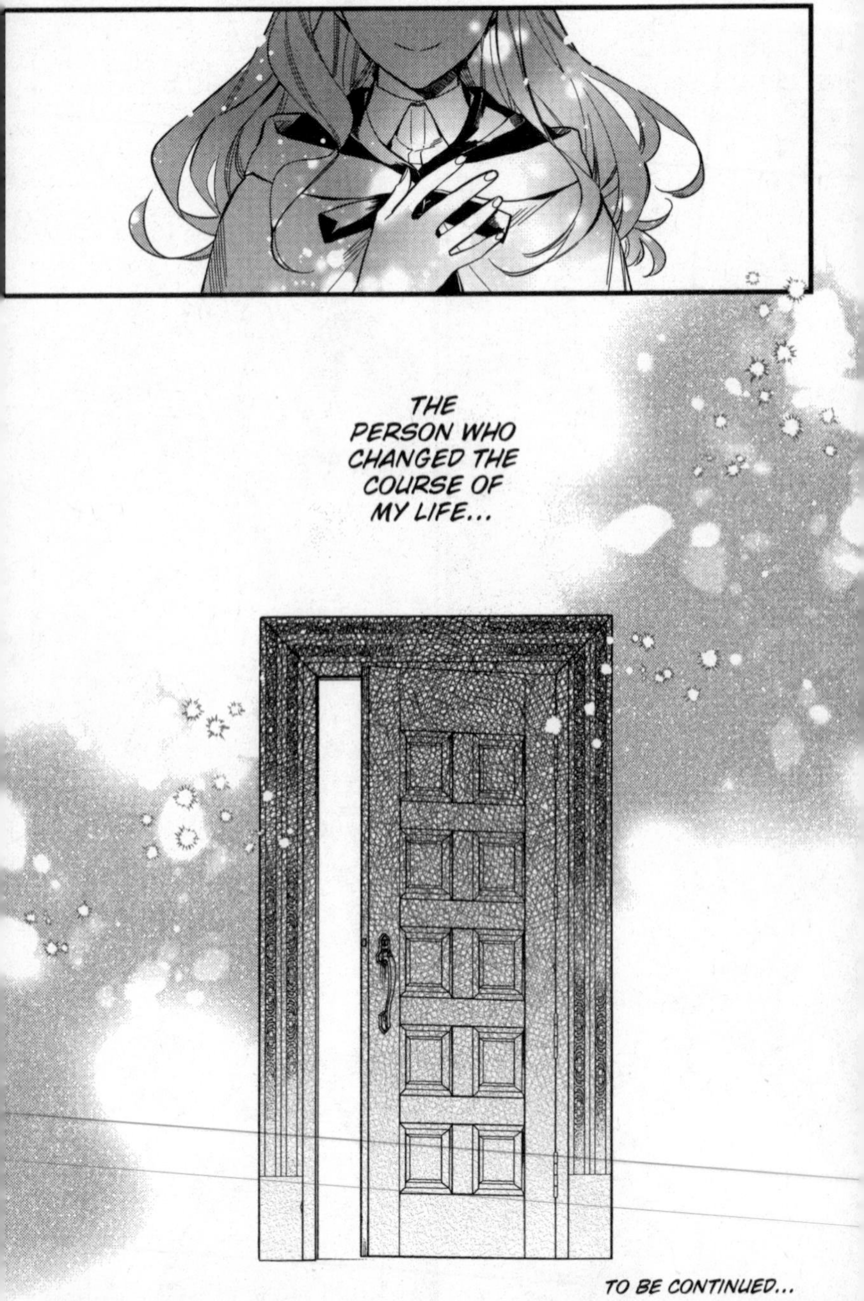
THE PERSON WHO CHANGED THE COURSE OF MY LIFE...
TO BE CONTINUED...

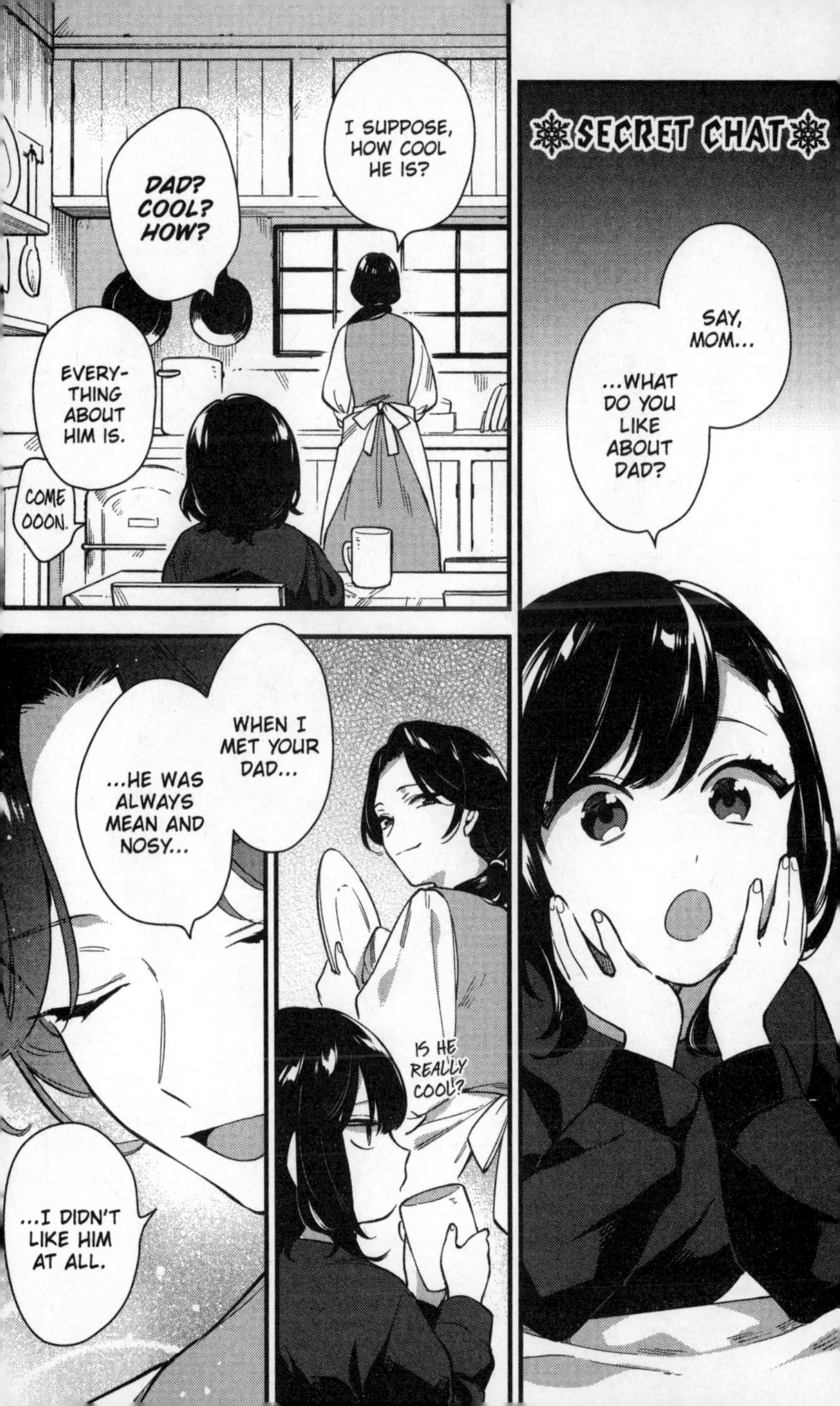
SECRET CHAT
SAY, MOM...
...WHAT DO YOU LIKE ABOUT DAD?
I SUPPOSE, HOW COOL HE IS?
DAD? COOL? HOW?
EVERY-THING ABOUT HIM IS.
COME OOON.
IS HE REALLY COOL?
WHEN I MET YOUR DAD...
...HE WAS ALWAYS MEAN AND NOSY...
...I DIDN'T LIKE HIM AT ALL.

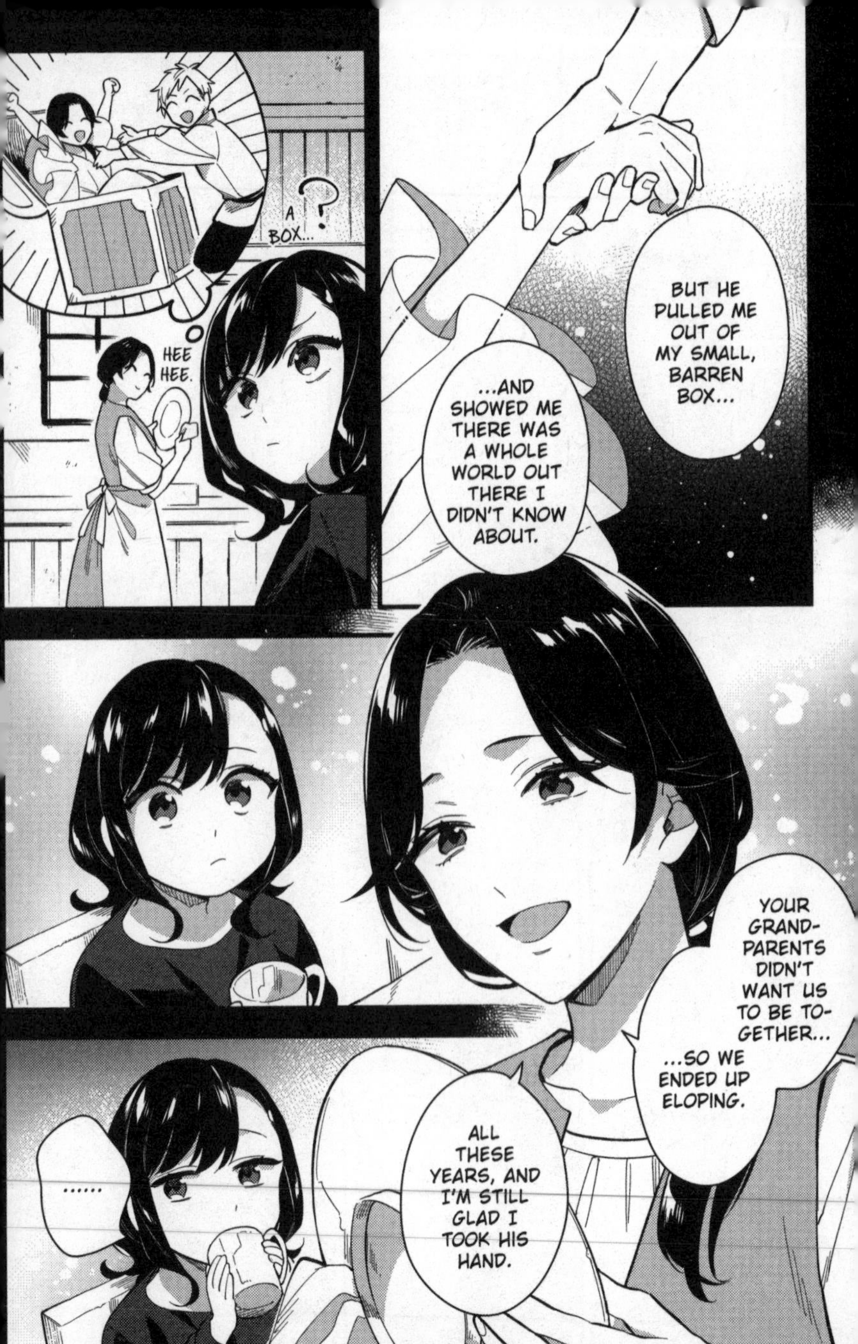
BUT HE PULLED ME OUT OF MY SMALL, BARREN BOX...
...AND SHOWED ME THERE WAS A WHOLE WORLD OUT THERE I DIDN'T KNOW ABOUT.
A BOX...?
HEE HEE.
YOUR GRAND-PARENTS DIDN'T WANT US TO BE TO-GETHER...
...SO WE ENDED UP ELOPING.
ALL THESE YEARS, AND I'M STILL GLAD I TOOK HIS HAND.
......

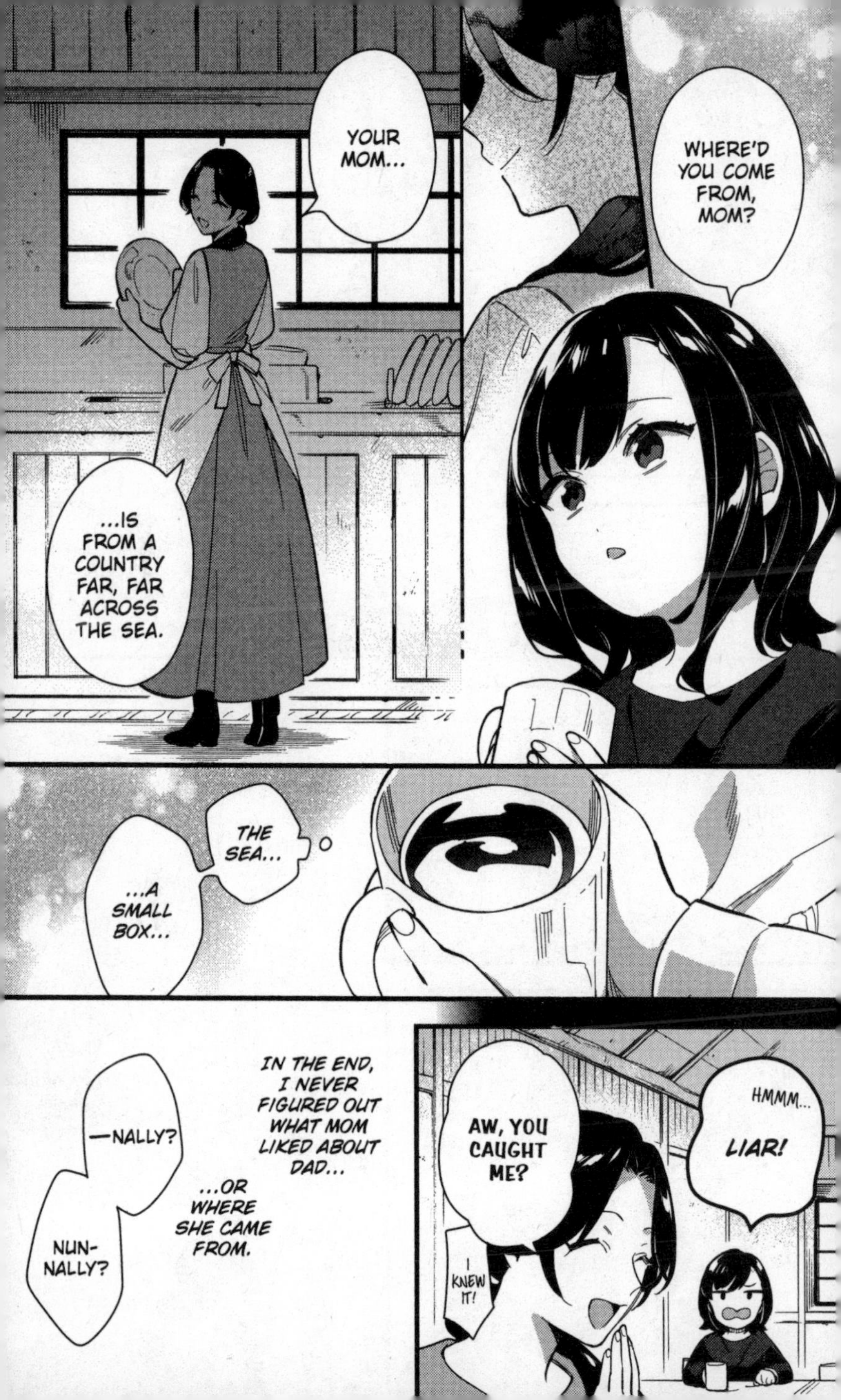
WHERE'D YOU COME FROM, MOM?
YOUR MOM...
...IS FROM A COUNTRY FAR, FAR ACROSS THE SEA.
THE SEA...
...A SMALL BOX...
HMMM... LIAR!
AW, YOU CAUGHT ME?
I KNEW IT!
IN THE END, I NEVER FIGURED OUT WHAT MOM LIKED ABOUT DAD...
...OR WHERE SHE CAME FROM.
—NALLY?
NUN-NALLY?

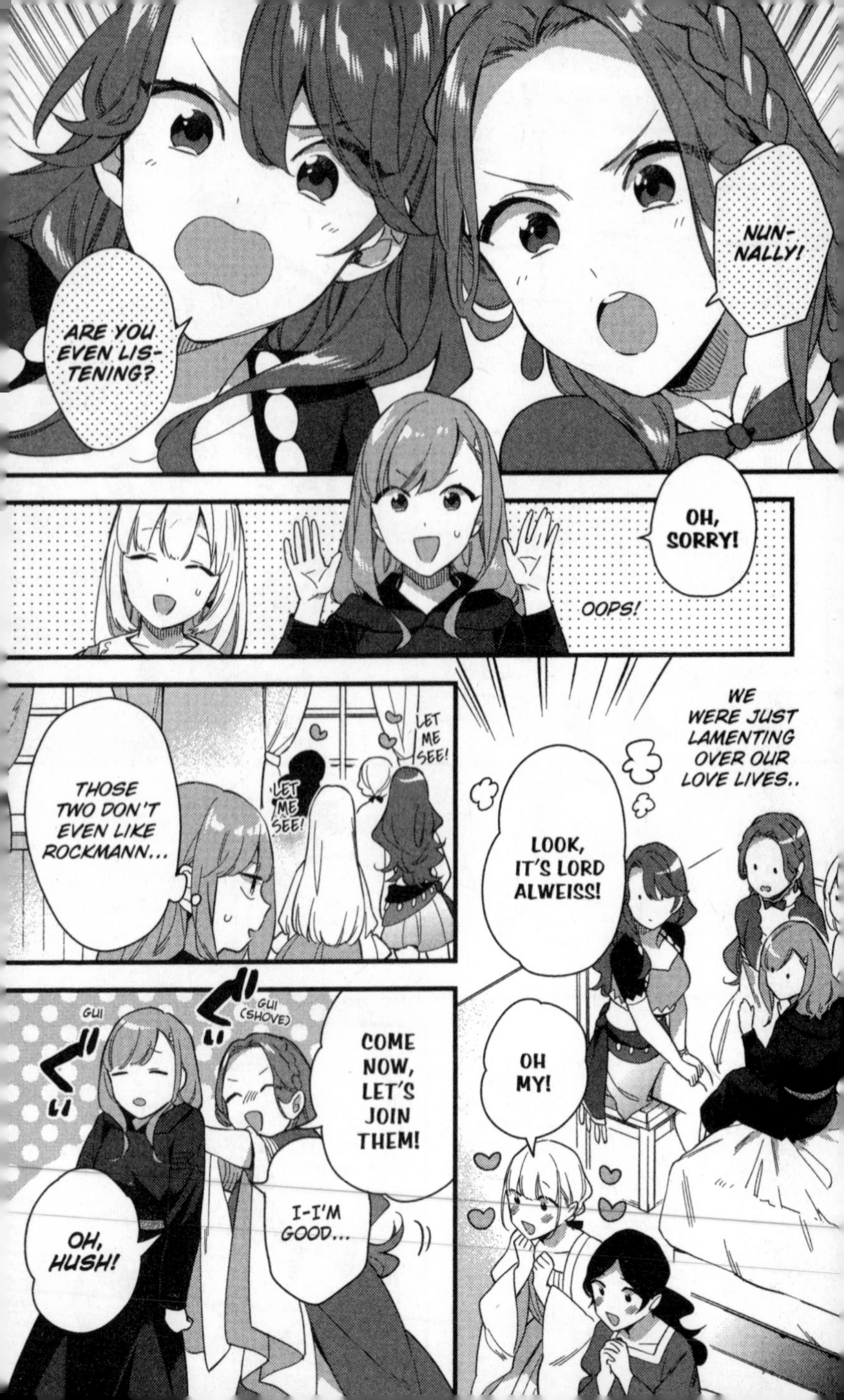
NUN-NALLY!
ARE YOU EVEN LIS-TENING?
OH, SORRY!
OOPS!
WE WERE JUST LAMENTING OVER OUR LOVE LIVES..
LOOK, IT'S LORD ALWEISS!
OH MY!
LET ME SEE!
LET ME SEE!
THOSE TWO DON'T EVEN LIKE ROCKMANN...
COME NOW, LET'S JOIN THEM!
I-I'M GOOD...
GUI (SHOVE)
GUI
OH, HUSH!

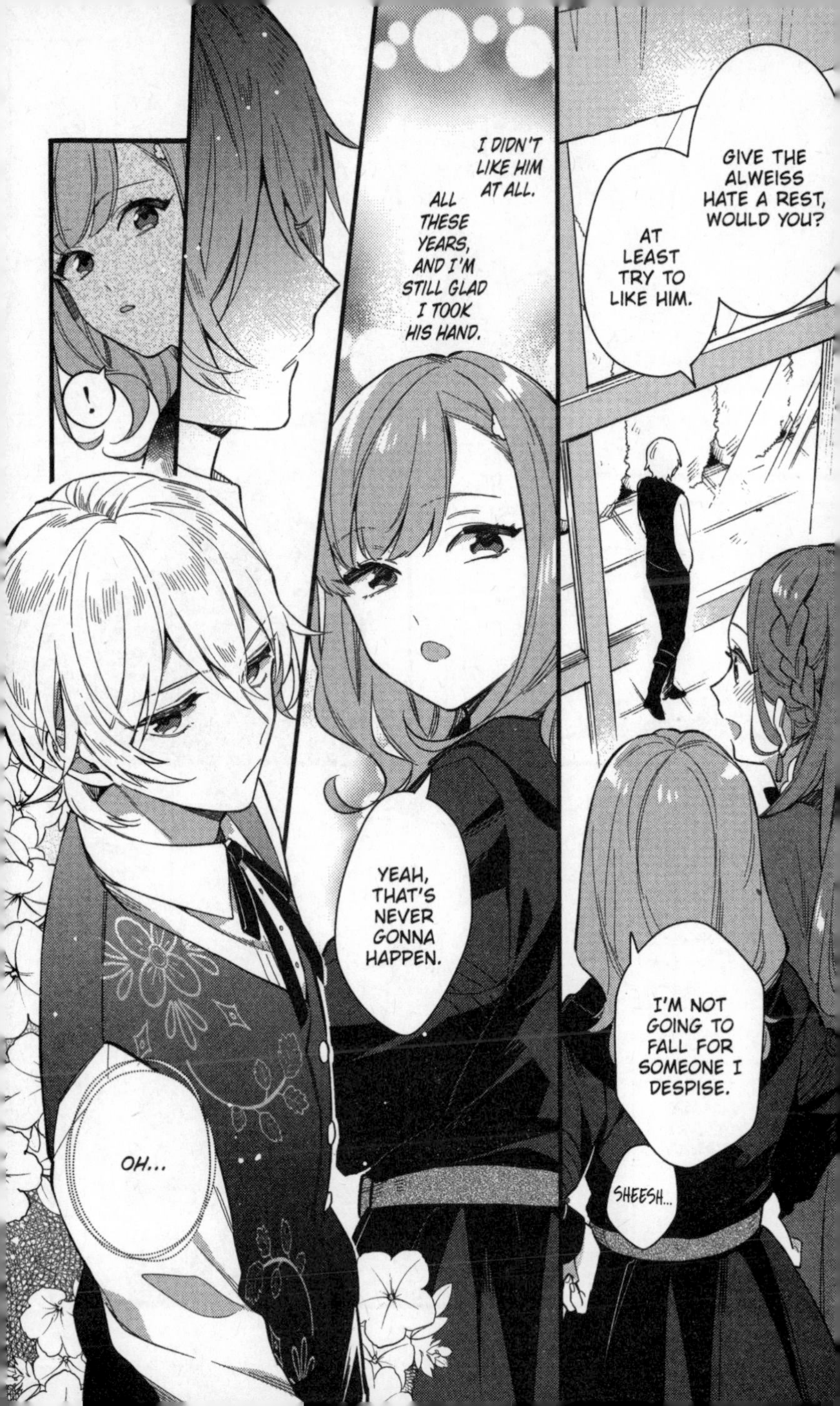
GIVE THE ALWEISS HATE A REST, WOULD YOU?
AT LEAST TRY TO LIKE HIM.
I'M NOT GOING TO FALL FOR SOMEONE I DESPISE.
SHEESH...
I DIDN'T LIKE HIM AT ALL.
ALL THESE YEARS, AND I'M STILL GLAD I TOOK HIS HAND.
YEAH, THAT'S NEVER GONNA HAPPEN.
!
OH...

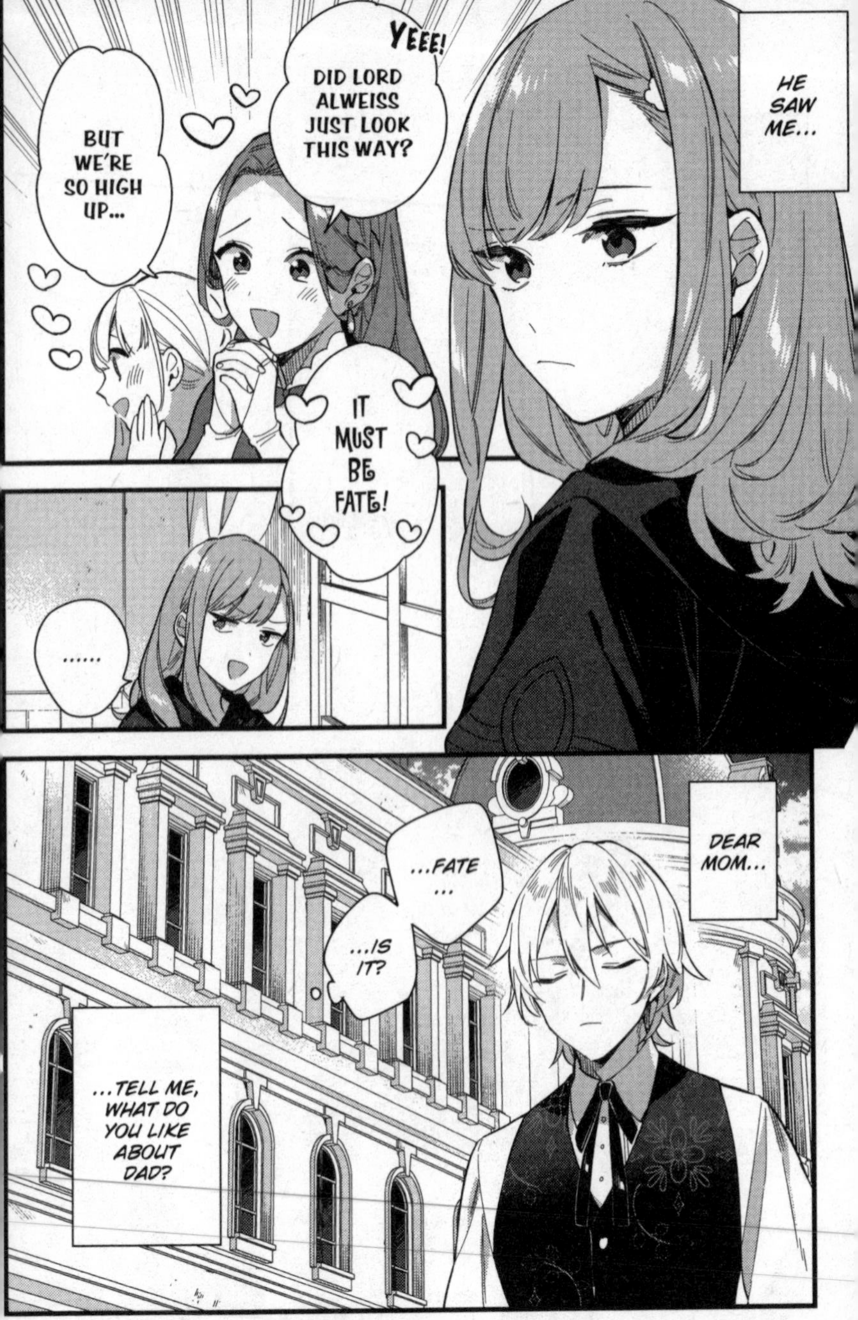
HE SAW ME...
YEEE!
DID LORD ALWEISS JUST LOOK THIS WAY?
BUT WE'RE SO HIGH UP...
IT MUST BE FATE!
......
DEAR MOM...
...FATE ...
...IS IT?
...TELL ME, WHAT DO YOU LIKE ABOUT DAD?

AN OPEN-AND-SHUT MATTER

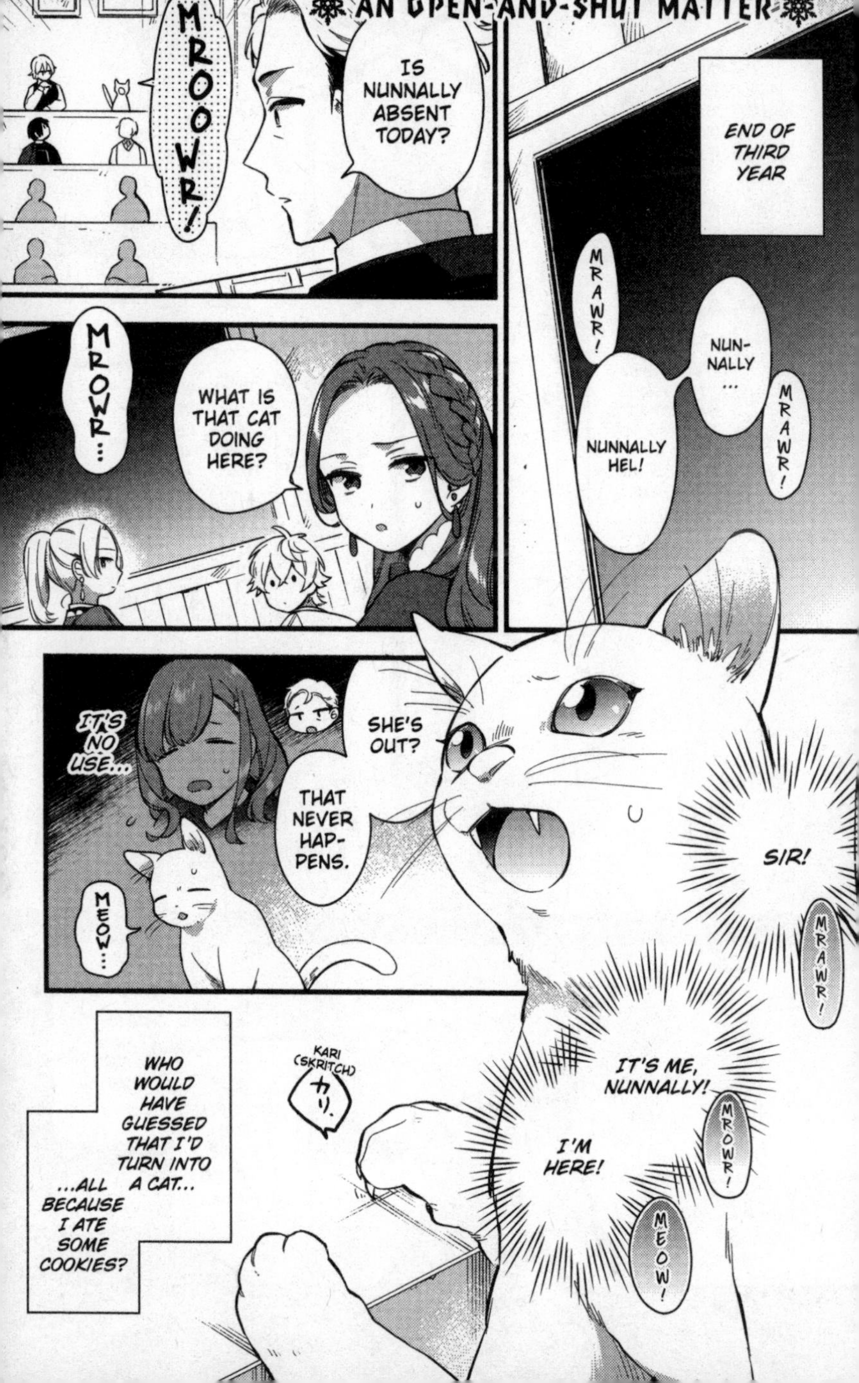
END OF THIRD YEAR
MRAWR!
NUNNALLY HEL!
NUN-NALLY...
MRAWR!
IS NUNNALLY ABSENT TODAY?
MROOWR!
WHAT IS THAT CAT DOING HERE?
MROWR...
SIR!
MRAWR!
SHE'S OUT?
THAT NEVER HAP-PENS.
IT'S NO USE...
MEOW...
IT'S ME, NUNNALLY!
MROWR!
I'M HERE!
MEOW!
KARI (SKRITCH)
WHO WOULD HAVE GUESSED THAT I'D TURN INTO A CAT...
...ALL BECAUSE I ATE SOME COOKIES?

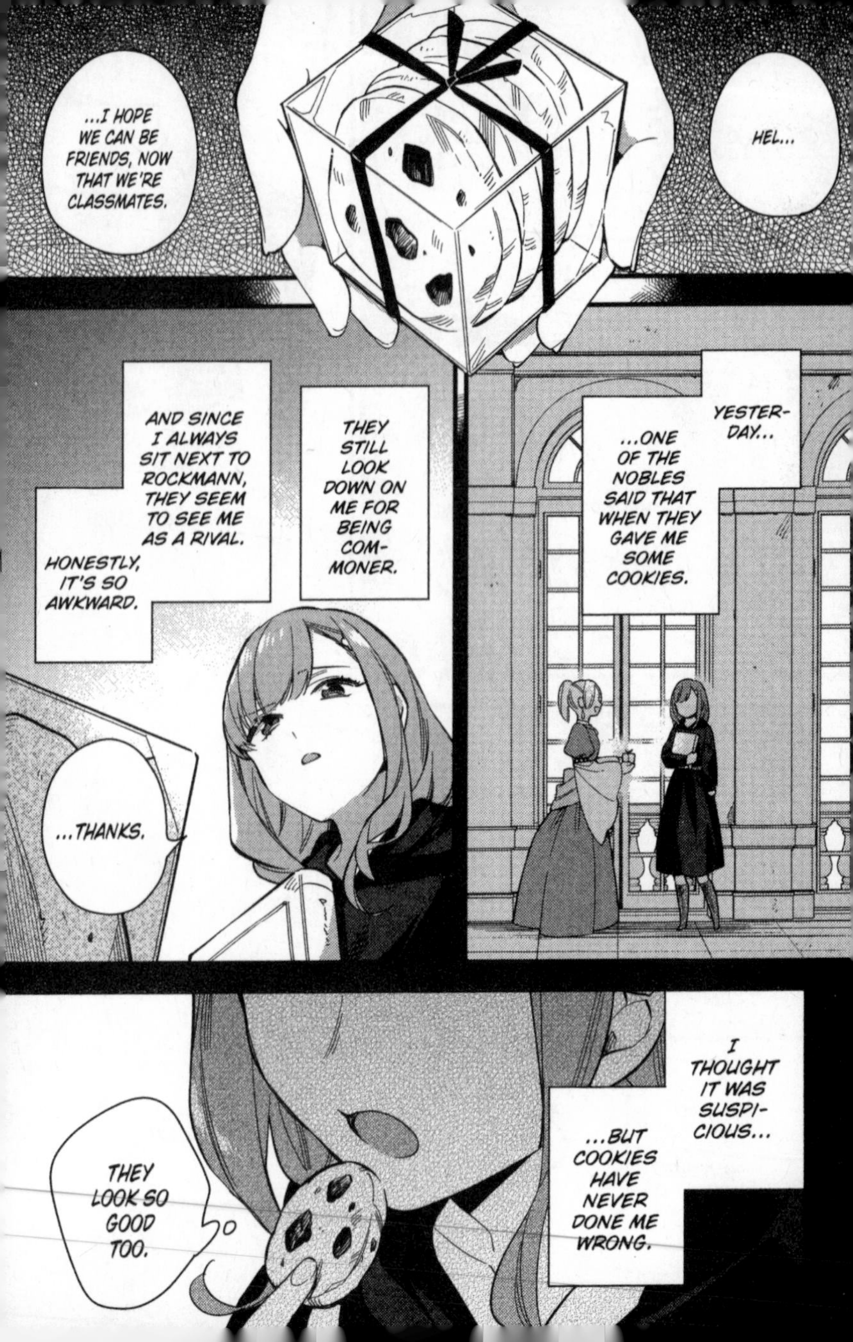
HEL...
...I HOPE WE CAN BE FRIENDS, NOW THAT WE'RE CLASSMATES.
YESTER-DAY...
...ONE OF THE NOBLES SAID THAT WHEN THEY GAVE ME SOME COOKIES.
THEY STILL LOOK DOWN ON ME FOR BEING COM-MONER.
AND SINCE I ALWAYS SIT NEXT TO ROCKMANN, THEY SEEM TO SEE ME AS A RIVAL.
HONESTLY, IT'S SO AWKWARD.
...THANKS.
I THOUGHT IT WAS SUSPI-CIOUS...
...BUT COOKIES HAVE NEVER DONE ME WRONG.
THEY LOOK SO GOOD TOO.

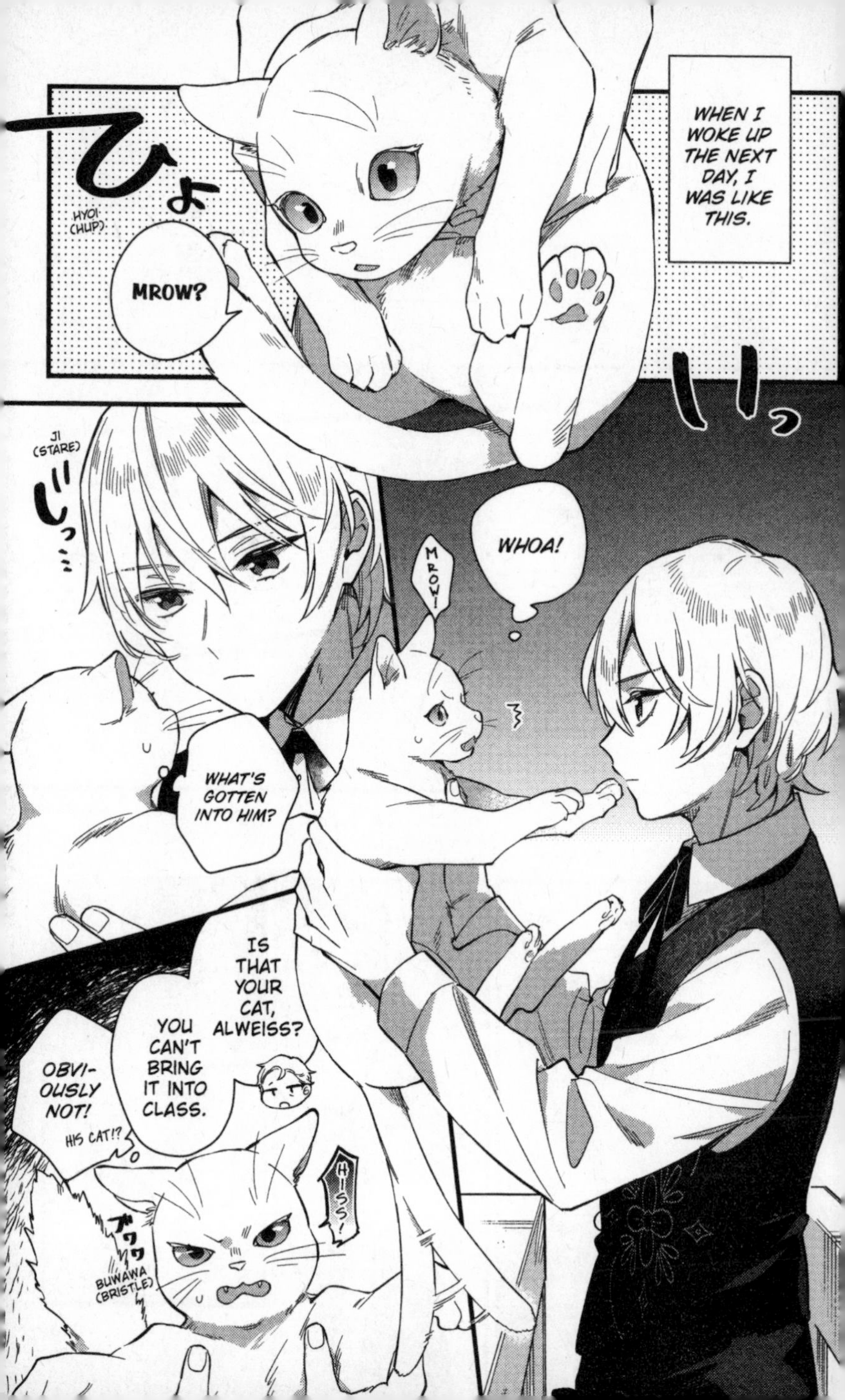
WHEN I WOKE UP THE NEXT DAY, I WAS LIKE THIS.
HYOI (HUP)
MROW?
WHOA!
MROW!
JI (STARE)
WHAT'S GOTTEN INTO HIM?
IS THAT YOUR CAT, ALWEISS?
YOU CAN'T BRING IT INTO CLASS.
OBVIOUSLY NOT!
HIS CAT!?
HISS!
BUWAWA (BRISTLE)

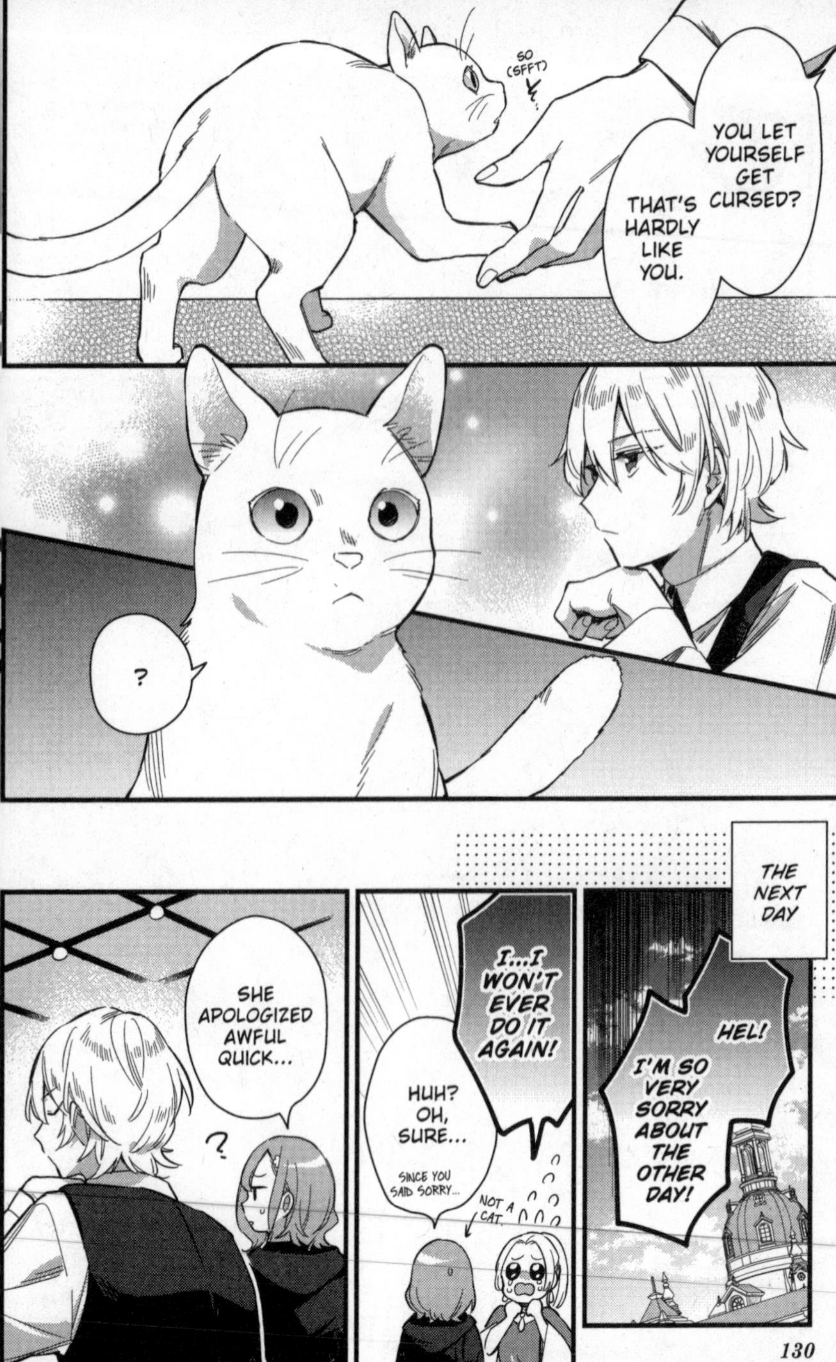
YOU LET YOURSELF GET CURSED?
THAT'S HARDLY LIKE YOU.
SO (SFFT)
?
THE NEXT DAY
HEL!
I'M SO VERY SORRY ABOUT THE OTHER DAY!
I...I WON'T EVER DO IT AGAIN!
HUH? OH, SURE...
SINCE YOU SAID SORRY...
NOT A CAT.
SHE APOLOGIZED AWFUL QUICK...
?

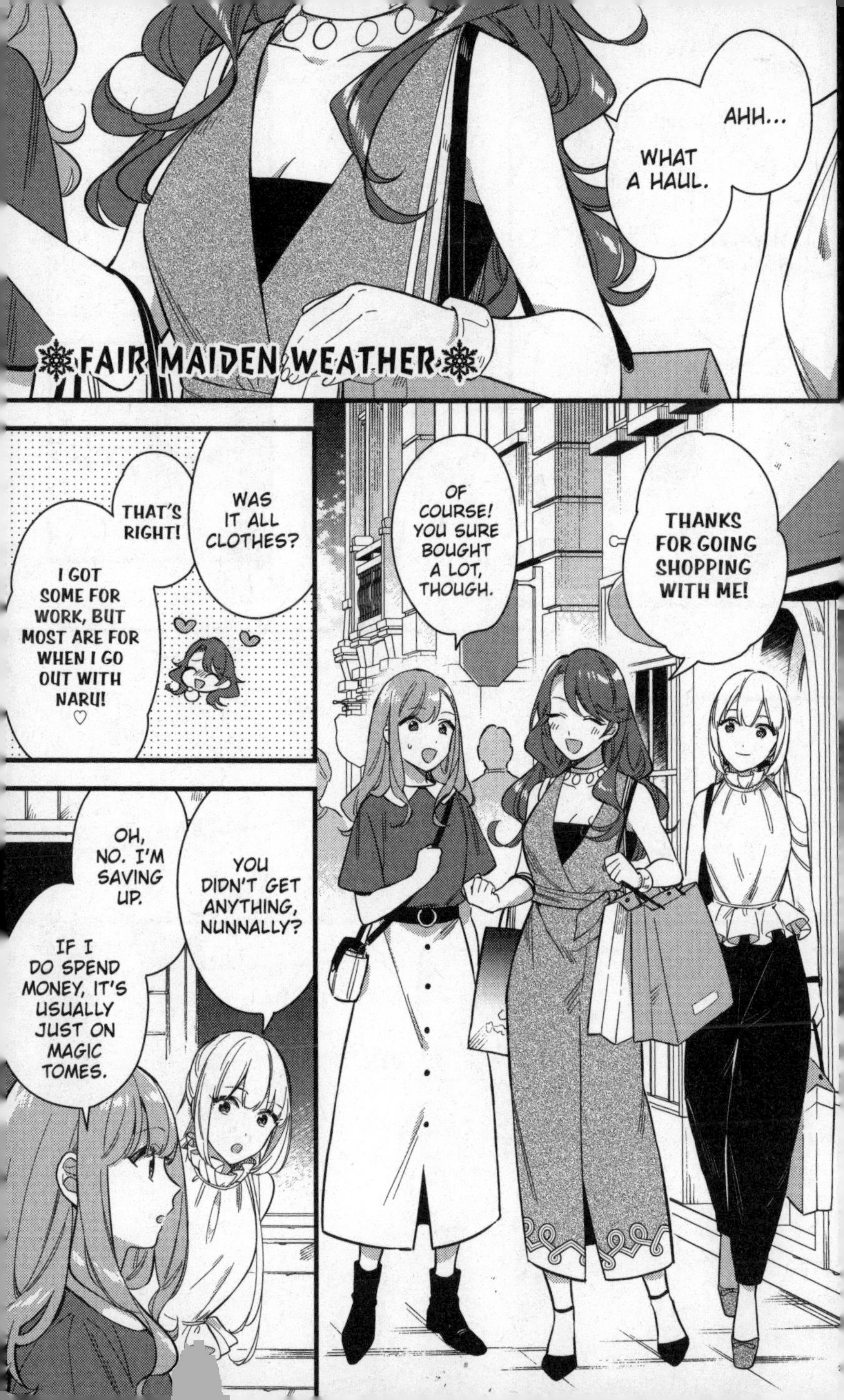
AHH... WHAT A HAUL.
FAIR MAIDEN WEATHER
THANKS FOR GOING SHOPPING WITH ME!
OF COURSE! YOU SURE BOUGHT A LOT, THOUGH.
WAS IT ALL CLOTHES?
THAT'S RIGHT!
I GOT SOME FOR WORK, BUT MOST ARE FOR WHEN I GO OUT WITH NARU! ♡
YOU DIDN'T GET ANYTHING, NUNNALLY?
OH, NO. I'M SAVING UP.
IF I DO SPEND MONEY, IT'S USUALLY JUST ON MAGIC TOMES.

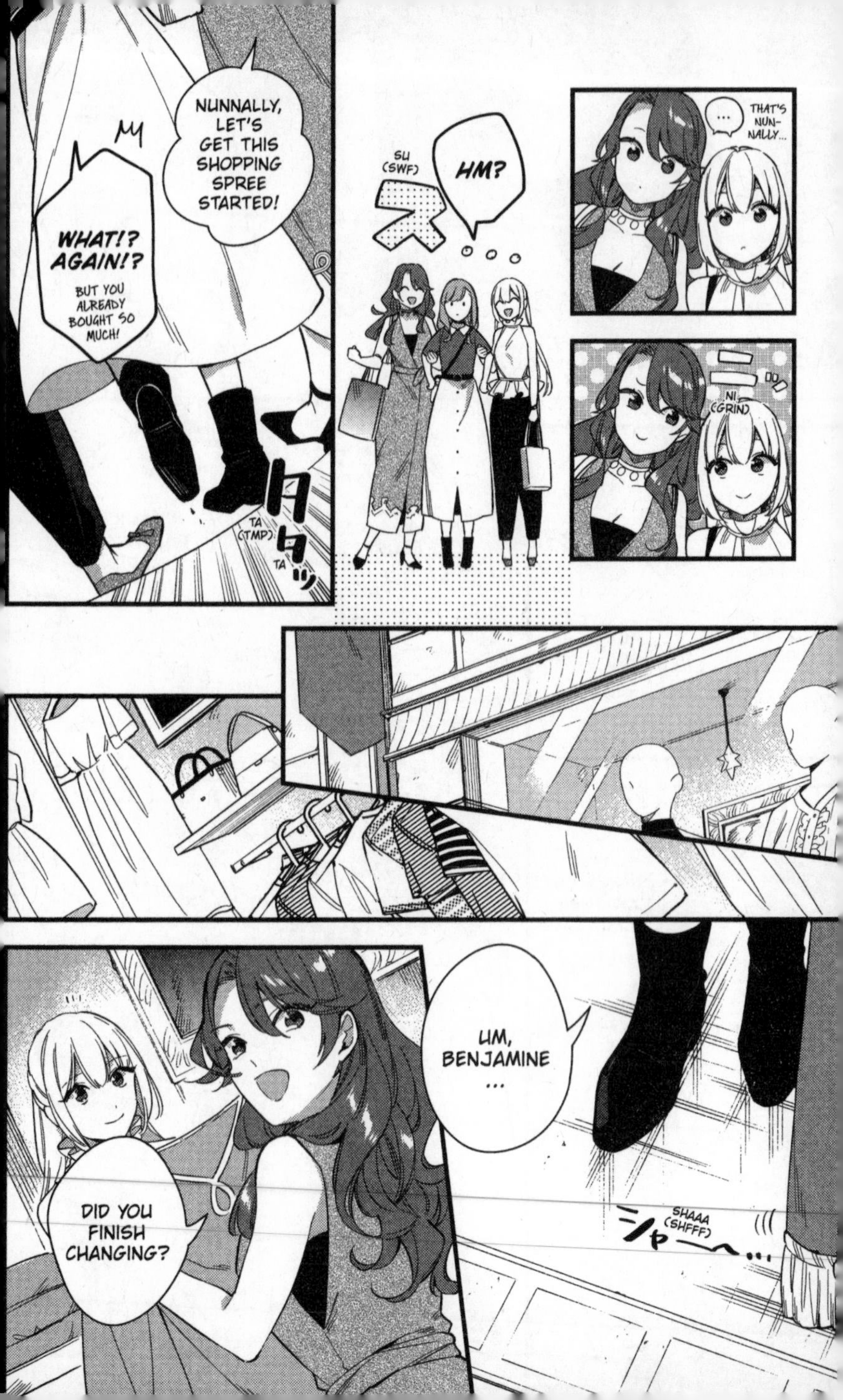
...
THAT'S NUN-NALLY...
NI (GRIN)
SU (SWF)
HM?
NUNNALLY, LET'S GET THIS SHOPPING SPREE STARTED!
WHAT!? AGAIN!?
BUT YOU ALREADY BOUGHT SO MUCH!
TA (TMP) TA
SHAAA (SHFFF)
UM, BENJAMINE ...
DID YOU FINISH CHANGING?

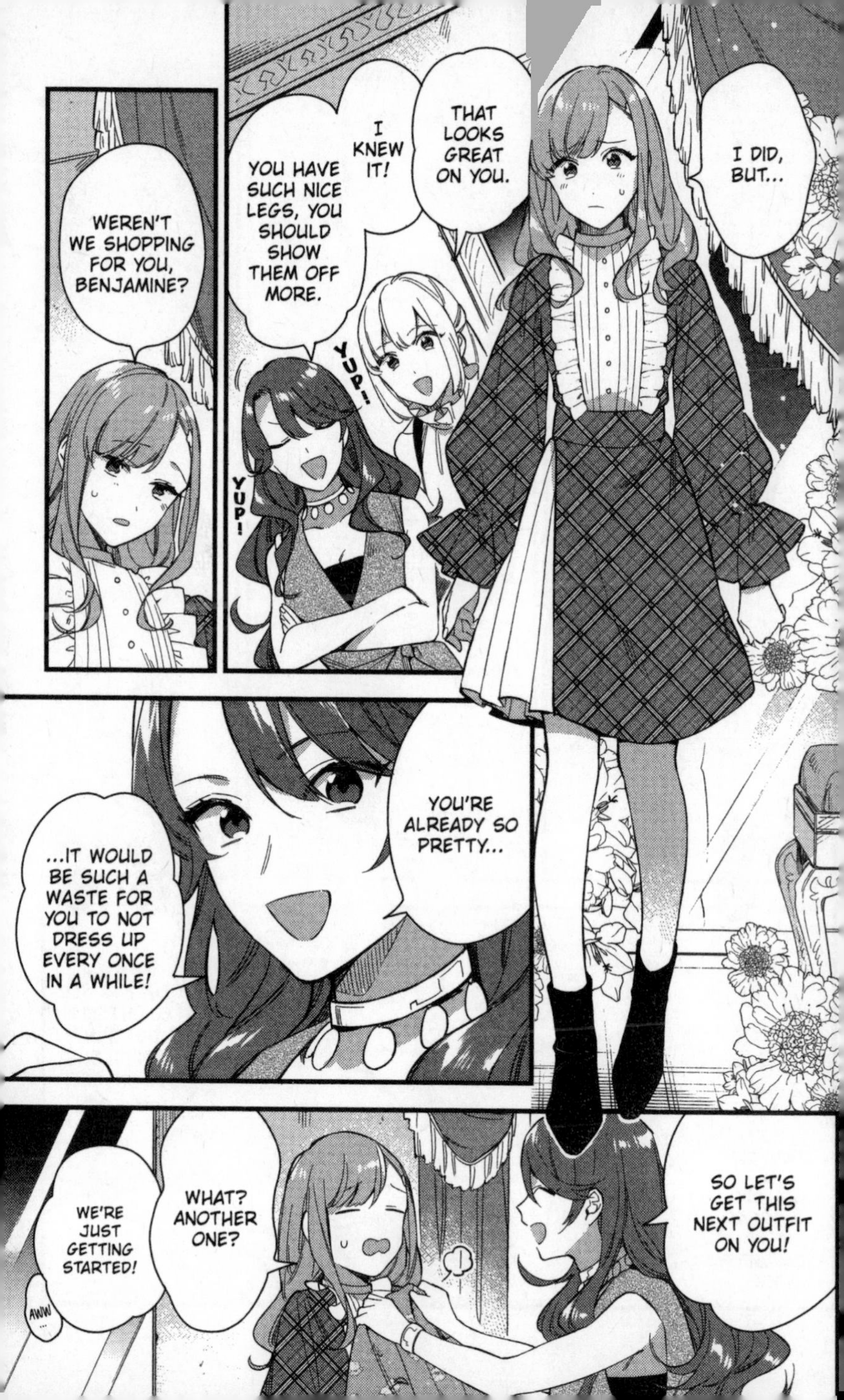
I DID, BUT...
THAT LOOKS GREAT ON YOU.
I KNEW IT!
YOU HAVE SUCH NICE LEGS, YOU SHOULD SHOW THEM OFF MORE.
YUP!
YUP!
WEREN'T WE SHOPPING FOR YOU, BENJAMINE?
YOU'RE ALREADY SO PRETTY...
...IT WOULD BE SUCH A WASTE FOR YOU TO NOT DRESS UP EVERY ONCE IN A WHILE!
SO LET'S GET THIS NEXT OUTFIT ON YOU!
WHAT? ANOTHER ONE?
WE'RE JUST GETTING STARTED!
AWW...

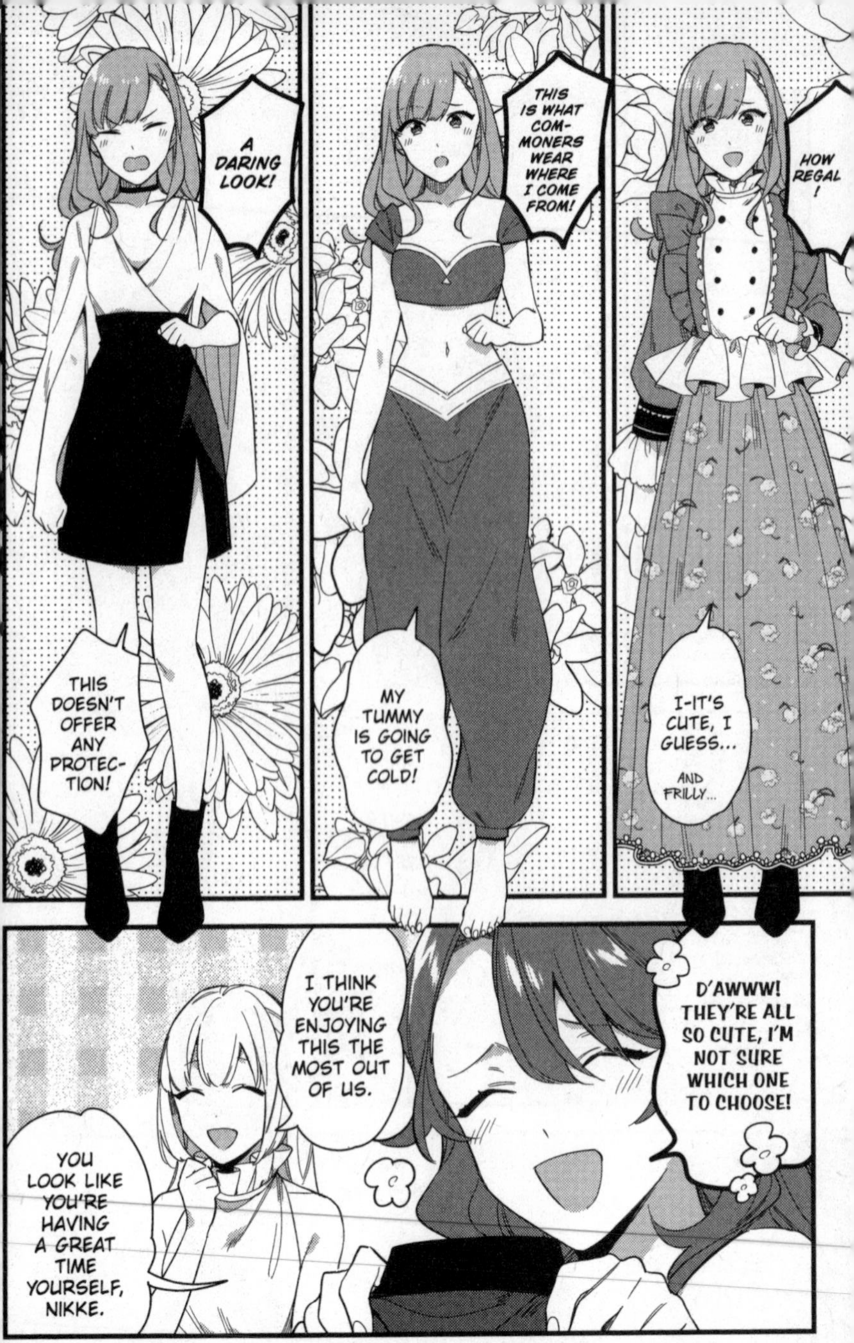
HOW REGAL!
I-IT'S CUTE, I GUESS...
AND FRILLY...
THIS IS WHAT COM-MONERS WEAR WHERE I COME FROM!
MY TUMMY IS GOING TO GET COLD!
A DARING LOOK!
THIS DOESN'T OFFER ANY PROTEC-TION!
D'AWWW! THEY'RE ALL SO CUTE, I'M NOT SURE WHICH ONE TO CHOOSE!
I THINK YOU'RE ENJOYING THIS THE MOST OUT OF US.
YOU LOOK LIKE YOU'RE HAVING A GREAT TIME YOURSELF, NIKKE.

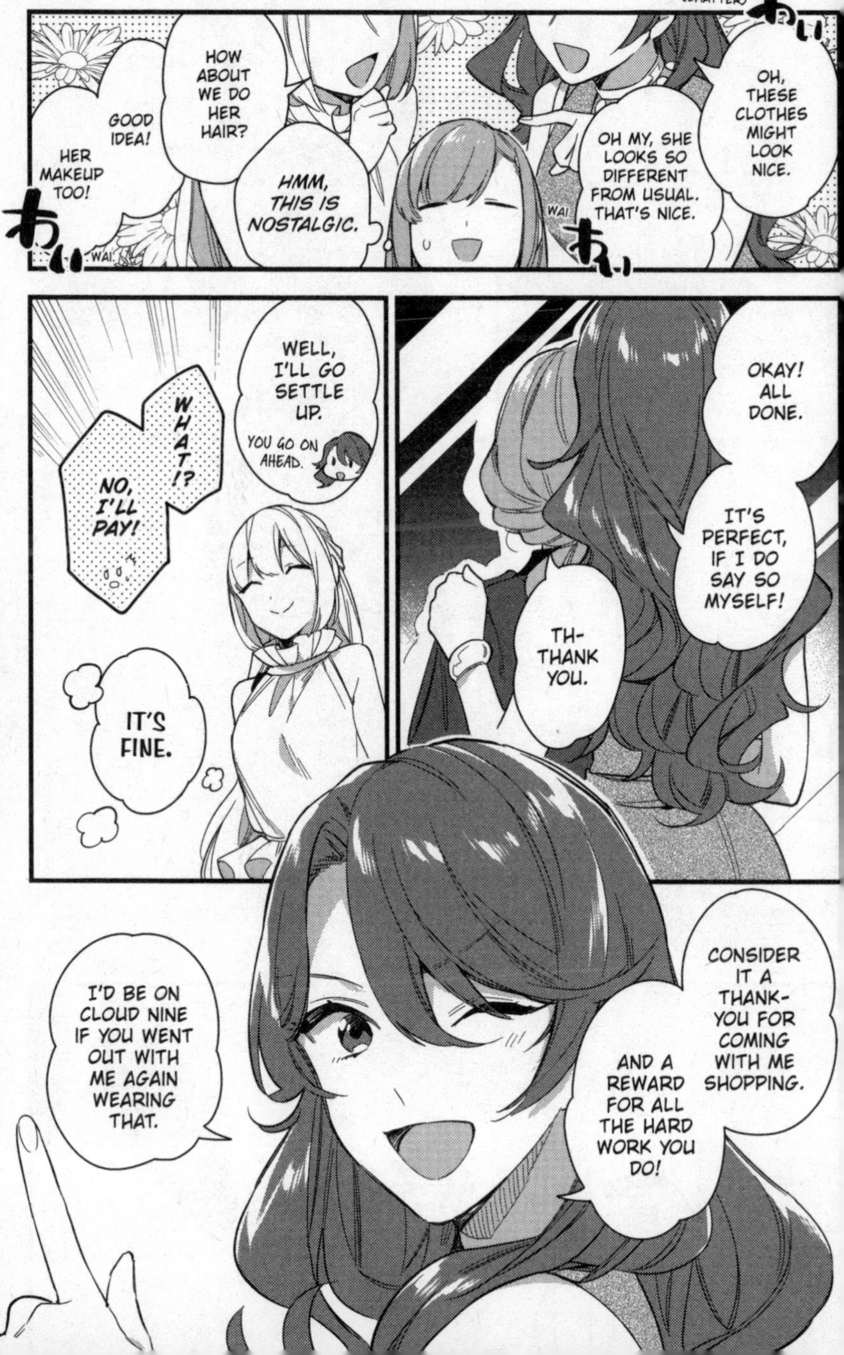
WAI (CHATTER)
OH, THESE CLOTHES MIGHT LOOK NICE.
OH MY, SHE LOOKS SO DIFFERENT FROM USUAL. THAT'S NICE.
WAI
HMM, THIS IS NOSTALGIC.
HOW ABOUT WE DO HER HAIR?
GOOD IDEA!
HER MAKEUP TOO!
WAI
OKAY! ALL DONE.
IT'S PERFECT, IF I DO SAY SO MYSELF!
TH-THANK YOU.
WELL, I'LL GO SETTLE UP.
YOU GO ON AHEAD.
WHAT!?
NO, I'LL PAY!
IT'S FINE.
CONSIDER IT A THANK-YOU FOR COMING WITH ME SHOPPING.
AND A REWARD FOR ALL THE HARD WORK YOU DO!
I'D BE ON CLOUD NINE IF YOU WENT OUT WITH ME AGAIN WEARING THAT.

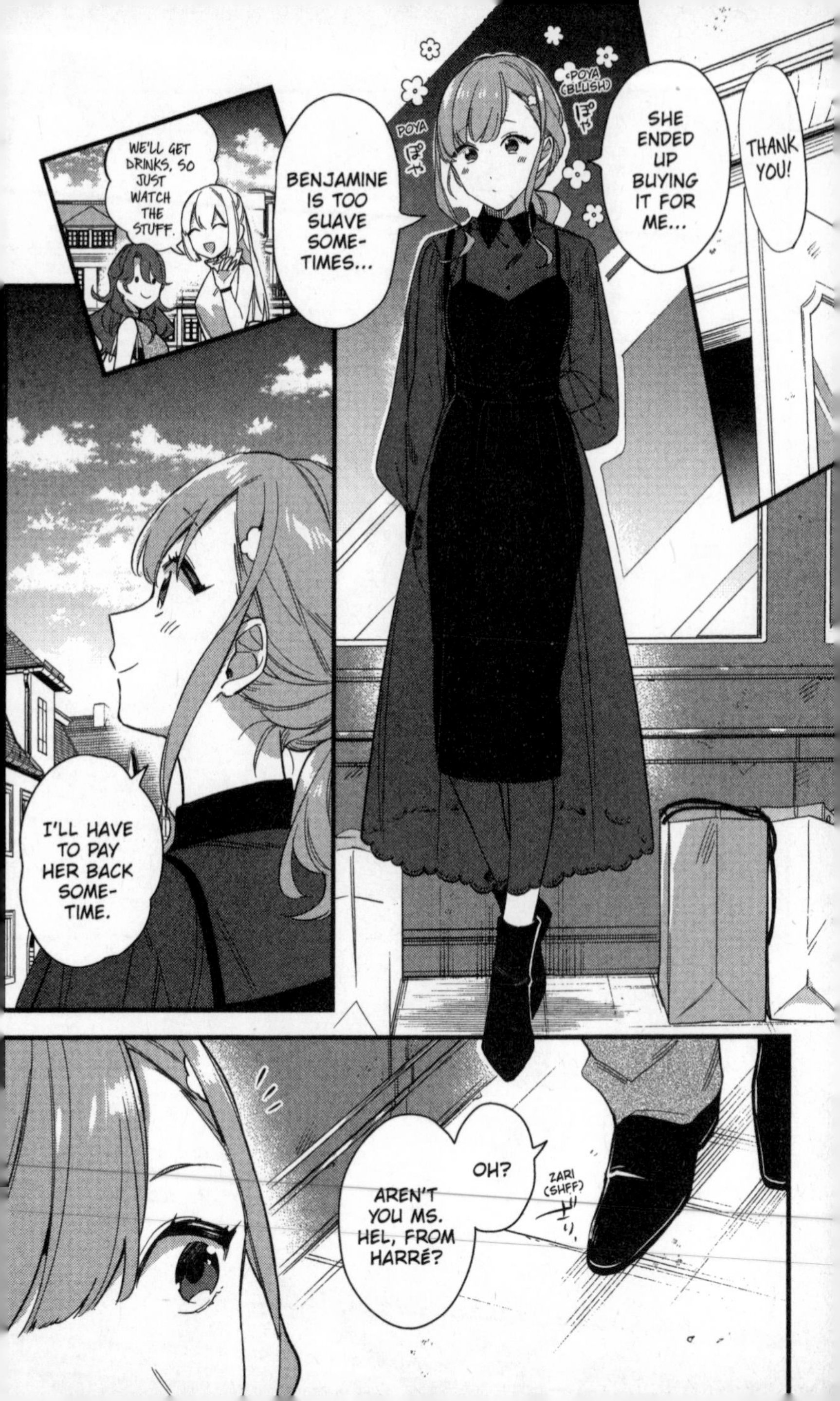
THANK YOU!
SHE ENDED UP BUYING IT FOR ME...
POYA (BLUSH)
POYA
BENJAMINE IS TOO SUAVE SOME-TIMES...
WE'LL GET DRINKS, SO JUST WATCH THE STUFF.
I'LL HAVE TO PAY HER BACK SOME-TIME.
ZARI (SHFF)
OH?
AREN'T YOU MS. HEL, FROM HARRÉ?

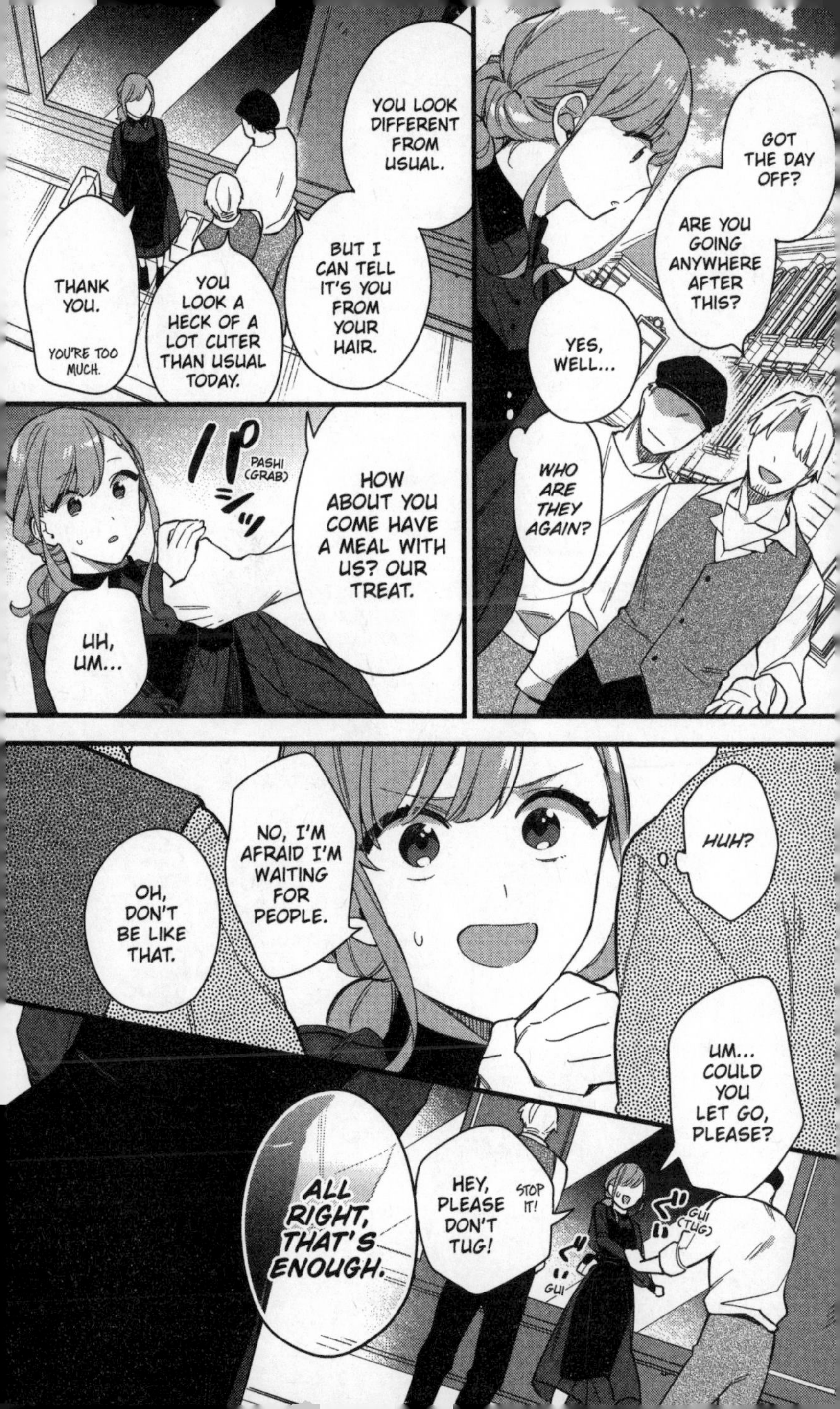
GOT THE DAY OFF?
ARE YOU GOING ANYWHERE AFTER THIS?
YES, WELL...
WHO ARE THEY AGAIN?
YOU LOOK DIFFERENT FROM USUAL.
BUT I CAN TELL IT'S YOU FROM YOUR HAIR.
YOU LOOK A HECK OF A LOT CUTER THAN USUAL TODAY.
THANK YOU.
YOU'RE TOO MUCH.
HOW ABOUT YOU COME HAVE A MEAL WITH US? OUR TREAT.
PASHI (GRAB)
UH, UM...
HUH?
NO, I'M AFRAID I'M WAITING FOR PEOPLE.
OH, DON'T BE LIKE THAT.
UM... COULD YOU LET GO, PLEASE?
GUI (TUG)
STOP IT!
HEY, PLEASE DON'T TUG!
GUI
ALL RIGHT, THAT'S ENOUGH.

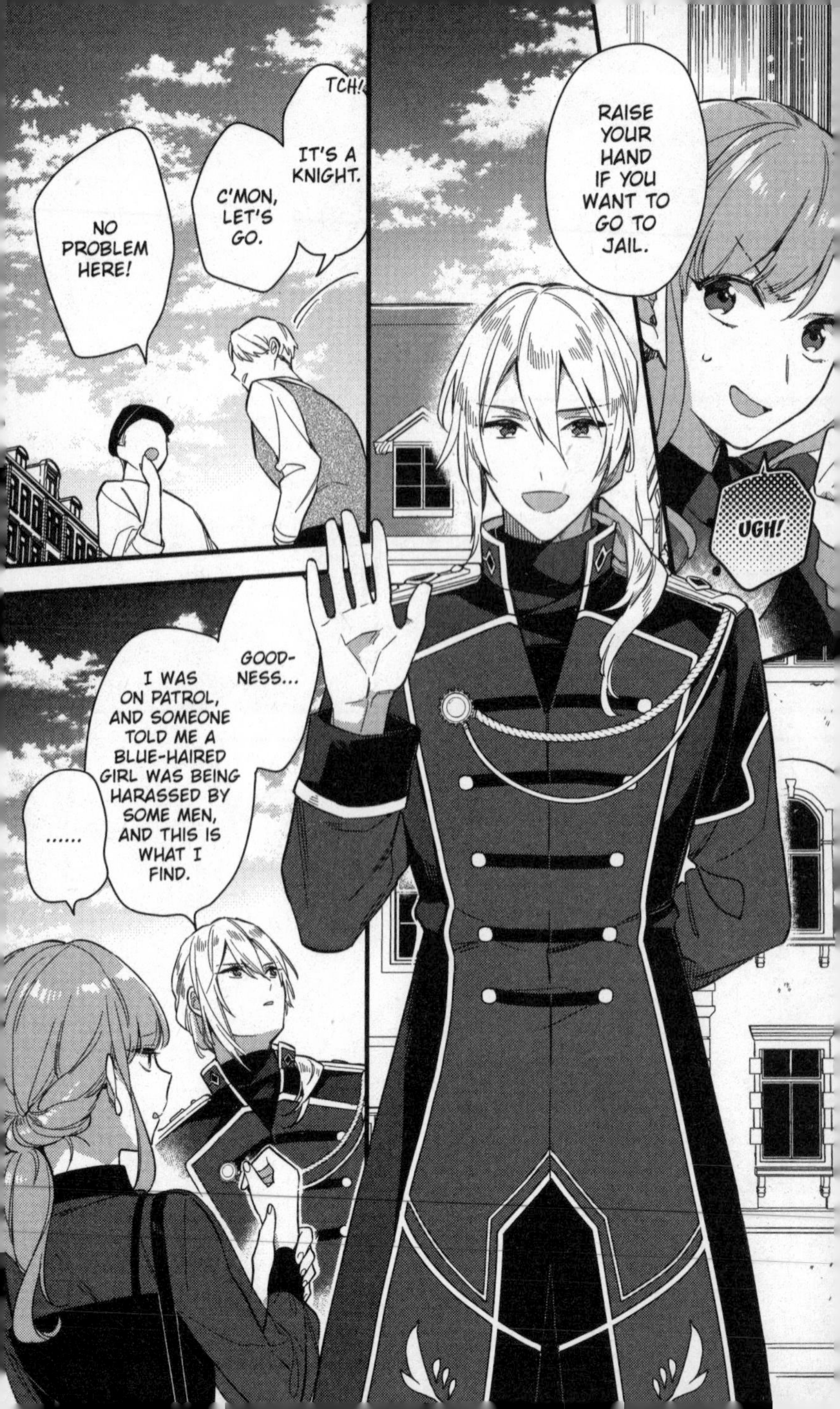
RAISE YOUR HAND IF YOU WANT TO GO TO JAIL.
UGH!
TCH!
IT'S A KNIGHT.
C'MON, LET'S GO.
NO PROBLEM HERE!
GOOD-NESS...
I WAS ON PATROL, AND SOMEONE TOLD ME A BLUE-HAIRED GIRL WAS BEING HARASSED BY SOME MEN, AND THIS IS WHAT I FIND.
......

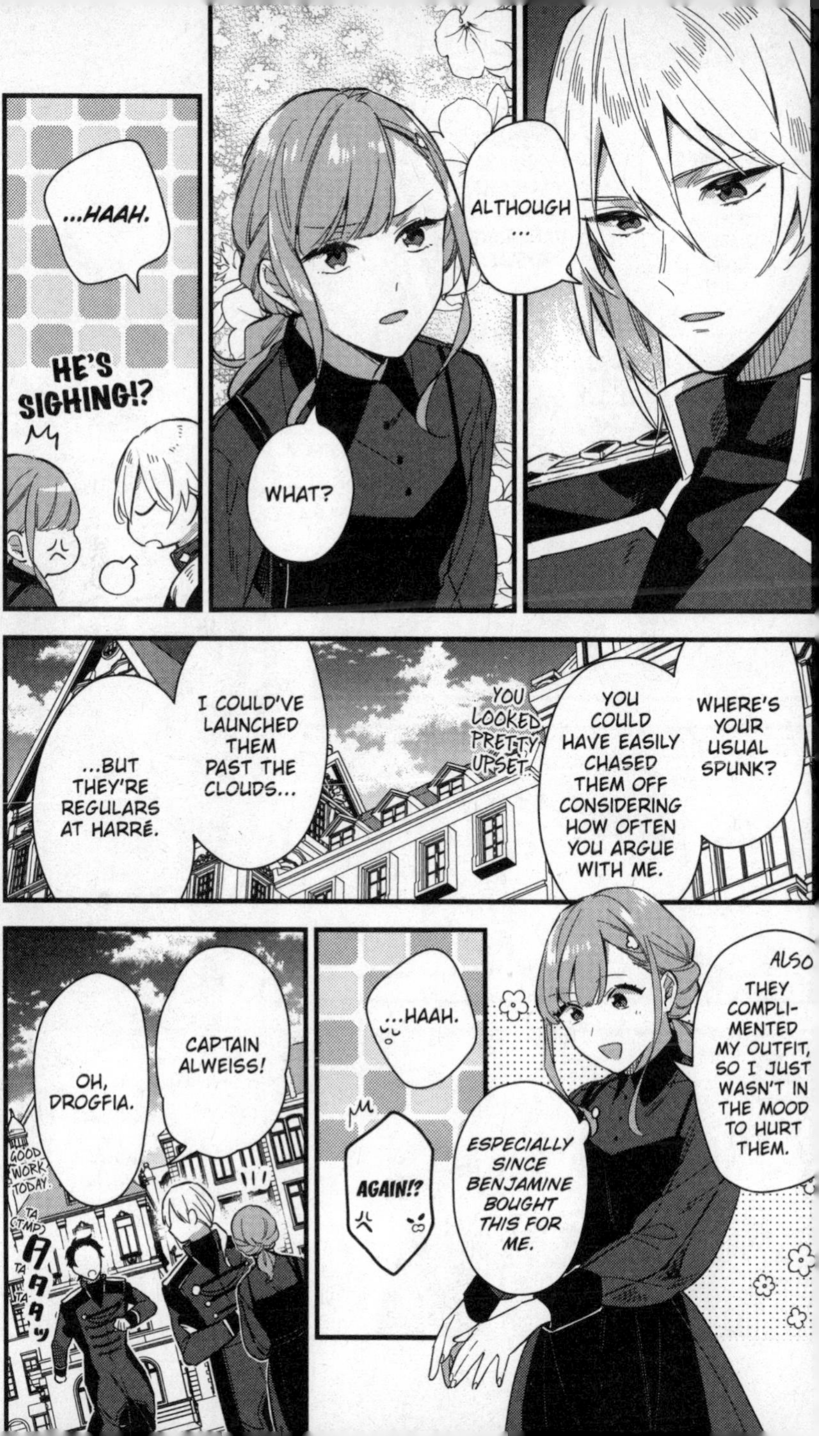
ALTHOUGH ...
WHAT?
...HAAH.
HE'S SIGHING!?
WHERE'S YOUR USUAL SPUNK?
YOU COULD HAVE EASILY CHASED THEM OFF CONSIDERING HOW OFTEN YOU ARGUE WITH ME.
YOU LOOKED PRETTY UPSET.
I COULD'VE LAUNCHED THEM PAST THE CLOUDS...
...BUT THEY'RE REGULARS AT HARRÉ.
ALSO THEY COMPLI-MENTED MY OUTFIT, SO I JUST WASN'T IN THE MOOD TO HURT THEM.
ESPECIALLY SINCE BENJAMINE BOUGHT THIS FOR ME.
...HAAH.
AGAIN!?
CAPTAIN ALWEISS!
OH, DROGFIA.
GOOD WORK TODAY.
TA (TMP) TA TA

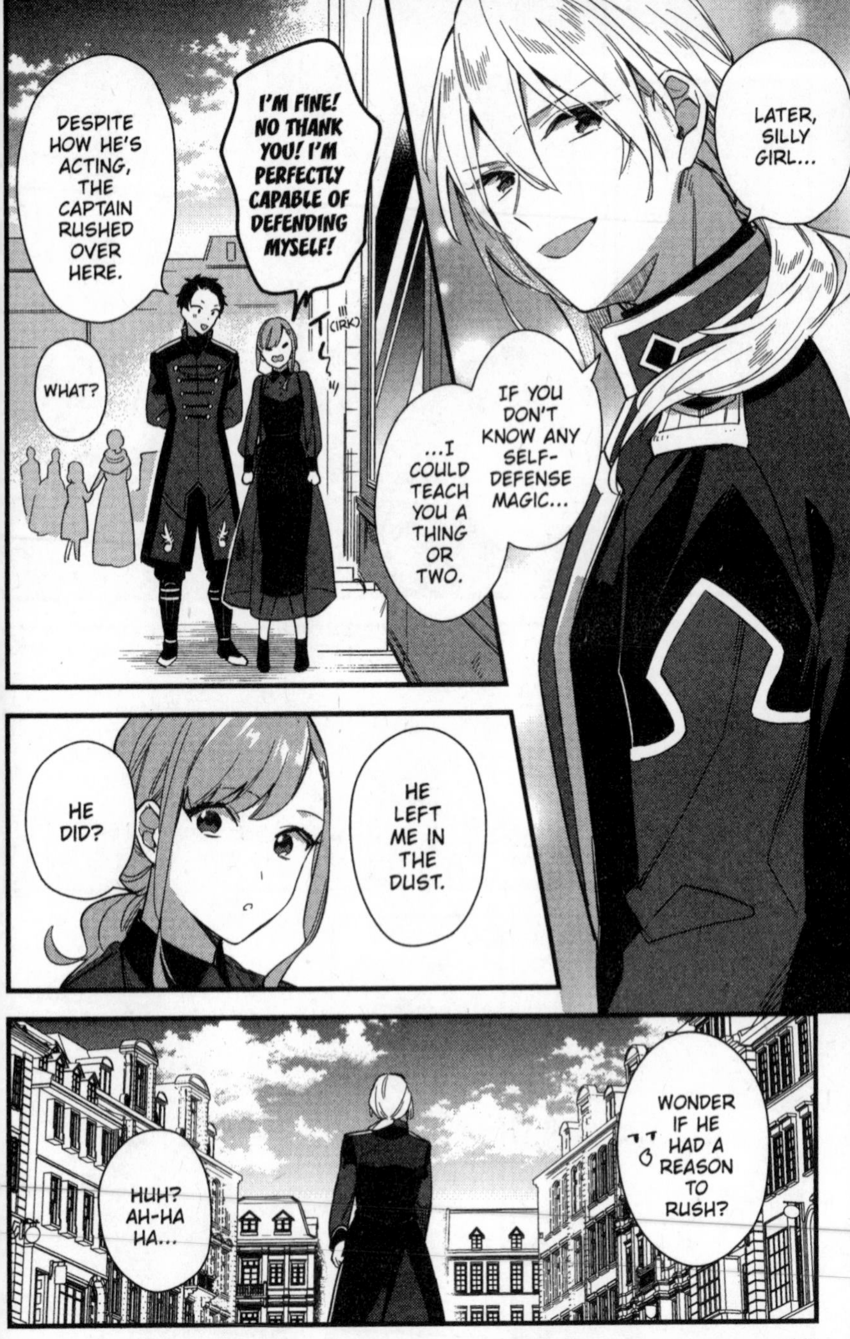
LATER, SILLY GIRL...
IF YOU DON'T KNOW ANY SELF-DEFENSE MAGIC...
...I COULD TEACH YOU A THING OR TWO.
I'M FINE! NO THANK YOU! I'M PERFECTLY CAPABLE OF DEFENDING MYSELF!
(IRK)
DESPITE HOW HE'S ACTING, THE CAPTAIN RUSHED OVER HERE.
WHAT?
HE LEFT ME IN THE DUST.
HE DID?
WONDER IF HE HAD A REASON TO RUSH?
HUH? AH-HA HA...

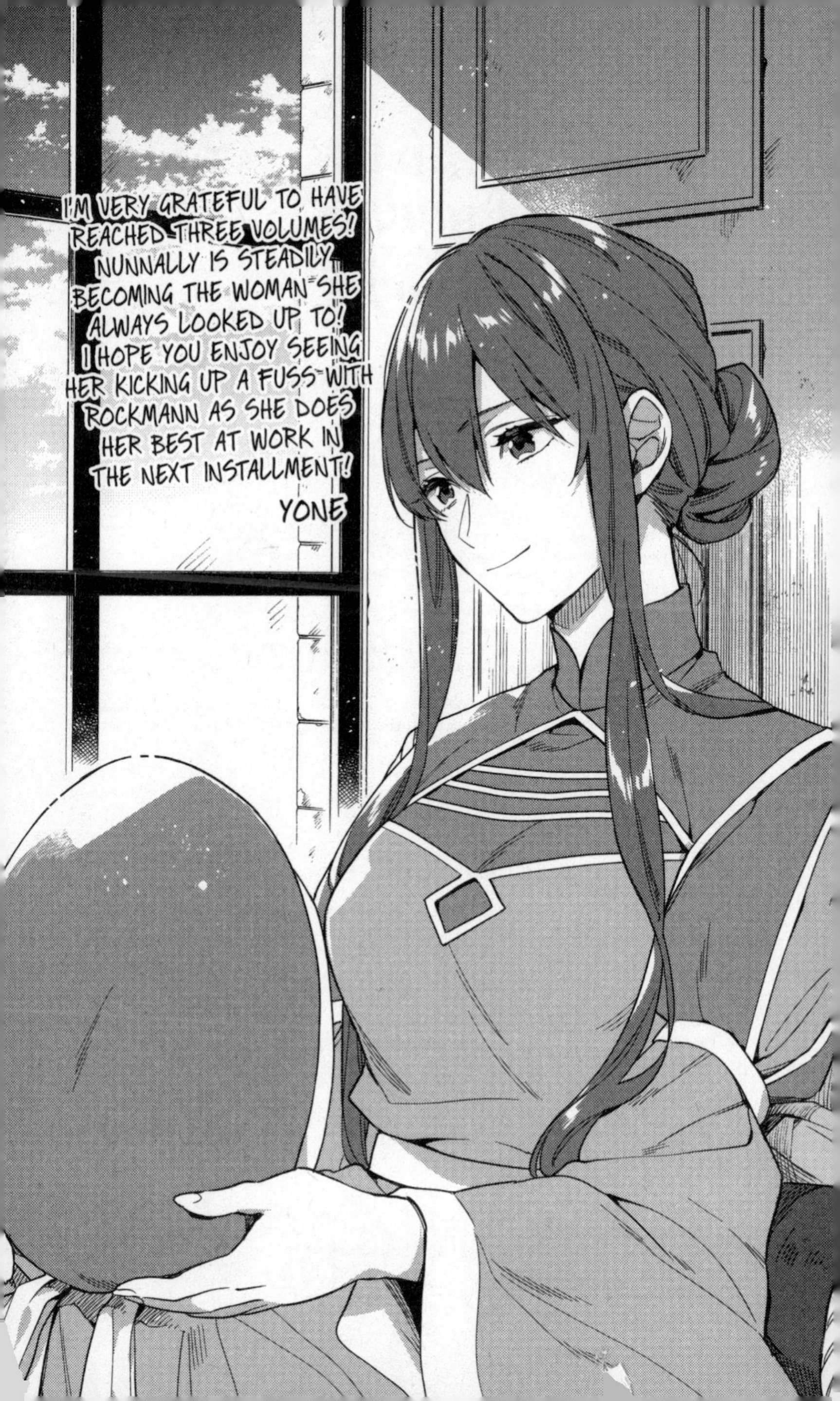
I'M VERY GRATEFUL TO HAVE REACHED THREE VOLUMES! NUNNALLY IS STEADILY BECOMING THE WOMAN SHE ALWAYS LOOKED UP TO! I HOPE YOU ENJOY SEEING HER KICKING UP A FUSS WITH ROCKMANN AS SHE DOES HER BEST AT WORK IN THE NEXT INSTALLMENT!
YONE

I Want to Be a Receptionist in This Magical World

3

Yone

Original Story:
MAKO

Character Design:
Maro

Translation: **Jan Cash** · Lettering: **Rachel J. Pierce**

This book is a work of fiction. Names, characters, places, and incidents are the product of the author's imagination or are used fictitiously. Any resemblance to actual events, locales, or persons, living or dead, is coincidental.

MAHO SEKAI NO UKETSUKEJO NI NARITAI DESU Vol. 3
©Yone 2020
©MAKO 2020 ©Maro 2020
First published in Japan in 2020 by KADOKAWA CORPORATION, Tokyo
English translation rights arranged with KADOKAWA CORPORATION, Tokyo
through Tuttle-Mori Agency, Inc.

English translation © 2024 by Yen Press, LLC

Yen Press
150 West 30th Street, 19th Floor
New York, NY 10001

Visit us at yenpress.com • facebook.com/yenpress
twitter.com/yenpress • yenpress.tumblr.com • instagram.com/yenpress

First Yen Press Edition: March 2024
Edited by Yen Press Editorial: Conner Worman, Carl Li
Designed by Yen Press Design: Liz Parlett

Yen Press is an imprint of Yen Press, LLC.
The Yen Press name and logo are trademarks of Yen Press, LLC.

The publisher is not responsible for websites (or their content) that are not owned by the publisher.

Library of Congress Control Number: 2023933180

ISBNs: 978-1-9753-5293-6 (paperback)
978-1-9753-5294-3 (ebook)

1 3 5 7 9 10 8 6 4 2

WOR

Printed in the United States of America